THE
PACKAGE KING

THE
PACKAGE KING

A RANK-AND-FILE HISTORY OF UPS

JOE ALLEN

HAYMARKET BOOKS
CHICAGO, ILLINOIS

Published in 2020 by
Haymarket Books
P.O. Box 180165
Chicago, IL 60618
773-583-7884
www.haymarketbooks.org
info@haymarketbooks.org

ISBN: 978-1-64259-164-4

Distributed to the trade in the US through Consortium Book
Sales and Distribution (www.cbsd.com) and internationally
through Ingram Publisher Services International
(www.ingramcontent.com).

This book was published with the generous support of Lannan
Foundation and Wallace Action Fund.

Special discounts are available for bulk purchases by organizations
and institutions. Please call 773-583-7884 or email
info@haymarketbooks.org for more information.

Cover design by Eric Kerl.

Printed in Canada by union labor.

Library of Congress Cataloging-in-Publication data is available.

10 9 8 7 6 5 4 3 2 1

CONTENTS

INTRODUCTION
TO THE 2020 EDITION

It's been nearly four years since the original publication of *The Package King*. I self-published the book in 2015 after writing a series of articles on UPS for the now-defunct *Socialist Worker*. My goal then was to make a small intellectual contribution to the reform movement in the Teamsters, specifically at UPS, and to help put into context the upcoming 2016 Teamster election and the 2018 contract battle at UPS. I was happy with the book, but it's up to others to judge whether it made the modest contribution I sought.

I've always marveled at how few books have been written about UPS, despite it being, by my calculation, the nation's first freight company and second only to the United States Postal Service as the country's oldest logistics company. For decades, UPS has been one of the country's largest employers and a ubiquitous presence in American life. It is one of the nation's most politically powerful corporations, shaping legislation in every state capital in the past fifty states, right up to Congress and the White House. Today it is the largest private-sector unionized employer in the United States. Yet UPS doesn't get the attention that its massive size and influence would seem to warrant.

I worked for UPS for a decade, dividing those years between the old Watertown Hub outside of Boston and the Jefferson Street Hub in Chicago. But I've deliberately avoided discussion of my work life at the company in *The Package King*. The reason for this is simple: I don't believe my particular work experience was fundamentally different from that of the millions of other workers who experience life inside the Big Brown machine. If there is something distinctive that I've contributed to the writing of this history, it's my socialist politics, which focus on the rank-and-file workers of UPS and the members of the Teamsters who work for change within the company.

Since the first publication of *The Package King*, I've kept up my writing on UPS, the logistics industry, and the Teamsters. I covered the 2016 Teamster election, the 2018 contract, and the issue of racism at UPS, along with other important topics, in a series of published articles. Some of these articles are compiled in this book's appendix. As the challenges facing logistics workers intensify, I hope that once again *The Package King* can make a small contribution toward the vital change necessary for workers—and not only those at UPS.

Joe Allen, Chicago, 2019

TROUBLED OVER WORK

When you are in a tough spot, one that forces you to balance profit or expediency and doing the right thing, I hope you remember this simple message: Good ethics are good business.

—Oz Nelson, former UPS CEO[1]

Homicides committed by disgruntled current and former employees at the workplace are on the rise. That kind of killing was virtually nonexistent before 1980.

—Fortune, August 9, 1993[2]

Joe Tesney went to work for the last time on September 23, 2014. He put on his distinctive brown uniform and drove to the United Parcel Service (UPS) hub in Inglenook, Alabama, on the outskirts of Birmingham, where he and another eighty package car drivers worked. Tesney was forty-five years old, with a wife and two children, and had worked at UPS for twenty-one years, nearly his entire adult life. He parked his car and slipped past security. He specifically chose to enter the building at a time when most drivers, loaders, and clerks would be gone. The building was relatively empty except for a handful of drivers and supervisors who were in their offices. Tesney entered his supervisor's office where he shot and killed two supervisors, Brian Callans and Doug Hutcheson, and then himself. Panic and chaos ensued. Dozens of police cars, ambulances, and other emergency vehicles descended on what had been just a few

3

hours earlier an obscure outpost of UPS's global empire.[3]

Police spokesperson Lt. Sean Edwards told the media that UPS had fired Tesney in the past month and he had received his termination papers the day before the shooting. Edwards said Tesney "was not expected to return to work because he was no longer employed there."[4] Various Alabama media outlets quickly contacted the only available relative of Joe Tesney who was willing to talk. "He was one of the best men I have ever known," said Tesney's mother-in-law, Wanda Binney. Asked whether she was surprised that Tesney could carry out such an attack, Binney responded, "Anybody but Joe. He's never hurt anyone in his life."[5] Tesney had been an active member of the NorthPark Baptist Church since 2003. His pastor, Bill Wilks, told the media that Tesney had been "troubled" over circumstances at work. "I think it's been an ongoing situation," Wilks explained. "In his own spirit, he's been troubled, and he's asked for prayer about that."[6]

Why was Tesney "troubled?" What was his "ongoing situation"? How does someone like Joe Tesney, who "never hurt anyone in his life," come to kill two supervisors and himself?

Brian Callans was in the wrong place at the wrong time on September 23rd. He was on vacation but fatally chose to make a quick stop at the Inglenook hub, where he met with fellow supervisor Doug Hutcheson. Hutcheson, according to one media source, "had investigated alleged wrongdoing by Tesney in the past and had recommended his firing."[7] What "wrongdoing"? Several media outlets reported that Tesney and UPS had been sued in civil court over alleged theft or negligent handling of an experimental racing radiator from HESCO, a design and testing shop, in November 2010.[8] Tesney stated that he mistakenly picked up the radiator during a stop at the company location. In September 2013, Jefferson County District Court Judge Jack Lowther ruled in favor of Tesney and UPS. That should have ended the issue for Tesney. But did it?

Soon after the Inglenook killings I talked to several former Teamster union representatives and stewards at UPS, and based on their experiences, they suspected that the lawsuit would have been a turning point in Tesney's relationship with UPS. "They put him on the 'least best' or 'shit list,' waiting for the opportunity to fire him, while subjecting him to constant auditing and other forms

of harassment," one former union rep said. A former union steward agreed: "I'll bet you that [Tesney's supervisors] kept muttering
under their breath, 'you see that guy? He's the one that cost us that
account.'" Was this the "ongoing situation" that Tesney talked to his
pastor about? Tesney's lethal outburst may seem to have come out
of nowhere, but some UPS insiders were actually surprised that an
episode of the kind had not happened sooner.

RAGE IN THE WORKPLACE

The Inglenook incident follows a pattern of rage workplace killings
that have become part of the American landscape. Mark Ames,
in *Going Postal: Rage, Murder, and Rebellion: From Reagan's Workplaces to Clinton's Columbine and Beyond*, puts the blame squarely on
Ronald Reagan: "It all started with his reign and his revolution—
specifically, with his reckless mass-firing of the striking air traffic controllers [Professional Air Traffic Controllers Organization
(PATCO)] in 1981."[9] Several forces combined to turn the American workplace into a living hell for many workers: the frenzy of
union busting, deregulation, the push for greater productivity, and
drastic wage and benefit cuts that followed Reagan's destruction
of PATCO. Neoliberalism (a deceptively benign-sounding label
for the destructive economic and political ideologies of the period)
came to dominate the world and was embraced enthusiastically by
US-based corporations, including UPS.

The title of Ames's *Going Postal* is, of course, based on a pop culture term for the string of mass revenge killings at post offices in the
1980s. But why the post office? Writing in 2005, Ames argued that
one reason "the whole rage murder phenomenon may have started
with post offices is that the eight-hundred-thousand-employee-strong
service, the nation's second-largest employer, was one of the earliest
and largest agencies in the post–New Deal era to be subjected to what
was essentially a semi-deregulation and semi-privatization plan, in
what the neoconservative American Enterprise Institute calls "the
most extensive reorganization of a federal agency."[10]

President Richard Nixon signed the Postal Reorganization Act
of 1970 into law following the historic US postal "wildcat" strike

(a strike conducted by rank and filers and unauthorized by union leadership). The act led to the creation of the modern United States Postal Service (USPS). The new model post office was demoted from a cabinet-level department to a corporate-like independent agency, and while the collective bargaining rights of postal workers were expanded (though these rights didn't include the right to strike), the change also unleashed neoliberal policies with deadly consequences.

UPS and the post office were, for decades, and still are, fierce competitors, and it is not surprising that UPS matched and then exceeded the post office in its brutal treatment of its workforce. UPS embraced neoliberal policies with gusto and became a trendsetter in corporate America. It led the way in the degradation of full-time into part-time jobs and the use of multiple-tier wage structures, one of the defining features of economic life that became the "new normal" for so many workers. UPS's peculiar military-style culture, which can be traced back to its founder, James (Jim) E. Casey, lent itself easily to the productivity push from the 1970s onward. UPS workers are some of the most productive workers in the world, with an array of resulting physical and mental health problems to show for it. One health study of UPS package drivers in 1992 reported "conflicting expectations emanating from differing supervisors and a disciplinary system in which [workers] were 'judged guilty, and sentenced before trial.'"[11] This is the world in which Joe Tesney suffered.

UPS's global workforce has grown today to over 440,000 employees, including the 250,000 US-based employees who are members of the Teamsters. Greg Niemann's *Big Brown: The Untold Story of UPS* reveals the wide, even surreal, gulf between the company's rosy self-image and the reality of life on the job.[12] Niemann's book is as close to an official company history as you can get.[13] "*Big Brown* is a must-read for anyone who's ever held a job or had a dream," gushes Paul Casey, a nephew of founder Jim Casey, on the book's back cover. Niemann, a former UPS manager and editor, is a proud company booster and seems overawed by the life and personality of Casey. He's a very good writer and competent historian, and readers can learn a lot from him, despite the sometimes syrupy, sugar-laden history of UPS that he serves up. I have used Niemann as a source and a foil throughout *The Package King*. But my book's most important contribution, I believe, is what it shows about how UPS has viewed the world and how it has tried to mold its employees to fit that view.

In a revealing passage halfway through *Big Brown*, Niemann describes the culture shock experienced by UPS's first German management team, composed entirely of Americans, when they began operations in West Germany in the mid-1970s:

> The work ethic in 1970s Germany was not the fine-tuned Swiss watch that the UPS pioneers had anticipated. The country's labor climate was institutionalized by German laws that called for extended vacations, much time off, liberal unlimited sick day policies, short work hours and weeks, and other inflexibilities. The hourly employees listened to the stress and pressure to *get the job done* as if it was Greek. According to Gale Davis, member of the initial startup team and later the German region personnel manager, "Most Germans felt that a better way to handle excessive work loads was to hire more and more people." Like most Europeans, the German population didn't even consider the concept of "living to work"; they only worked to live and strived to work as little as possible. You can imagine how this lassitude and lack of commitment struck UPS managers who lived and breathed "brown."[14]

Niemann expects his predominately American readers to have knee-jerk sympathy with UPS and its hostility to unions, social welfare programs, health and safety laws, and even extended vacations. The team's bewilderment at demands to hire more workers to handle "excessive work loads" is almost comical. Yet the most shocking detail is that management expects workers to "live to work." I'm not suggesting that we are going to replace "going postal" with "going brown," but UPS's treatment of its workforce will have its reckoning. The company's bosses, however, seem oblivious to the realities of the culture they have fostered.

THE GRINCH THAT STOLE CHRISTMAS

UPS escaped deep media scrutiny of its workplace practices following the Inglenook killings. However, media coverage was showered on the company in 2013, the previous year, when it had failed to deliver millions of packages in time for Christmas. A last-minute avalanche of packages, especially from online retail giant Amazon, overwhelmed UPS's delivery system, making a mockery of its guarantee of on-time delivery. It was the company's biggest public relations black eye in recent memory. A snarky *Wired* reporter commented, "Santa can deliver millions of packages in time for Christmas, but apparently, UPS can't."[15] The British *Daily Mail* told its US readers, "the United Parcel Service has turned into the Grinch that stole Christmas for thousands of families who didn't get their packages in time for the holiday."[16] Larry Ledet, fifty-five, who had driven a UPS truck for twenty-seven years, turned to Facebook to defend UPS workers against the torrent of customer and business media complaints, writing, "I'm a driver, got off at 10:10 last night, 60 hr weeks, I'm tired. Mother Nature, a booming economy and no one visiting malls any more caused this.....no reason 4 anyone to be mad...Merry Christmas."[17]

The 2013 Christmas fiasco accelerated discussion of Amazon getting into the delivery side of its business. UPS attempted to prevent another Christmas debacle in 2014 and spent over $500 million to modernize its facilities. It also hired an additional 95,000 seasonal workers to ensure it made Christmas deliveries on time.[18] It managed to do so but was criticized by financial analysts for excessive spending.[19] UPS's brand is very important to it, and the company is regularly recognized by *Fortune* as one of the "World's Most Admired Companies" in its industry. But the holiday debacle affected its reputation. In 2015, when *Fortune* was compiling its upcoming list, UPS's problems of the two previous Christmas seasons impacted its rating. It was placed thirty-fourth, far down the list from its archrival, FedEx, which was awarded the twelfth spot. *Fortune* had this to say about UPS: "The Georgia-based delivery company makes deliveries in more than 220 countries and territories. The busy 2015 holiday season turned out to be a mixed blessing: While the company is delivering more packages than it used to, that also means it has higher costs, which led to charging customers surcharges for peak shipping."[20] UPS just couldn't make the business media happy.

The company made the news again in February 2014 when it brazenly fired 250 drivers in New York who had walked off the job for ninety minutes to protest the unjust firing of popular union activist Jairo Reyes, a twenty-four-year veteran of the company. UPS was forced to back down when it became clear that Teamsters Local 804, which represented the "Maspeth 250," as they became known, wouldn't surrender. Tim Sylvester, president of Local 804, launched a campaign that subjected UPS's workplace practices to public scrutiny. Notices of termination were withdrawn on Wednesday, April 9, including that of Jairo Reyes, who was awarded back pay.[21] However, the very next day, members of Teamsters Local 89 at UPS's massive "Worldport" in Louisville, Kentucky, led by Fred Zuckerman, voted down the local supplement to the National UPS Master Contract by a 94 percent no vote. Teamsters General President James P. Hoffa, who has a reputation for being pro-company, spent a year and a half in brush fire wars as eighteen local supplements and riders to the national contract were repeatedly voted down during the first round of voting. Eventually a frustrated and angry Hoffa unilaterally implemented the UPS national contract and remaining supplements on a restive rank and file.[22] Not surprisingly, Zuckerman and Sylvester challenged Hoffa for leadership of the Teamsters in the 2016 international union election.[23]

WHAT HAVE UPS'S BILLIONS DONE TO US?

The Package King is a critical history of one of the most iconic US brands and the evolution of the modern logistics industry. It also tells the story of how UPS workers responded to this industry at crucial turning points. The book follows in the tradition of twentieth-century socialist author Upton Sinclair's *The Flivver King: A Story of Ford-America*. Sinclair's book was published originally by the UAW in 1937, and the 200,000 copies that the union sold for twenty-five cents a piece were part of a campaign to organize the auto giant. Sinclair tells a thinly fictionalized story of Henry Ford and the world he made. On *The Flivver King*'s original cover, the UAW posed the following questions: "What is Henry Ford? What have the years done to him? What has his billion dollars made of him? [. . .] Here also are his workers. What has the billion dollars done to *them*?" That last question could be easily asked of UPS today.[24]

At the time of UPS's founding over one hundred years ago, no one could have predicted that a small Seattle-based bicycle messenger service would grow into a global behemoth of staggering size and importance. Nor could anyone have predicted that the small presence of UPSers in the Teamsters would grow into a "union within a union."[25] With nearly 250,000 members, UPS is the single largest Teamster employer and the largest private sector, unionized employer in the United States; its growth has reshaped the Teamsters into this country's most notorious union. The conflicts within the Teamsters—between the rank-and-file members and Teamster officers, between reformers and the "old guard" (mobbed-up, conservative officers), and between local and international officers—have played a major role in shaping the posture of the union toward UPS and, in turn, the relationship between the company and the union. UPS's enormous political influence has also played a detrimental role in blunting the aspirations of UPS workers and reformers in the Teamsters. The persecution of Ron Carey, the only reformer to lead the union, is the most egregious such example. Carey's saga will be examined in later chapters.

"THE OTHER ARMY"

Despite its history of internal conflict, United Parcel Service remains the world's largest package delivery company, with 99,892 package cars, vans, tractors, and motorcycles. It is, writes journalist Margot Roosevelt, a "Fortune 50 company that moves 6 percent of the US Gross Domestic Product and 2 percent of the world's GDP."[26] Its 237 planes fly to 220 countries a day and deliver 4.6 billion packages and documents.[27] The ubiquitous UPS drivers on the streets of the United States (and increasingly throughout Europe), with their military-style brown uniforms, could easily be mistaken for soldiers assigned to civilian work. When journalist Alex Frankel asked a long-time driver if her job reminded her of the military, she replied without hesitation, "'I call it 'the other Army.'"[28] And as with combat veterans, what happens to workers at UPS doesn't stay at UPS—it impacts livelihoods and communities far beyond the hub gates.

Literally millions of Americans have worked at UPS, and, along with military service and serving in prison, employment at the shipping behemoth has been become a rite of passage for many. The company is one of the largest contributors to national political candidates, and its immense lobbying power can be felt through many organizations, including the American Legislative Exchange Council (ALEC), the Business Roundtable, and the American Trucking Associations. There are few political issues in which UPS doesn't see itself as having a direct interest, whether it is the Trans-Pacific Partnership treaty or voting rights. The company has played a major role in shaping the economic and political world we live in today.[29]

"Working at UPS should be the best job in America—and it just isn't," a member of the Teamsters UPS National Negotiating Committee remarked during a break in national negotiations in 1997. The UPS negotiator, who had been a driver for a short period, didn't dispute the issues that the union raised in negotiations; he simply responded, "You can't argue with success—we must be doing it right."[30] The tension in this exchange, between the frustration of individual workers and the rise of a powerful company, is at the heart of *The Package King*.

The Package King provides a deep look into the sometimes turbulent history of UPS and the inner workings of the world of logistics and the big data metrics that shape the modern workplace.[31] Whether you are a logistics worker, a consumer, a trade union activist, or a student of the modern economy, I hope this book provides a new way of looking at the rise of one of the world's most important corporations—and how it might be changed for the better.

Joe Allen, September 2015

CHAPTER 1
THE PACKAGE KING

Ah, packages!

—James E. Casey

There are few things in life that get a UPS supervisor or manager more excited than the sight of thousands of packages or Next Day Air envelopes careening down the myriad belts crisscrossing the sorting and distribution centers of the world. Their eyes widen and their breath quickens. You can see the dollars signs popping up in their eyes like old-fashioned cash registers as each package passes them by. Packages of every shape and size are the nuggets of gold from which the UPS fortune is made. They are more important than the physical and mental health of the workers who sort, load, unload, repair, clerk, and deliver them. While UPS may enshrine its corporate "mission" in such noble-sounding words as "service" and "integrity"—as if the company is charged with promoting the common good—it is, first and foremost, in the business of making money off its workers.[1]

This obsession with packages over people is nothing new. It goes right back to the company's hallowed founder, James (Jim) E. Casey. "Casey is a package," one exasperated retail store manager told the *New Yorker* in 1947. "Casey once told me that he had never drunk a glass of milk in his life," the head of a department store told the reporter, "and I thought for a minute he might stop talking about those goddamn packages and tell me why he never drunk a glass of milk. But no! He went right into night loading operations in Chicago."[2] On another occasion, Casey, while visiting a store, dropped into the wrapping room and looked around ecstatically at the sight. "Casey's eyes sparkled and he began to twitch. 'Deft fingers!' he said. 'Deft fingers wrapping thousands of bundles. Neatly tied. Neatly addressed! Stuffed with soft tissue paper! What a treat! Ah, packages!'"

What sparked the interest of the *New Yorker*, a highbrow cultural magazine, in Jim Casey and UPS? It appears to have been the messy, spontaneous (wildcat) strike on the streets of Manhattan that shut down UPS operations for fifty-one days in the fall of 1946. Back then, UPS did the home deliveries for New York's leading department stores, such as Lord & Taylor. Customers would buy their items, and the department store would package and wrap them, then hand them over to UPS for home delivery. The strike prevented New York's middle-class shoppers from getting their goods, and this disruption caught the eye of the editors at the *New Yorker*.

The magazine assigned Philip Hamburger, who would stay at the *New Yorker* for a total of six and a half decades, to interview Casey and get a feel for the company that had become so indispensable to New York's retail businesses.[3] This wasn't the first time the *New Yorker* had written about UPS. In December 1934, a few years after UPS made the leap from the West Coast to New York City, Casey was featured in the "Talk of the Town" section of the magazine, and the editors gave the story the distinctly condescending title of "Errand Boy."[4] The short piece noted that Casey began his career doing "errands" but that the nature of his role had changed considerably. "He's sort of an errand king now, the head of the United Parcel Service, which delivers packages by the millions in this city and elsewhere."

The 1934 article picked up on the military, or even cult-like, policies that UPS adopted for its employees. "The employees are about as regimented a bunch of people as you've ever heard of. For his first few weeks [an employee is] tutored in driving, delivery, and courtesy. This involves a hundred and thirty-eight rules." The article even mentioned a UPS summer "camp" for employees, saying that "when business is slack, the unmarried deliveryman may spend [his] time at a camp in Connecticut which the company operates. . . . Several hundred go there every year for a month or two."[5] What went on in these summer camps may be lost to history, but their existence shows that UPS sought to create a private world were employees were encouraged to adopt the values and personality traits of Jim Casey.

By the time Casey was interviewed by Hamburger in 1947, the founder's stature had risen in New York. Reflecting that change, Casey was bumped up to the "Profiles" section of the *New Yorker*, a space usually reserved for major figures of the business and political world. He was no longer a new face in town but the leader of a major, growing business. Late in 1946, UPS delivered its one-billionth package and by 1947 employed 2,800 people with 1,700 trucks in New York alone. It operated in seventeen major cities across the United States and delivered one hundred million packages a year. What makes Hamburger's profile of Casey so interesting, from the vantage point of seven decades later, is that it is a rare, unvarnished, early look at the man—a portrait of Casey very unlike the legendary image that would later be manufactured. The founder comes across as an austere disciplinarian with a more than slightly loopy fascination with packages.[6]

"Casey is a tall, spare man of fifty-nine, with high cheekbones and, most of the time, a rigidly detached expression," reported Hamburger. He found Casey hard to interview, describing him as "taciturn" and somewhat reluctant to answer questions. However, when they moved from Casey's fourth floor office at the old Manhattan hub on First Avenue to view the endlessly moving belts of the package sorting system below, Casey perked up. "He becomes animated in the presence of packages." Hamburger was himself impressed by the "surf-like rumble of the parcels"—a sound recognizable to anyone who has spent time in a UPS hub. It became clear that "Casey's life is devoted almost entirely to packages." This vocation for package delivery was combined with a deliberate faux modesty about it all. "'Anybody can deliver a package,'" Casey told Hamburger. But the *New Yorker* writer had a keen eye and wasn't buying Casey's claim. "He does not believe it," said Hamburger.

A TIBETAN MONASTERY

Hamburger also noticed that Casey "packaged" the idea of UPS, not unlike the thousands of items that his drivers picked up every day at fashionable New York department stores. "Over the years," Hamburger wrote, "Casey has taken what might look to outsiders like the simple job of handling and delivering packages and turned it into a semi-religious rite." A "simple job" is an understatement, but "turning it into a semi-religious rite" is right on the money. Every aspect of the company image was carefully crafted, from the crisply pressed, brown uniforms to the company slogan, "Safe, Swift, Sure."

The mystique of the UPS driver was an important selling point. UPS drivers, an incredulous Hamburger wrote, "are governed by a series of regulations that could easily be mistaken for the house rules of a Tibetan monastery." Before hitting the road each day, drivers had to carefully study illustrated cards that scolded them to "check and double check: Are your shoes shined? Is your hair cut? Are you clean-shaven? Are your hands clean? Is your uniform pressed?" If this is a childish way to treat grown men, it didn't seem to bother Casey, who made periodic visits to UPS hubs to enforce the rules like a general inspecting his troops. "On one such visit," said Hamburger, "he stood by as a station supervisor assembled a group of drivers and package sorters and examined their shoe shines and haircuts." He then declared, "The spokes of our wheel spell service" and left the building.

Casey was determined to find the right people to be his drivers, and it began during the hiring phase:

> Applicants for United Parcel Service jobs must, first of all, impress . . . with their neatness and courtesy. If they pass muster on those counts, they are subjected to intelligence tests. No one at United Parcel, least of all Casey, is searching for a genius-type deliveryman. The personnel department has discovered that high-scoring applicants are inclined to be temperamental and to mislay their bundles. Assuming that the results of an applicant's test place him somewhere in the broad category between wizard and idiot, and that a job is available, he is hired.[7]

Hamburger's snarky tone aside, he does capture Casey's search for moldable personalities that he could lay his hands on and shape into perfect drivers. This shaping process continued after work hours. "A man who gets a job at United Parcel finds that his education has just begun. The leisure hours of an employee are supposed to be crowded with self-improvement projects," explained Hamburger. This included reading the UPS newsletter, *The Big Idea*, which was filled with homilies to the UPS way of doing business, employee profiles, and Casey witticisms.

Casey never tired of trying to "improve" his drivers. His obsession with packages never flagged, either. In one memorable scene, Hamburger captured both Casey's obsessions and bigotries very well:

> Recently, he stood silent with a friend, watching thousands and thousands of packages. He was silent for several minutes. Then his face lighted up. He seemed exhilarated. "Packages for everybody!" he exclaimed suddenly. "Packages for Chinatown—a difficult area. Drivers have trouble remembering who they left the package with—everybody looks alike! Packages for Harlem—hardly any charge accounts in Harlem! Packages for the West Side—democratic neighborhood. Give packages the kind of welcome packages deserve! Packages for Greenwich Village—very odd packages!"[8]

SEATTLE ORIGINS

UPS founder Jim Casey was born in the remote windswept mining town of Candelaria, Nevada, in 1888. His Irish immigrant father, Henry, was a failed prospector, and, like many others, he developed a debilitating lung disease from his years in the mines that disabled him for the rest of his life. The dominant figure in the Casey family was his mother, Annie. From an early age, young Casey had to work to help keep the family afloat. The Casey family moved to Seattle, which became the launching pad for the company that became known as United Parcel Service.

What was the allure of Seattle for the Casey family? Seattle was a boomtown in the late 1890s because it was the jumping-off city for the Klondike Gold Rush, the last great gold rush on the North American continent. Many Americans are familiar with this historic event through the work of Jack London. Seattle became the bustling way station for those heading north to the inhospitable and unforgiving environments of the Yukon Province of northwestern Canada and Alaska. Eventually 100,000 prospectors made their way north, many of them outfitted by local businesses with clothing they needed to survive the coming harsh winters, as well as mining equipment and food supplies. The city boomed with legitimate and illegitimate businesses that serviced the needs of these would-be prospectors.

It was in this busy city that Casey began his career as a messenger at the age of eleven, delivering tea (and opium). He was mentored by an elderly Irishman who taught him the delivery business.[9] In 1907, Casey, along with his friend Claude Ryan, founded the American Messenger Service, the very beginning of UPS. Casey's brother George joined them a few years later.

In the years leading up to the First World War, Seattle and the larger Pacific Northwest was a bastion of US radical politics and working-class militancy. In 1912, Eugene Debs, the presidential candidate of the Socialist Party, received 900,000 votes nationwide, with 40,000 coming from the state of Washington.[10] The Industrial Workers of the World (IWW), popularly known as the "Wobblies," organized thousands of timber workers throughout the Northwest. The decade following the end of the Klondike Gold Rush saw the economy of the region stagnate, but it began to boom again with the outbreak of war in Europe in 1914. When the United States declared war on Germany in 1917, the economy boomed even further, resulting in skyrocketing inflation that ate away at workers' living standards. An even bigger threat to the lives of radicals, trade unionists, and "suspect" ethnic minorities was the legal assault on their constitutional freedoms by the state and federal governments and their vigilante allies. Despite this hostile atmosphere, the union movement represented by the American Federation of Labor (AFL) grew by 400 percent from 1915 to 1918, while radical and revolutionary ideas spread throughout the working class. The Russian Revolution of 1917, the first successful workers' revolution in history, received widespread support throughout the Pacific Northwest.[11]

THE GENERAL STRIKE

This tense political atmosphere exploded in the great Seattle General Strike of 1919, when the working class ran the city from February 6 to February 11. An elected strike committee representing 110 local unions ran the city for five days. It was an incredible display of the potential of workers to run society, not simply negotiate a place in it. Striking trade unionists inspired non-union workers to join the strike. Many strikers and supporters were veterans of the First World War and wore their military uniforms on the picket lines and at demonstrations.

The radicalism of the Seattle working class during the general strike made a deep impression on Jim Casey, who renamed his company United Parcel Service in the historic year of 1919. UPS company historian Greg Niemann argues that Casey was very aware of the politics of his hometown: "The Pacific Northwest of Jim's early years had a robust social movement, and Seattle . . . was already known across the country as a haven of left-wing politics."[12] The Seattle radicals of Casey's youth, writes Niemann mockingly, "called for the emancipation of the working class from the 'slave bondage of capitalism,'" and "wanted the working class in possession of economic power, to control business enterprise without regard to capitalist masters." Casey "couldn't have helped but notice the unrest and reasons underlying the working-class argument. Flyers, demonstrations, meetings, and strikes were commonplace in those early years of the twentieth century. For Jim, already in the messenger and delivery business, the working classes were potential customers and employees."[13]

Whether Casey truly understood the "unrest" is subject to debate. Niemann never quotes him directly. Casey's opinions are inferred from Niemann's interviews with UPS managers and some family members. Yet it may be true that Casey had some grasp of working-class concerns. In 1919, Casey "invited the Teamsters to represent the several dozen United Parcel Drivers and part-time hourly package-handling employees in Oakland."[14] The Teamsters had a conservative, pro-business reputation and were the best option, from the perspective of UPS, to represent the company's employees.

However, the entire labor movement came under siege during the early 1920s to mid-1920s. After an initial burst of strike activity and the growth of union membership following World War I, the movement shrank under the impact of an aggressive "open-shop" (non-union) campaign by employers, a Red Scare, and violent repression from state and local governments, and with the help of vigilantes.[15] Along with repression and threats, some employers used methods drawn from modern sociology and psychology in hopes of blunting the development of a militant class-consciousness and making workers impervious to radical ideas.[16]

UPS was no exception. Employee-corporate relations campaigns encouraged a "family" atmosphere where employees could make suggestions about better operations—without actually changing the totalitarian relationship between boss and worker. The company newsletter, *The Big Idea*, was first published in 1924, and employee stock ownership was introduced in 1927 with these conservative goals in mind.[17]

AN ENGINEERING ROAD TRIP

During the twenties, UPS expanded along the West Coast to include locations in Oakland, Los Angeles, Portland, San Francisco, and San Diego. The company brought these policies to each new location. The national headquarters of UPS also moved to Los Angeles and remained there until the 1930s. This explosive growth forced a rethinking and redesign of the UPS package sorting and distribution system. Casey reached outside the company for an industrial engineer and hired Russel Havighorst in 1923. Havighorst had worked as an industrial engineer for both General Motors and Ford. The auto industry was seen as the most modern and cutting edge of all US industries with its assembly line method of production. This was probably a big selling point for Havighorst who started out as an assistant delivery supervisor in Los Angeles. Havighorst replaced the "large, partitioned, crescent-shaped tables sorting was typically done on, and . . . installed a specially designed belt conveyor and bin system, manned by sorters who sent packages down a wooden chute to bins organized by drivers' routes."[18]

Havighorst moved on to San Francisco to redesign the hub and the interior of package cars. Not satisfied, Casey and Havighorst hit the road in 1926 to tour the era's leading industrial operations.[19] They traveled the breadth of the United States, making inspection stops at leading department stores that had their own package delivery operations. During the trip, write business historians Mike Brewster and Frederick Dalzell, Casey and Havighorst took notes, sketched layouts and machinery, and ran calculations about resources spent and time and money saved."

The two men toured Henry Ford's massive River Rouge plant in Detroit, US Steel in Pittsburgh, and even an Armour meatpacking plant in St. Louis. But it appears that two stops in Chicago, at Marshall Field's and Sears Roebuck, made the biggest impression. While at the Marshall Field's warehouse, Casey and Havighorst "marveled at the nine-belt sorting system and 3,500 trunks in which the parcels were sorted." Sears Roebuck also caught their imaginations: "We can only touch upon the wonders at Sears Roebuck," Havighorst later wrote. "The success of their entire operation may be said to be due to ideals of the very highest order reinforced by an iron-clad time schedule which holds everyone strictly to its limitations as those of the old German Imperial Army."[20]

UPS was developing on the basis of these ideas and inspiration. What did this mean for UPS workers? And what was the response of the Teamsters to changes within the company?

DAVE BECK

UPS had a cozy relationship with the Teamsters for many years, and the person largely responsible for this was Dave Beck, an ambitious union politician. Beck and Jim Casey shared much in common. Beck was also born in the West—in Stockton, California, in 1894, into an extremely poor family. Like the Casey family, the Becks also moved to Seattle for better prospects.[21] From Seattle, both Casey and Beck launched national careers, one in business and the other in the labor movement. Dave Beck first became a Teamster in 1914, driving a laundry truck at the age of eighteen. He joined the navy after the United States entered the war in 1917 and was stationed in England. He returned to Seattle just in time to attend a meeting of his old Teamster local union, the Laundry and Dye Works Drivers Local 566, where he argued *against* joining the general strike—in the end Local 566 was the only Teamster local union in Seattle not to join. Beck was proud of his scabbing: "I don't know what I said, but I know damned well that I stood them on their feet, and how good that felt to a punk kid in a sailor outfit."[22]

Seattle historian Nard Jones wrote, "If the General Strike made a deep impression on the average citizen it made even a deeper one on Beck."[23] It made Beck into a professional anticommunist and an opponent of militant trade unionism. During the 1920s, Dave Beck emerged as a Teamster leader in Seattle and was poised to become the most powerful Teamster official on the West Coast. Trucking historian Donald Garnel chronicles his methodical rise to power:

> Upon his return from the war, Beck resumed laundry wagon driving and became extremely active in Local 566. He was elected to the executive of his local union and through his position regularly attended the Joint Council meetings. In 1923, Beck was elected President of Joint Council 28, an unpaid position, which nevertheless offered him many opportunities to use his skills at oratory. His appetite for leadership whetted, he decided to run for secretary-treasurer of his local, and won. Early in 1925, Beck took over as principal officer of Local 566.[24]

Dan Tobin, the conservative if not outright reactionary president of the International Brotherhood of Teamsters (IBT), took a liking to Beck and appointed him an international organizer, which supplemented his income and widened the scope of his duties and influence on the West Coast. Beck pursued incredibly conservative, pro-business policies that ultimately had a terrible impact on the rank and file of the union. "I have no use for class warfare," he once said.[25] According to historian Dan La Botz, Beck viewed "employers as collaborators, rather than as adversaries" and identified "with the boss and his problems, rather than with the worker and his problems. Guided by this philosophy of collaboration, Beck visited all the Teamster union halls urging wage cuts in 1929 when the Crash occurred and the Great Depression began."[26]

It wasn't until the mid-1930s that Dave Beck and Jim Casey met face-to-face to discuss the future of the Teamsters at UPS. The city was rocked by the San Francisco waterfront strike that later spread along the West Coast in 1934. The strike was led by Harry Bridges, a well-known radical trade unionist from Australia who was closely allied to the Communist Party USA. Bridges's union, later known as the International Longshore and Warehouse Union (ILWU), not only transformed the notoriously terrible conditions of the San Francisco waterfront but may also have served as a threat to the position of the conservative Teamsters in the delivery and warehousing industries.

Faced with this upsurge of radical trade unionism, Jim Casey chose to bargain with the Teamsters throughout most of the West Coast. However, he hit a major roadblock in Los Angeles, home to the headquarters of the United Parcel Service in the 1930s. LA was a violently anti-union city during this era, as Niemann notes: "The *Los Angeles Times* and the Los Angeles Police Department were already working to put down labor strikes and reforms. Up to this point only the San Francisco Bay Area drivers were unionized, but union organizer Dave Beck wanted to unionize UPS."[27]

Beck told his biographer John McCallum in 1978 that he well remembered "dealing with the Casey brothers": "[W]e organized UPS in Seattle, Tacoma, Portland, and on down the coast to San Francisco–Oakland. But when it came time to go into Los Angeles, we hit a brick wall. I mean, we couldn't make a dent."[28] Jim Casey apparently feared being ostracized by the powerful Merchants and Manufacturers' Association, which vigilantly policed all businesses to make sure that Los Angeles remained union free.

"YOU FIGURE IT OUT"

Beck met with Casey to sell him on the idea of organizing UPS in Los Angeles, but the fearful Casey refused to budge. He threw the ball back into Beck's court, saying, "I don't know, you figure it out." Beck responded by directing Casey to go to the Merchants and Manufacturers' Association and tell its leaders that when UPS contracts expired throughout the West Coast, "we are either going to work for UPS in Los Angeles on the same conditions as in other cities or we are *not* going to work for you in any other city." The association received the message and promised to underwrite any strike by the Teamsters in Los Angeles. Casey grasped that it was better to sign with the Teamsters than to fight them all over the United States. "From that day to this," Beck declared, "we've been organized with no interruptions or major labor disturbances of any significance. Soon after, we did identically the same thing with all the major companies there."[29]

These highly effective strategies and tactics were taken straight from the playbook of Minneapolis Teamsters led by the revolutionary socialists Farrell Dobbs, Carl Skoglund, and the Dunne brothers.[30] Beck would play a central role in expelling these socialists from the Teamsters in the early 1940s, but he was not averse to stealing their strategies, while rejecting their politics. Beck became more remote and conservative as he grew more powerful. Historian Murray Morgan, in *Skid Road: An Informal Portrait of Seattle*, captured the changing personality and lifestyle of the once-poor Dave Beck:

> His observance of the rituals of being rich became more conspicuous. His clothes grew richer and better tailored, his office larger and more deep-toned, his cars longer, his phone conversations curter, his invitations to the annual Round Up Party at the Washington Athletic Club—a must for business and political leaders—more peremptory. It was during this period that Dave Beck moved from the modest frame house, which had pinned him to the middle class, into a new Sheridan Beach estate with private pool, private cinema, even sumptuous private quarters for his private bodyguards.[31]

Wealth and power brought on arrogance and contempt for the union members that Beck claimed to represent. "Why should truck drivers and bottle washers be allowed to make decisions affecting [Teamster] policy?" he reportedly once asked. "No corporation would allow it."[32]

Beck's smug elitism was unfortunately not unusual among trade union officials, especially in the increasingly corrupt and mobbed-up Teamsters. Beck is a largely forgotten figure in Teamster history, but his greatest legacy was bringing all UPSers on the West Coast into the union during the 1930s.

It was also during this period that UPS made a leap into the crowded and competitive retail market of New York and came into contact with Teamsters Local 804, which would prove itself over time to be one of the most independent-minded and militant local unions in the country.

CHAPTER 2
UPRISING IN NEW YORK

. . . the atomic bomb of industrial disputes . . .
—**Joseph M. Proskauer, lawyer for New York City's department
stores, describing the UPS strike of 1946**[1]

New York beckoned UPS. It was the largest US city and retail market, as well as the financial and corporate capital of the country. For Casey and the company's top management, it would have been impossible for UPS not to be in New York if they aspired to be a national company. In 1930, UPS set up its delivery operations in Manhattan and became the premiere delivery service for all of New York's leading and popular department stores and specialty shops.

The timing of the jump to New York was inauspicious given the onset of the Great Depression that followed the stock market crash of 1929, but there was an opportunity in the crisis for companies like UPS. Many of New York's department stores had their own in-house delivery services that provided free delivery of store-bought goods, and, according to historian Susan Porter Benson, "during the Depression [store managers] asserted firmly that it was time to eliminate the 'frills' of more prosperous times."[2] Buying these burdensome in-house department store delivery operations was one important way by which UPS grew during its first decade and a half in the New York City metropolitan area.

Along with leaping into New York's bustling and crowded retail industry, Casey moved the national headquarters of UPS to New

York, to a location above the hub at 331 East 38th Street, where it remained for many years to come.[3] UPS was no longer a provincial business. By the end of the 1930s, the company would succeed in making itself an indispensable part of New York's retail industry and serve as the delivery company for over 350 of the city's leading retail businesses.[4]

"SNOOTY"

Casey also brought to New York his strangely austere and obsessive personality, which became increasingly out of sync with the reality of his ballooning personal wealth. He moved into the Waldorf-Astoria Hotel on Park Avenue, which was at the time the most luxurious and internationally famous hotel in the United States. He shared a floor with the visiting Duke and Duchess of Windsor, the future king and queen of England. Greg Niemann writes in *Big Brown* that Casey was somewhat embarrassed by his growing wealth and concerned that the Waldorf was too "snooty" a place for him. He even polled his management staff and asked them about the propriety of his living at the hotel. His grand residence notwithstanding, Casey maintained a "frugal," "thrifty" image. Niemann portrays his sparse, saintly New York office as "a small stark room, occupied only by a green metal desk, several chairs, and a coat tree. Except for the few papers he was working on and a metal model of a UPS package car, the desk was always bare."[5] This image of modesty is still prized by UPS.

After the company began hiring drivers and package handlers, UPS signed a contract with Local 804 that established cooperation between the company and union officials that had been pioneered on the West Coast and was closely identified with Seattle Teamster leader Dave Beck. The International Brotherhood of Teamsters had granted a local union charter that created Local 804 in the 1930s.[6] Although it was not chartered to exclusively represent UPS workers, the local counted over 1,800 New York UPSers in its ranks by the end of the 1930s.[7] During the next several decades the absolute number and proportion of UPSers in Local 804 grew, making it the giant UPS local it is today.[8] During this decade, the Teamsters

Union as a whole was going through a fundamental transformation of its membership and structure. The US working class in the 1930s engaged in history-changing struggles that created the first stable mass industrial unions in the country's history. The Teamsters were not immune to this change, but it came not from the crusty leadership circle around Teamster president Dan Tobin but from the pioneering revolutionary socialist leaders of the Minneapolis Teamsters.[9]

Niemann makes the fanciful declaration that "the 1930s were a time of great labor unrest in the United States, [but] UPS weathered through because of a corporate culture based on family-like relationships."[10] However, the reality was very different; relations between Local 804 members and the New York management of UPS have always been stormy, and conflicts have been fought out on the picket line. One of the first Local 804 strikes took place on Monday, November 13, 1939, after members walked off the job the previous Friday night to protest the suspension of "John Fargos, a twenty-year-old belt boy, employed to sort merchandize."[11] From the one-sided, pro-company press account, UPS appeared to have violated the grievance procedure in disciplining a union member and, in response, union members walked out—despite the no-strike agreement in their contract. Union members went back to work with the disciplinary case slated for arbitration. This one small incident shows what many UPS Teamsters recognize to this very day: the ongoing battle between union members and management over workplace rights.

During World War II, as inflation ate away at the living standards of working-class people across the country, the leaders of the two large union federations, the AFL and the CIO, pledged not to strike for the duration of the war effort. This signaled to corporate America that most union leaders would not strike to defend their hard-won gains of previous years. In spite of this enormous pressure, Local 804 members went on strike against UPS for two and a half weeks in June 1942, stopping the deliveries of 100,000 packages at 375 stores in the New York metropolitan area. The strike, according to the *New York Times*, followed the "suspension of 315 drivers for refusal to do overtime."[12] Then, very quickly, other issues, including wage increases to keep up with wartime inflation and jurisdictional disputes with other local unions, came to the forefront.[13] On May 16, 1945, a week after the end of World War II in Europe, 1,400 Teamsters went on strike against UPS throughout New York City, Long Island, Westchester, and parts of New Jersey and Connecticut. The Teamsters had been working without a new contract. The key issues were wage increases, better working conditions and medical benefits, and the suspension of sixty-five workers for refusing to work a sixth day.[14] The strike ended with the suspended workers compensated for lost time and the issue of excessive overtime subject to contract negotiations.[15]

A WORKING-CLASS CITY

These skirmishes between UPS and Local 804 were part of a larger emerging battle between capital and labor to shape the post–World War II world. In 1946 the battle exploded into open warfare. Historian Sharon Smith observes that workers "who had risked their lives fighting in the war returned home to a recession economy and, in many cases, to find that they'd lost their jobs. Those who still had jobs faced sharply lower wages. During the war years, productivity had risen 11 percent, but average hourly raises had totaled only 0.6 percent. In addition, four million women workers who had landed industrial jobs during the war years were thrown out of work immediately afterwards." Overall, notes Smith, the "first six months of 1946 marked 'the most concentrated period of labor-management strife in the country's history,' according to the U.S. Bureau of Labor Statistics."[16] The big battalions of militant unionized workers in steel, auto, packinghouse, and electrical industries were all on strike at the same time in 1946.

New York rivaled all of the great industrial cities of the Midwest for the militancy displayed by union workers during this period. "At the end of World War II," according to historian Joshua Freeman,

> New York was a working-class city. In 1946, of the 3.3 million employed New Yorkers, less than 700,000 were proprietors, managers, officials, professionals, or semiprofessionals. The other 2.6 million men and women neither owned the businesses for which they worked nor had substantial authority over their operations. They were, to use an old-fashioned term, proletarians. By them-

selves they made up one-third of the city's population of nearly eight million. Along with their husbands, wives, and children they were a clear majority.[17]

There were few categories of workers that weren't impacted by the strike fever that gripped New Yorkers. Freeman notes that "New York strikes during the year after the war included a week-long walkout by ten thousand painters; a four-week strike by seven thousand members of the American Communications Association that disrupted telegraph communication into and out of the city; and a 114-day strike against the Brooklyn-based Mergenthaler Co., the largest maker of linotype equipment in the country."[18]

Within this heady atmosphere, UPS bought Macy's delivery service. Macy's, the jewel in the crown of New York's retail trade, was the city's oldest and most venerated department store.[19] Macy's sold its delivery service as part of a postwar cost-cutting plan. It would have seemed a rather innocuous change, but new and long-standing grievances exploded into public view after the purchase. Historian Daniel Opler describes the dramatic effect the change had on workers:

> Unlike Macy's delivery workers, who were members of RWDSU [Retail, Wholesale and Department Store Union] Local 1, UPS had a closed-shop contract with the AFL-affiliated Teamsters. The delivery workers, furious that their union had been changed without their consent, declared themselves on strike, and many workers in Local 1-S adamantly refused to cross the picket lines at both the main 34th Street store and the Parkchester branch. The strike quickly became a bitter and violent one, with frequent battles outside Macy's warehouses as police tried to escort UPS trucks past picket lines. On at least one occasion the UPS truck drivers got to the Macy's warehouse by ramming through a line of picketers, landing two strikers in the hospital. On other occasions, mounted police rode into the crowds outside the store with horses, scattering strikers so that the UPS trucks could get through the line. Bitter though it was, the strike was also brief. Within two weeks, Macy's managers backed down and agreed to pay the delivery workers any difference between what the workers had made working for Macy's and what UPS paid its employees."[20]

A temporary truce was worked out between the new members of

the Teamsters and Macy's. However, the Local 804 executive board appeared oblivious to the rage boiling underneath them.

Militant strikes continued to rock New York. A "series of trucking strikes culminating in a September 1946 walkout by twelve thousand Teamsters [led] to empty grocery store shelves and factory closings," writes Freeman.[21] On September 13, 1946, the Teamsters held a wildcat strike at UPS. "Deliveries of consumer purchases by 375 large retail stores in the metropolitan area, including all the major department stores, were halted," according to the *New York Times*, "when 1,000 of the 1,700 drivers and helpers of the United Parcel Service staged an outlaw strike in a dispute over payment for time lost because of the general truckmen's strike."[22] The executive board of Local 804 attacked the actions of its members as "foolish and futile" and sent letters to 3,000 members of the local, ordering them to return to work. The same *New York Times* article reported that "a rank and file committee, which claimed to represent the 800 former Macy's drivers and helpers, called on officials of the [United Parcel] service on Wednesday and demanded to be paid, asserting that the service and the former employer had made a separate commitment to the former Macy's employees."

"A PROTRACTED UNION REBELLION"

The Local 804 executive board spurned a meeting with the rebel rank-and-file committee, even though many of the grievances of the strikers were directly related to a recently concluded agreement between the local union and UPS.[23] In the days that followed, the rebel rank-and-file committee spread the "outlaw strike" to more than 2,000 UPS drivers and package handlers. Leonard Geiger, a former Macy's worker and official of the RWDSU who demonstrated immense skills mobilizing and leading this rebellion inside Local 804, led the rebel committee. The continuing citywide Teamster strike was the biggest display of Teamster power in many years in New York City.[24] The tenacity and determination of the UPS strikers impressed the reporters of the *New York Times*:

> Three hundred and seventy-five of the leading retail stores of the area, which previously had escaped the more serious effects of the

teamsters' strike, faced a week of curtailed businesses as the outlaw strike among United Parcel Service employees spread to 2,000
employees and moved into the status of a protracted union rebellion. . . . The metropolitan area's retail stores . . . were drawn deeper
into the strike picture when more than 2,000 shouting, stamping
employees of the United Parcel Service, members of Local 804 of
the Teamsters Union, refused to go back to work and voted to press
their demands against the service through an insurgent "rank and
file" committee.[25]

Edward Conway, president of Local 804, proved helpless in
the face of the revolt of most his membership and refused to meet
with Geiger and others on the insurgent rank- and-file committee.[26]
Despite the intervention of Teamster president Dan Tobin, who
ordered the strikers back to work, and hysterical attacks in court by
department store attorney Joseph Proskauer, who called the strike
"the atomic bomb of industrial disputes," the strikers remained firm.

In early November 1946, a settlement was reached.[27] The rebel
strikers won "a 33 and a half cent hourly wage increase, a forty-four-
hour work week, night differentials and arbitration of differences
concerning retroactive pay, new wages for inside works, and the date
of a future wage reopening, if any." However, on the issue of "voluntary overtime—one of the most difficult issues in the dispute—the
company retained considerable latitude."[28] It was the longest strike
at UPS until 1976.[29]

After the 1946 strike, Geiger was appointed an organizer for
Local 804, and in 1949, he was elected president. Geiger quickly
accommodated himself to the most backward forces in the union.
He became first an ally of Dave Beck and then of Jimmy Hoffa.
In March 1957, the US Senate's "Rackets Committee" broadcast
lurid revelations of corruption and gangsterism in the Teamsters
on national television and radio, and news of the findings was soon
splashed across all of the nation's major newspapers. At the same
time, Geiger attempted to push through a dues increase of one dol-
lar per month for all members of Local 804. Inflamed by these revelations and their own officers' "outlandish living," over 1,500 Local
804 members attended their union meeting. Geiger, who had led
a rank-and-file rebellion a decade earlier, now faced a rebellion of
his own. It was a rowdy meeting. He tried to delay the vote but was

shouted down by the membership. "Vote, vote, vote!" they shouted until a vote was called. The dues increase was defeated 1,400 to 100.[30] The members of Local 804 were proving to be as independent-minded and militant as ever. Geiger would be dead from a heart attack within five months.[31]

Among the newly hired drivers at UPS in the final years of the Geiger administration was Ron Carey, whose father, Joseph, was a veteran UPS driver. Ron Carey was just out of the marine corps when he was hired in Queens in 1956, and in 1958 he became a union steward. It would take the better part of the next decade before Carey was elected president of Local 804 in 1967.[32]

BIG BROWN

From the late 1950s through 1970, UPS came into focus as the company we recognize today, with its massive fleet of distinctive dark brown trucks, which are omnipresent in America's commercial and residential neighborhoods. "Big Brown," the popular nickname coined at the time for UPS, captured its well-crafted image as a powerful, efficient, and profit-driven machine. However, inside UPS hubs across the country and for its drivers on the streets, the company's aggressive management, relentless drives for higher productivity, and peculiar military-style culture put enormous pressure on workers in order to capture more of the shipping market. The goal of UPS management was nothing less than to become the world's biggest shipping company.

In this quest UPS had an important ally: the bulk of officials in the Teamsters union. Until the late 1970s, there was no national contract between UPS and the Teamsters. UPS management dealt on a daily basis with local Teamster officials, whom they viewed as little more than low-level supervisors, answerable only to them, and whom they expected to police the union rank and file. This set the stage for a huge rift between Teamster officers and members at UPS. Stan Weir, writing in his classic account of the rank-and-file revolts of the 1960s, "USA: The Labor Revolt," declared from the vantage point of 1967:

> The rank-and-file union revolts that have been developing in the

industrial workplaces since the early 1950s are now plainly visible. Like many of their compatriots, American workers are faced with paces, methods, and conditions of work that are increasingly intolerable. Their union leaders are not sensitive to these conditions. In thousands of industrial establishments across the nation, workers have developed informal underground unions. . . . Led by natural on-the-job leaders, they conduct daily guerilla skirmishes with their employers and often against their official union representatives as well. These groups are the power base for the insurgencies from below that in the last three years [1964 to 1967] have ended or threatened official careers of long standing.[33]

Where do UPSers fit into this picture drawn by Weir? Many UPSers (and Teamsters in general) by the late 1950s were increasingly dissatisfied with the state of their union. Congressional investigations, federal prosecutions of Teamster officials (including the conviction of Teamster president Dave Beck for corruption), media exposés of widespread corruption, gangsterism in the union, and sweetheart deals with the bosses shocked and angered rank-and-file members who spent their days, unlike many of their union officers, doing difficult and exhausting work.[34]

In New York, the death of Teamster Local 804 president Leonard Geiger in August 1957 opened up a period of political rivalry and strike action in the local union. Geiger, a former Macy's department store employee and militant strike leader in 1946, was elected president in 1949 and became extremely unpopular with his members during the course of the 1950s. A clear rift had opened between the rank-and-file members of Local 804 and their officers that would not close anytime soon. In December 1957, Jack Mahoney was elected president of Local 804 and Thomas Simcox vice president.[35] Neither Mahoney nor Simcox could satisfy their members' desire for a cleaner, more militant union. Soon after his election to local president, Mahoney came under intense pressure to distance himself from his deceased and discredited predecessor, Leonard Geiger, in upcoming contract negotiations with UPS. Negotiations broke down, and Local 804 went on strike in the run-up to Christmas in 1958—UPS's busiest and most vulnerable time of the year due to the pressure to deliver packages by the holiday deadline.

TWENTY WILDCAT STRIKES

A. H. Raskin, the *New York Times*'s revered labor reporter, captures something of the stirrings going on in the local union at the time, but he didn't see the big picture. Raskin was a liberal sympathetic to the labor movement, but the Christmas strike led him to bemoan the "cost of democracy" in the unions. "The United Parcel Service strike provides a reminder," he wrote, "that increased union democracy sometimes can have its painful side for employers and the public." Unfortunately, for Raskin, Local 804 members had "taken to heart the maxim that the rank and file should be supreme in its own organization."[36] While Raskin decried former Local 804 president Geiger as "a virtual czar in the local union," he didn't want a return to czardom. Still, he wasn't happy: "Since [Geiger's] death, rival factions have been having a field day in the organization, and rank-and-file expression has become a watchword. In the last year there have been twenty wildcat strikes. In negotiations with the United Parcel Service, eleven shop stewards were added to the union's executive board to assure more direct representation for the workers."[37]

Rank and filers' demands, which included the right to a veto power over where new UPS hubs were to be built, baffled Raskin. The virtues of union democracy, Raskin complained, "become somewhat cloudy when union officers and their rank-and-file watchdogs in collective bargaining indicate such fear of being accused of 'selling out' that their demands never drop out of the stratosphere of unattainability."[38] Labor reporters may not be interested if a union leader "sells out," but rank and filers who elect and pay such people usually are. A new era of labor militancy was just beginning, but Raskin couldn't see it yet. He was mainly annoyed that his packages weren't getting delivered.

Jack Mahoney served one term as Local 804 president and was replaced by his vice president, Thomas Simcox. Simcox served two terms in office, but he was also unable to satisfy the demands of his increasingly militant and independent membership. The disputes between UPS and the rank and file of Local 804 also began to move from a local conflict to an issue with national implications for the Teamsters and UPS. In the early morning hours of Monday, May 13, 1962, Local 804 and several other New York–area local Teamster unions went on strike against UPS. "The decision followed the overwhelming rejection of a final company offer made to three of the four locals involved. The membership of Local 804, in secret balloting, turned it down by a vote of 2,273 to 93," according to the *New York Times*.[39] The *Times* also reported that Local 804 president Simcox "had indicated opposition to the strike," and that the "strike decision represented a repudiation of James R. Hoffa, international union president."[40]

Hoffa had sent his personal representative Fleming Campbell to a joint meeting of Locals 804 and 183 but received a hostile reception. "His plea to the members to accept the employer offer was shouted down by most of the 1,500 men present."[41] The old contract had expired on March 31, but it was extended while negotiations continued. The younger workers, drivers, and package handlers alike in Local 804 were eager to take on the company and began to act independently of the local officials. They staged short-lived wildcat strikes the previous Tuesday and Wednesday but returned to work soon afterwards.[42] The strike lasted seven weeks into the beginning of July, and there were several attempts to bring the strike to an end. But it was the younger workers who led the way in voting down a company offer that would have permitted UPS to hire part-time evening workers; a "reasonable performance" clause was also objected to. The vote was a close one: 1,195 against and 1,011 for. The younger workers were the margin of difference in voting down the offer because, according to *Times* reporter Ralph Katz, "the younger men feared an extension of the use of part-time workers."[43]

Unfortunately, the younger workers in Local 804 couldn't overcome the intransigence of their president, Thomas Simcox, the pressure from UPS and Hoffa, and the unwillingness of older workers to stay on the picket line, so the membership of Local 804 "accepted terms they had twice previously rejected for settlement of the long walkout."[44] Though a new militancy was on display by the young workers of Local 804, the introduction of part-time work was an ominous development. Hoffa had negotiated a contract that same year that introduced part-time work into UPS hubs in Southern California. Though Local 804 had its own separate contract, Simcox had capitulated to the demands of Hoffa and UPS for the expansion of part-time work that would eventually destroy most full-time jobs inside UPS hubs during the next two decades. Among the younger drivers and package handlers who participated in these struggles was Ron Carey.[45]

"CONCERNED ABOUT THE WAY THINGS WERE BEING HANDLED"

The Carey family's lineage at UPS was much longer than those of many UPS senior managers. Joseph Carey retired in January 1976 after forty-five years on the job as a driver in the Bronx, placing him among the first generation of UPS drivers hired in New York after the company made the leap from the West Coast. Ron Carey was hired as a driver in 1955, and two years later was elected a shop steward; soon after, he enrolled in a nighttime college labor-management relation class.[46] If you add up the time that the two Careys worked at UPS, plus Ron Carey's time as a local union president and international union officer, it comes to a working relationship with the company that totalled nearly sixty-seven years. Ron Carey had a deeper knowledge of UPS and its operations than many other Teamster officials or activists of his generation.

In 1963, however, the year following the defeat of the strike, Carey was twenty-eight years old and an eight-year veteran of UPS, who was "concerned about the way things were being handled" by the Simcox administration, according to journalist Steven Brill. Carey had "always dreamt" of running for business agent, a sometimes elected and usually appointed union representative who processes grievances and other contract violations. He finally ran in 1963 and lost. Two years later, he ran again and lost. The third time proved to be a charm. In 1967, Carey challenged the Simcox administration with his "Security and Future" slate for the Local 804 executive board, with Carey as the candidate for president, the most powerful position in the local union. He defeated Simcox but not without a last-minute effort by UPS to knock Carey out of the race. Carey later recounted to Brill in *The Teamsters*, the book that gave Carey his first national exposure, that a friend in UPS management tipped him off that "the company was happy with people who were then running Local 804, and that they were going to get Carey out of his UPS job so he wouldn't be eligible to run."[47]

Carey expected the worst, and when he was asked to step into the dispatch supervisor's office, he brought along a briefcase with a tape recorder in it. The meeting began with the supervisor declaring, "Ron, I'm afraid we're going to have to ask for your resignation." Carey asked why should he resign, and his supervisor replied, "because we have evidence, Ron, that you've been having an affair with another woman. And, if you don't resign, we're going to have to turn that evidence over to your wife."

He then asked the supervisor to repeat what he said, and then opened the briefcase to reveal the tape recorder. This clumsy attempt at blackmail not only failed, according to Brill, but Carey "won a lot of votes that year by playing the tape at meetings during the campaign."[48] Carey's election proved a turning point in the history of Local 804 that would have long-term consequences for the entire Teamsters union.

UPS PLAYS HARDBALL

UPS's clumsy attempt to knock Carey out of the race for local union office was not its only effort that year to clamp down on militancy in the Teamsters. In Philadelphia, long a stronghold of anti-Hoffa Teamsters, Locals 107 and 169 held a strike against UPS in May 1967 and stayed on the picket line for three months. Two months earlier, Hoffa entered federal prison in Lewisburg, Pennsylvania, and the future of the union was very much up in the air. UPS used the opportunity to strike back at the Philadelphia Teamsters. It announced on July 12, 1967, that it was "discontinuing operations" in the Philadelphia area and fired 1,500 of its employees.[49] UPS returned to doing business in Philadelphia three years later, in June 1970. It is hard to imagine UPS doing such a thing today given how integrated it is with the retail and industrial economy and its long-term relationship with key customers. Yet UPS used this and many other hardball tactics repeatedly through the years to keep the Teamster rank and file under control.

Where else did we find Stan Weir's "natural on-the-job leaders" conducting "daily guerilla skirmishes with their employers and often against their official union representatives as well" at UPS in the late 1960s?[50] In Louisville, Kentucky, Vince Meredith, the chief shop steward at UPS, built a virtual "union within a union" at Local 89 with a network of supporters across the state.[51] In Chicago, two young African American hub workers, Bennie Jackson and Freeman Wilson, organized and led a wildcat strike at UPS's metropolitan hub, located south of the Loop, on Jefferson Street, in 1969. The strike was notable not only for taking on Louie Peick, the mobbed-up and extremely dangerous leader of their Local 705 but also for the strikers' decision to go to the nearby University of Illinois at Chicago (UIC) campus to appeal for support from the campus's radical student movement.[52] It was one of the first connections between student radicals and workplace militants at UPS and a political development that would have a profound impact on Teamsters politics in the 1970s.

CHAPTER 3
THE RISE OF
THE "QUIET GIANT"

Plenty of people have seen United Parcel Service's brown trucks. Few realize that UPS is one of the biggest shipping companies in the country.
—Forbes, 1970[1]

UPS faced a crisis in the late 1940s and early 1950s. The company's traditional business model was increasingly out of sync with the rapidly changing retail business market. The crisis was so severe that the very future of the company was at stake. Yet not only did UPS survive the crisis, it dramatically shifted its business strategy, and during the two decades that followed, it emerged as one of the rising giants of the shipping industry.[2] What was the source of the crisis, and how did UPS survive it and prosper?

Following the end of World War II, the domination of the retail trade by big city department stores came to an abrupt end as the US population migrated to the suburbs.[3] The suburban shopping mall, ubiquitous today, was a new and conspicuous symbol of the changing shopping habits of Americans during the period of postwar economic prosperity. Historian Lizabeth Cohen, in her seminal book *A Consumers' Republic: The Politics of Mass Consumption in Postwar America*, points out that in the two-decade period from 1939 to 1961, the suburban share of the total metropolitan retail trade leapt from a miniscule 4 percent, in 1939, to a commanding 60 percent, in 1961.[4] The new suburban shopping malls were specifically built with massive parking lots to accommodate this new generation of car-owning shoppers.[5] Suburban as well as urban shoppers increasingly took their packages home with them, virtually eliminating the need for home deliveries by specialty delivery companies like UPS.

PARCEL POST

Until 1961, UPS still emblazoned their drivers' caps with the slogan "The Delivery System for Stores of Quality"—a quaint reminder of how UPS had established itself. However, the retail business had dramatically changed. UPS founder and still-serving CEO Jim Casey saw the potential for a different type of business market that the company could gobble up, observing that "the vast field of distribution for wholesalers and manufacturers appears to be wide open for us."[6] This is not to say that UPS didn't maintain profitable connections with many high-end department stores.[7] The future of UPS lay in becoming a general freight company, a "common carrier" shipper in the industry lingo, a much broader business that connected manufacturers, wholesale distributors, and customers. Within this market UPS specialized in the delivery of small parcels ("parcel post") packages weighing one pound or more. UPS already had a certain expertise in this market because of its years in the department store delivery business.

Parcel post became a battlefield in the 1950s and 1960s between UPS and its competitors—the United States Post Office being the biggest—and other long-established firms like Railway Express Agency.[8] The post office had begun a package service back in 1913 and had a virtual lock on the market. But in a blunder of historic proportions, it announced in 1952 that it would no longer accept parcels over twenty pounds. This ceded to UPS what eventually became a huge market.[9] In order to capture this market and win the right to do business in the forty-eight contiguous states, UPS needed to become a truly national company.

The freight industry, like many other businesses during the 1950s and 1960s, was far more regulated by the federal and state governments than can be imagined today. This stricter regulation was an important contributing factor in the strength of the Teamsters.[10] The federal Interstate Commerce Commission (ICC), for example, was created in 1887, but its jurisdiction was expanded to regulate the interstate trucking business. The equivalent agencies on the state level regulated the conduct and scope of freight companies for intrastate trucking. Many right-wing ideologues and their corporate masters portrayed these decades of business regulation as a long dark night of tyranny and persecution of business. But consumer advocate and later presidential candidate Ralph Nader exposed this corporate grousing (and later right-wing fantasy) as the fiction that it was. In 1970, a team of his young lawyers ("Nader's Raiders") issued a scathing report on the ICC, charging that the eleven commission members were "political hacks" appointed to their positions as "political payoffs," and were "unqualified and weak." The so-called regulators gave the freight companies pretty much what they wanted, and in return the freight companies offered the ICC commissioners what Nader called "deferred bribes." Eleven out of the twelve commissioners, who had left the commission from 1958 to 1970, got jobs as lawyers directly or indirectly representing the freight companies before the ICC.[11] The so-called regulation of the freight industry was a racket, the worst type of "crony capitalism."

"AN ALMOST ANONYMOUS CHARACTER"

In 1953, UPS acquired common carrier franchises in Chicago and New York. It already had that status in Los Angeles, inherited from a merger long ago. "Also in 1953, in California," according to business historians and journalists Mike Brewster and Frederick Dalzell, "UPS received authorization to extend its reach into the wholesale trade in San Francisco and Oakland, and to connect its Los Angeles and San Francisco markets with wholesale service."[12] This was a huge boost to its West Coast operations, and by 1962 California became the most populous state in the country, a potentially huge new market for the company's services. When UPS celebrated its twenty-fifth anniversary of doing business in the New York metropolitan area in July 1955, it coincided with its 750 millionth delivery in the New York area. It was a moment of transition in the company's history, with the future far from certain. The *New York Times* reported on the events and picked up on a characteristic of the company that would be its trademark for the next two decades: "In keeping with the almost anonymous character of United Parcel Service, the identity of the specific milestone package will be unknown to the store, the customer and the company itself."[13]

This "almost anonymous character" was a glimpse into the methodical, stealthful way that UPS built itself into the country's leading shipping company. It avoided media coverage, did little advertising, and revealed next to nothing about its top officers outside the company. UPS systematically worked its way state by state and through the ICC until it snuck up on its competitors.

The federal government also aided the development of UPS as a national company—and other interstate freight companies as well—with the construction of the massive interstate highway system. Begun during the administration of World War II hero Dwight D. Eisenhower, the interstate system is the vast network of freeways that connects all parts of the continental United States. The Federal Aid Highway Act of 1956 authorized the construction of the highway system, and the total cost of construction was estimated to be over $425 billion by 2012. The system of highways has a total length of 46,000 miles.[14] UPS could not have emerged as the giant of the shipping industry without this huge subsidy from the federal government; no consortium of private investors could have built such a system. As late as 1991, UPS remained critically dependent on the interstate highway system when it built its vast Chicago Area Consolidation Hub ("CACH"). The size of thirty-seven football fields, the hub is located fifteen miles southwest of Chicago, just off Interstate 294.[15] The CACH employs around 11,000 people, and as many as 1.3 million packages pass through the facility each day, making it the most important ground package hub in the UPS system.[16]

As the 1950s transitioned into the 1960s, there were two important developments at UPS. Company founder James E. Casey retired as chief executive officer in 1962. However, Casey would remain on the board of directors until his death in 1983 at the age of ninety-five. For many workers at UPS, Casey's retirement was a turning point, marking the moment when working conditions began rapidly deteriorating. The sixties also saw UPS emerge from the fringes of the freight industry with an explosive growth in business and profitability. UPS doubled its revenues between 1964 and 1968, from $200 million to $400 million, and simultaneously doubled its profits to $5.5 million. As an enthusiastic *Forbes* reporter wrote in a 1970 profile of the company, "there doesn't seem to be any prospect of a slowdown ahead."[17] By 1970, UPS did business in thirty-one states and had just gotten permission from the ICC to add nine more midwestern states to its growing empire. Over the next decade UPS completed its conquest of the forty-eight contiguous states, and then Alaska and Hawaii.

It was getting harder to conceal UPS's prominence in the industry. "Plenty of people have seen United Parcel Service's brown trucks. Few realize that UPS is one of the biggest shipping companies in the country," *Forbes* wrote, dubbing the company the "Quiet Giant." The *Forbes* profile also revealed some of the thinking of top management: UPS "officials believed only one parcel shipping company could exist in the United States, and it hoped that keeping a low profile would prevent anyone from copying its methods." The *Forbes* profile also praised UPS for its "uncommon shrewdness," in scaling "its operations to fit its basic market. REA [Railway Express Agency] and the truckers can have the big-ticket shipments. UPS won't take any package that weighs more than 50 pounds—its average package weighs 10 pounds and is about the size of a briefcase. This means every package can be sorted on a conveyor belt and easily carried by a single deliveryman. Its average charge is only about 80 cents."[18]

The biggest losers in the package wars were the US Post Office and REA. By 1969, while the post office continued to deliver one billion packages annually, UPS had made its way to delivering 500 million packages annually, a staggering amount, and that share would continue to grow. In effect, UPS became the *other* post office. In 1968, UPS's revenue was $400 million, or 55 percent greater than the largest freight company, Consolidated Freightways. That same year REA lost $40 million.[19] A major reshuffling of position was taking place in the shipping industry. UPS had made a successful shift during the 1950s and 1960s from being a relatively small, very specialized delivery company, and now it was on its way to becoming a giant in the industry.

REBELLION IN LOCAL 804

Rebellion had been brewing for years in New York's Local 804 against the complacent pro-company leadership of Thomas Simcox before Carey took office in early 1968. Soon afterwards, he found himself not only in a contract fight with UPS but also facing a hostile Teamster officialdom that conspired to undermine him. Just to make sure that everyone understood where the power brokers in the Teamsters stood, Teamsters General President Frank Fitzsimmons appointed Carey's defeated opponent Thomas Simcox to a newly created job with the New York Joint Council of the Teamsters. Journalist Steve Brill wrote that the appointment "did not sit well with the members who had voted him out or with the insurgents who had replaced him."[20] But there was little they could do about it. The Jimmy Hoffa–crafted Teamster constitution of the late 1950s gave the general president of the Teamsters extraordinary powers, and what he couldn't do "constitutionally," his Mafia friends would do by other means.[21]

In his 1978 book, *The Teamsters,* Brill captures this transition period in Carey's life with all its excitement, uncertainty, and looming difficulties with the Teamster old guard. "He had come to the UPS talks that day in 1968," recounted Brill, "a thirty-three-year-old package driver who had hardly had time to get used to not wearing brown all day. He was eager to deliver on the campaign promises his 'Security and Future' ticket had made for tough but reasonable negotiating that would produce better wages and benefits with fewer strikes."[22] Carey was especially determined to win a "twenty-five-and-out" retirement clause in the contract that would allow UPS workers to retire after twenty-five years of service with a full pension. Many UPS contracts had a thirty-and-out deal. Yet when Carey appeared at contract negotiations, he found that the nefarious Fleming Campbell and another staffer had been appointed by the mobbed-up New York Joint Council to "help" him, according to Brill.

"Help," of course, meant undermining. After suffering their annoying presence for several meetings and their pathetic attempt to force him to accept an inferior contract, Carey stuck to his demands, and the New York Joint Council representatives stormed out of negotiations, calling him a "psycho."[23] Despite his effort to win better benefits without strikes, Carey called a strike on May 2, 1968, and four thousand UPS workers hit the picket line. Along with the demand for a twenty-five-and-out retirement clause, Carey was also resisting the further increase in the number and proportion of part-time workers.[24] Several weeks into the strike, Teamsters General President Fitzsimmons made a last-ditch effort to derail Carey and ordered a vote on UPS's last proposal. Fitzsimmons was calculating that the weeks on strike had made the strikers weary and eager to get back work. He was wrong. Carey told his members that it was Fitzsimmons's idea and that he was opposed to the company's offer. The membership overwhelmingly rejected the offer, and the strike lasted nine weeks. Carey won a big victory after UPS capitulated to the union's demands.

1968

The year 1968 was a tumultuous one for Ron Carey and Local 804, but it was also part of a wider transformation of American society. Civil rights, Black Power, the Vietnam antiwar movement, and women's liberation revolutionized political, cultural, and workplace life in the United States. Women entered the workforce in larger numbers in fields that weren't traditionally considered "women's work," such as auto, steel, and in fast-growing UPS. Vietnam veterans, who had their fill of the petty tyranny of military life, were not willing to put up with it again on the job. Many radicals who cut their teeth in the civil rights and antiwar movements began to look toward the rank-and-file struggles of US industrial workers as the next step in their political evolution. As early as 1966, for example, Kim Moody, a leader in the Independent Socialist Clubs and one of the future founders of *Labor Notes* magazine, put forward a position paper at that year's SDS convention entitled "Toward the Working Class" in which he argued that "the working class is not the only group that must struggle to revolutionize American society, but it is a group that cannot be left out of this struggle."[25]

Carey was no political radical; in fact, he told Steve Brill that he considered himself a political conservative. (Carey voted for Nixon in 1972 and Ford in 1976.) Historian Nelson Lichtenstein has argued that the radicalism of the era gave "a radical edge to many shop floor struggles, especially after 1967."[26] No one, including Ron Carey, who wanted to lead a clean, fighting local union against the machinations of the Mafia and UPS could be unaffected by it. In 1970, Carey led an unlikely political strike—one of several of the era—after Republican Richard Nixon tried to whip up public support for his policies in Vietnam (while simultaneously demonizing the antiwar movement) by asking his "silent majority" to wear American flags to publicly display their patriotism. UPS drivers in Carey's local began to spontaneously wear American flag pins or buttons on their uniforms during work hours. In response, many black UPS drivers began wearing black liberation buttons on their uniforms. Management ignored the pins until customers began to complain about them, and then UPS fired twenty workers for wearing various buttons. A wildcat strike began on July 28, 1970, in support of the fired drivers, and soon after, Carey made the strike official.[27]

BLACK POWER

The strike lasted eleven days. The courts came down hard on the local union and its top officers, including Carey, who were heavily fined for violating the no-strike clause of the local contract. Carey and striking workers rallied at New York City Hall where he told the crowd, "We are fighting for the American flag and the pride of a man in his country or his race."[28] In the settlement that followed, UPS rehired the fired workers and allowed American flag buttons to be worn, but the question of other buttons was submitted to arbitration.[29] Carey ended up paying only a $500 fine. The "political edge" to workplace struggles that Lichtenstein talked about was primarily due to the increasing presence and radicalism of black workers in industrial workplaces. Carey's local by 1970 was 35 percent black.[30] Carey frankly admitted to Steve Brill that he followed the lead of a black shop steward on the button fight. "A shop steward, a black guy, at UPS had told the men they could wear the Black Power emblem, and I felt I couldn't afford not to back him."[31] Even though Carey expressed regret about the "button strike," it was an important fight for free speech in the workplace and probably saved him from being seen as another racist Teamsters official, as so many were.

In a funny twist of fate, while black workers in the late 1960s and 1970s were the most militant force in workplace struggles, UPS was under enormous pressure to hire black workers (and later women) to positions that they were previously denied because of past racist and sexists hiring practices. According to Robert Putnam and Lewis Feldstein, "in the mid-1960s, the United Parcel Service was overwhelmingly an organization of white males, many of them Irish Catholic, many with a background in the military."[32] Greg Niemann also pulls no punches about UPS's racist policies: "By a long-standing tradition many companies did not hire minorities and UPS was one of them. UPS found it easier to go along with the majority of white America, and its managers indulged in stereotyping minorities rather than hiring them."[33]

The first phase of the civil rights movement had won significant legal victories for African Americans and women, though these victories went unrealized in many workplaces. Also, civil rights activists beginning in the early 1960s began to focus on major corporations who refused to hire black workers, including UPS.[34] UPS, which was primarily based in large urban areas, was conspicuous in its absence of black drivers in cities with large and growing black populations. During the urban rebellions that followed the assassination of Martin Luther King Jr. in April 1968, UPS package cars were kept off the streets and did not service their customers in Cleveland, Los Angeles, Baltimore, and Washington, DC.[35]

"SHAPING CHANGE"

While Niemann doesn't pull his punches on the past hiring practices of UPS, he tries his best to explain the company's changing approach to "responding sagaciously to change, and to *shaping* change." "Shaping change" can mean a lot of things, including undermining change or muting its effects. Aside from activists pounding on the door and demanding the hiring of black workers and women, another big motivating factor in changing UPS's hiring policies was a fear of lawsuits. The Equal Employment Opportunity Commission (EEOC), led by William H. Brown, a well-known African American attorney from Philadelphia, won a landmark case against corporate goliath AT&T. "The case was settled in early 1973," according to Niemann, "with a very expensive consent decree. It was a wake-up call to American industry."[36]

How expensive? AT&T was required to distribute $15 million to 13,000 women and 2,000 minority men, according to the EEOC, along with "$30 million in immediate pay increases for 36,000 women and minorities whose advancement in the Bell system had been hampered by discrimination."[37] UPS was not interested in suffering the same fate as AT&T, and its hiring policies changed dramatically.

To facilitate these changes, UPS put a more "progressive" face on the company. In 1972, James P. McLaughlin, whom Niemann describes as a "liberal," was promoted from chief operations officer to UPS president. Walter Hooke, a liberal labor relations expert brought in from outside the company in the early 1960s and promoted to national personnel manager in 1968, received greater support for the needed changes to hiring policies. William H. Brown, the feared chair of the EEOC, who had successfully defeated AT&T, returned to private practice in 1973, joining the Philadelphia law firm of Schnader Harrison Segal & Lewis LLP, UPS's long-standing legal counsel. Bernie Segal, a senior partner at the firm, had served on the board of directors of UPS for many years.[38] Segal could himself boast impeccable liberal and civil libertarian credentials. He worked with the Kennedy administration to initiate the Lawyers' Committee for Civil Rights Under Law to support civil rights activists in the Jim Crow South and the expansion of legal services to the poor, chairing President Lyndon Johnson's advisory committee on the National Legal Services Program. As a young lawyer in Philadelphia in 1953, he was part of a legal team that defended Communist Party members indicted under the repressive Smith Act.[39]

UPS "LIBERALISM"

But there were well-defined limits to Bernie Segal and UPS's "liberalism" in this era. Philadelphia was the same city where, in 1967, the company had tried to smash the militant Local 107 of the Teamsters by pulling out of the city, closing up its operations, and refusing to do business there for nearly three years. Segal barked that he hoped that Local 107 "will have control of its members the way other Teamster Unions do throughout the country."[40] It apparently was one thing to support civil rights outside the workplace, but quite another for workers to have power in the workplace, and if you had to use gangsters to keep the militants in line, so be it. William Brown was hired by Segal's firm, and, "shrewdly," according to Greg Niemann, "UPS had Brown assigned as counsel, developed a strong relationship, and in 1982, invited him to serve on the UPS board of directors. Mr. Brown was the first minority to do so."[41] In effect, UPS bought the coach of the competing team and put him to work for their side.

During this same era, UPS also began cultivating relationships with conservative, if not outright reactionary, institutions in the black community in order to mute the impact of more pro-union or radical influences. Walter Hooke, as early as 1962, began a relationship with the Urban League, one of the oldest and most pro-corporate organizations in the black community. Niemann recounts his time working as a UPS consultant at the Congress of Racial Equality (CORE) in Harlem during the early 1970s. CORE had been a heroic civil rights group that after 1968 saw its membership disintegrate under the leadership of the corrupt Roy Innis, who turned sharply to the right politically and became notorious for selling CORE's name for all sorts of corrupt corporate activities. Innis gained notoriety for supporting the infamously racist "Subway Gunman" Bernie Goetz in the 1980s.[42] UPS tried desperately to "shape change" for its own interests in this era, but despite its best efforts, the inclusion of more African Americans and women actually helped spur a greater militancy inside its hubs across the country.

CHAPTER 4

UPSURGE AT
THE TIGHTEST SHIP

Use the Union's Power
> —the slogan of *UPSurge*, a rank-and-file newspaper

UPS was shaken by an unprecedented militancy in its workforce from 1968 through 1976, when local and region-wide strikes shut down the company for months on end. This period of workplace rebellion throughout the Teamsters—what historian and former Teamster reform activist Dan La Botz calls "The Tumultuous Teamsters of the 1970s"—produced one of the most dynamic, though short-lived, rank-and-file movements of its time: UPSurge.[1] The very name UPSurge was a play on the company's ethos, according to *UPSurge* editor and package driver Anne Mackie, inverting its meaning from robotic efficiency to in-your-face rebellion.[2]

However, UPS didn't sit idly by when faced with this new rank-and-file challenge. It struck back hard with lockouts, aggressive bargaining, and the surveillance, harassment, and firing of activists. It also changed the nature of the workforce through the vast expansion of part-time work inside the hubs in an effort to weaken the union's rank and file.

By 1970, UPS was the single largest Teamster employer in the United States. Despite this large and growing presence, UPSers were not considered "real Teamsters" by the mobbed-up officers that

49

lorded over the membership, or even by many older Teamster rank and filers. UPSers were mocked as "Buster Browns" (because of the color of their uniforms and shoes) or were considered "lightweights" because of the small packages they handled.[3] The military-like dress uniforms of UPS drivers, complete with an uncomfortable bow tie, were a daily reminder of the arcane dress style of the company and a source of amusement to other Teamsters. The dress code produced one of the most significant battles at UPS in the late 1960s in Louisville, a strike led by Vince Meredith.

In 1964, Meredith began working as a package car driver in Louisville. Born in 1931 during the depth of the Great Depression, he joined the newly formed US Air Force when he turned nineteen. Meredith was stationed at one of the many bases that made up the archipelago of US military bases across occupied Japan. "He came to love the country," according to La Botz: "[He] learned to speak the language, and fell in love with a Japanese woman named Chiyo, and he decided he wanted to marry her. The chaplain warned him against marrying a Japanese woman, telling him that they would never be accepted in the United States. He re-enlisted and went back to Japan. Finally, he overcame the obstacles. 'It took me about thirty-eight months all together to get married: two tours.'"[4] Meredith's fights with such a powerful institution as the air force prepared him for his future battles with UPS.

After Meredith went to work at UPS, management eyed him for a supervisory position, but when he was offered the job, he turned it down. He later told La Botz in a interview in the late 1980s that he turned it down because "I'd seen too much" and UPS "don't show respect for a person." Meredith was elected a union steward within five months of being hired and eventually rose to chief steward.[5] Today looking back at pictures of UPS drivers with their bow ties can bring a smile to one's face—the images are a quaint reminder of a bygone era. But at the time they were a day-long annoyance to anyone who had to wear them while doing hard physical labor. The bow tie had to go, but it would take the threat of a statewide strike to get rid of it. Meredith described the scene:

> That bow tie was the hardest thing to get out of that first contract I negotiated. They give us a dollar-an-hour raise, in three years, and

didn't want to take the bow tie off. It was a strike issue, and we voted ninety-nine percent across the state of Kentucky to strike if we didn't lose the bow tie. Finally the division manager of the state of Kentucky came into the negotiations and said, "Take off the goddamned bow tie," and he walked out. And after that, in the next contract, across the whole United States the bow tie was gone.[6]

Meredith, like Ron Carey, was another one of Stan Weir's "natural on-the-job leaders." He refused an offer from the Local 89 president to become an appointed business agent after Meredith pointedly asked him, "'If you ask me to do something that I consider morally wrong, would I have to do it?' And he answered, 'Yes.' And I said, 'Well, I don't need your job.'"[7]

"We were the first ones in UPS to ever use the roving picket line," Meredith told La Botz. There were a half dozen wildcat strikes in Louisville, including the one to return Meredith to work, in the late 1960s and early 1970s, and not one union member lost their job—quite a stunning achievement.[8] Meredith and his crew during this time created their own defense fund to make sure that no Teamster ever lost a day's pay if UPS unfairly disciplined them. It was funded by weekly contributions and administered by Meredith and his supporters.[9] It was an unusually highly organized workplace, one that Teamster activists across the country came to admire and tried to emulate. Meredith made several efforts to start a national network of UPS stewards and other activists, but "it just wouldn't jell." So when UPSurge came onto the scene in the seventies, Meredith was elated. "I thought it was a godsend." La Botz believed that "Vince Meredith brought to UPSurge what was probably the best organized, strongest and most militant group of workers in the country."[10]

INTERNATIONAL SOCIALISTS

There would have never been an UPSurge without the International Socialists (IS). The IS emerged out of the great radicalization of the 1960s, first as the Independent Socialist Club (ISC) at the University of California at Berkeley during the historic Free Speech Movement in the fall of 1964. It later grew into a national organization and changed its name to the International Socialists. The IS established a national office in Detroit and started a weekly newspaper, *Workers' Power*, that was devoted to covering the rank-and-file struggles of US workers. The political inspiration for IS was veteran revolutionary Hal Draper, author of the pamphlet *The Two Souls of Socialism* and popularizer of the term "socialism from below," which captured the revolutionary democratic spirit of Karl Marx's belief that socialism could only be achieved through the "self-emancipation of the working class."[11] The IS adherence to "socialism from below" merged naturally with the rank-and-file rebellion spreading across the US working class.

In 1973, the postwar economic boom came to a screeching halt. The bosses responded to the economic crisis with a concerted offensive to drive down wages, increase productivity, and weaken union organization. Discontent among the rank and file grew, and strikes spread across the country as workers fought back against employers' offensives.[12] It took many changes in the political scene and in the labor movement over the next decade, but by the mid-1970s, the Teamsters became a major focus of the IS's trade union work. The Teamsters were especially militant in the Detroit area. Many ISers got Teamster driving jobs or dock work in the freight industry in preparation for the upcoming 1976 National Master Freight Agreement (NMFA) negotiations.

However, women in the IS who wanted to be politically active in the Teamsters, like Anne Mackie, found it easier to get a driving job or hub job at UPS in the 1970s, rather than in freight, the traditional stronghold of the Teamsters. Mackie began her political life as an antiwar activist at the University of Washington, and later in the feminist movement in Seattle. She joined the IS in the early 1970s and moved to Portland, Oregon, to be a public school teacher. Mackie left her teaching job and easily got a package car job at UPS. Mackie recalls, "I was a package car driver in Portland for about a year and things were much more liberal out there. It was the party line [for UPS] and they were going to do it. So they treated me fairly well."[13] The IS, however, wanted to concentrate its members in the Midwest, so Mackie left Portland for Cleveland, Ohio, where she got another package car job right away, something that would be virtually impossible to do today. In Cleveland she found a different atmosphere than she'd faced in liberal Portland—one much more hostile toward women. "I already knew the package car game and no matter how much they wanted to get rid of me—they couldn't. Because I was competent and knew how the system worked."[14] So, UPS was stuck with Anne Mackie.

Mackie, with a coterie of other ISers (mostly women), founded UPSurge, the powerful rank-and-file group. UPSurge launched in 1975, the same year that IS members who worked in the freight industry started Teamsters for a Decent Contract. For historian Cal Winslow, UPSurge was different from previous organizational efforts: "It was first of all organized to fight the company. Its initial focus was preparation for the 1976 central states contract negotiations. It began in the central states and was built on an informal shop stewards' network with roots in decades of militant activity. In the sixties and seventies there were continuous conflicts and strikes, official and unofficial, including traveling wildcat pickets in 1973."[15]

UPSURGE

The Teamsters had a regional contract due to expire at UPS on May 1, 1976, that covered thirteen states in the Midwest. UPSurge wanted to organize a national campaign to put on the agenda much needed rank-and-file demands. Mackie remembered being overwhelmed by the tasks at hand. "I said to myself, 'Oh, fuck. I'm taking on the Teamsters union, and United Parcel!'" Despite some initial anxiety about the work ahead, Mackie and others were undeterred. "We just went for it." Mackie's infectious optimism was typical of many of the early UPSurge activists. "We, socialists, brought this passion, a desire to confront the company," she declared. "To stand up for women's rights, black rights, and union rights on the job. To hand out the newspaper *UPSurge*. We even went through a National Labor Relations Board (NLRB) lawsuit to hand out the newspaper. We were passionate. And I was feeling passionate about messing with them, and it [UPSurge] just took off."[16]

UPSurge needed a way to go beyond its initial base in Cleveland to reach UPS's rapidly expanding national workforce. Mackie decided that a national newspaper was the way to do it. The newspaper was to have the same name as the embryonic organization and the slogan "Use the Union's Power" emblazoned on its masthead. "We printed 3,000 copies and stuffed them into the back of tractor-trailers in the Cleveland hub," Mackie recalled.[17] The first issue of *UPSurge* debuted in September 1975 with the headline "Driver Shafted—for 30 Bucks," along with a host of local UPS news stories from across the country, an account of how a speedup in San Francisco was stopped, and a major story on part-timers. The front page also included a statement from the editorial board of *UPSurge*: "You have a right to read and distribute this newspaper!"[18]

The most important part of the first issue was on the inside pages, a feature called "Our Big Idea." The name was both a play on the name of UPS's venerated company newsletter and an eight-point program to launch UPSurge as a national organization in preparation for the upcoming 1976 contract battles. Mackie declared, "They had a magazine called *The Big Idea*. So we put out a list called 'Our Big Idea.'"[19] UPSurge eventually produced twenty-seven, mostly monthly editions of the newspaper during its lifetime. Soon after the first edition, *UPSurge* began making its way across the country, and the demand for it exploded. By the second issue, the circulation had jumped to 6,000, and after four months the UPSurge office in Cleveland was printing 10,000 copies. Its circulation eventually climbed to 15,000.[20] When the first edition reached Vince Meredith in Louisville, he quickly contacted UPSurge. A retired Meredith told *Socialist Worker* reporter Lee Sustar in 1997, "I had been in contact with other stewards around the country. But the *UPSurge* newspaper gave us the backbone to fight UPS—and the union, too."[21]

INDIANAPOLIS 600

When some members in Meredith's Louisville hub raised a concern about socialists being the backbone of UPSurge, he responded, "I always told people if there were socialists and communists in UPSurge, it was because they were fighting for the things that UPS workers needed."[22] UPSurge formed an organizing committee, with Meredith playing a prominent role. The focus in the Midwest was on the big central states' UPS contract that covered thirteen states. UPSurge and Teamsters for a Decent Contract called for a Midwest contract conference to be held in Indianapolis, Indiana, in late January 1976. They wanted, according to Mackie, to "create momentum around 'Our Big Idea.'"[23] UPS rank and filers poured into Indianapolis, and the conference surpassed all expectations. Looking back three decades later, Cal Winslow writes that the "founding 'convention' of UPSurge . . . was astonishing. Six hundred and fifty UPSers gathered in a Holiday Inn in the western suburbs of the city. The meeting was part business, part protest rally, part celebration—it was certainly unparalleled in UPS history."[24] Anne Mackie thought that, at most, 250 people would attend, based on their existing contacts and subscription list for the newspaper. UPSurge later reported that participants came from as far away as Portland, Oregon, and Boston, Massachusetts. Every major city in Ohio had a representative, and Detroit had so many attendees that they chartered a bus flanked by a car caravan.

Over 150 UPSers turned out from Indianapolis—quite an accomplishment in itself—and Vince Meredith and his crew brought half of Louisville's "full-time employees and all seven stewards."[25] UPSurge had clearly tapped into something much larger than they'd known. Mackie later wrote that it "was one of the largest rank-and-file Teamster meetings since the founding of this union." In his welcoming speech, Meredith, the chief steward from Louisville, captured the feeling of this historic gathering and used the occasion to mock UPS's arrogance: "Can't you imagine what UPS would have said a few months ago if they were told we were planning a national convention? They would have treated it like a joke. Well, do you think they are laughing tonight?"

UPSurge made no economic demands at the conference. It took the lead from Meredith who advised, "vote the first [offer] down; the second one is always better."[26]

"OUR BIG IDEA"

Instead, the conference focused on demands first articulated in "Our Big Idea": Full-time wages and benefits for part-timers, an "innocent until proven guilty" grievance procedure, an end to military-style dress and appearance, a national contract with rank-and-file control of bargaining, elected business agents and stewards, and an end to discrimination against racial minorities and women, among other demands. These demands were directed at the Teamsters as much as they were at UPS and were designed to strengthen the union in the workplace.[27] Meredith warned the Teamsters and UPS, "we have no intention of ratifying a lousy contract. We're going to negotiate this one on the picket line." Mackie told the crowd, "this will be a Teamsters union that knows the only way to get anything out of the companies is to use the union's power. This means a Teamsters union that recognizes that confrontation not collaboration and no backroom deals is the way to win for the membership."[28]

Everyone left the conference in high spirits. UPSurge felt like a crusade and a social movement. UPSurge activists pledged to organize campaign meetings in their home cities and popularized the slogan "Ready to Strike" to show their determination to win. Meredith's threat "to negotiate on the picket line" was no bluff. In no small part due to UPSurge's pressure on the Teamsters, the union called a strike in the central states that lasted two weeks, as well as a strike later that summer on the East Coast that lasted thirteen weeks. After the Teamsters ordered the strikers back to work in the central states, Mackie said, "then we had a wildcat."[29] UPSurge led wildcats in several cities in the Midwest, including Cleveland.

UPSurge was the last great rank-and-file movement of the 1970s. After 1978, political life for radicals and rank-and-file activists became much more difficult in the trade unions. The legacy of UPSurge, however, lasted long after the demise of the paper and the organization. Many UPS-based union reformers continued as members of Teamsters for a Democratic Union (TDU) and played critical roles in Ron Carey's election as the first reform leader of the Teamsters in 1991, and later in the historic 1997 UPS national strike. Yet possibly the greatest legacy of UPSurge was its vibrancy during that moment of transformation of the workplace when it challenged policies that today are the norm across the United States.

"WE RUN THE TIGHTEST SHIP
IN THE SHIPPING BUSINESS"

UPS polished its image with its first-ever national television advertising campaign starting in the late 1980s.[30] The first of these commercials set the tone for the rest: A group of eager Japanese businessmen request to tour a mythical UPS facility in Somewhere, USA, during the height of the mania for Japanese management techniques. The well-dressed characters look curious and awed by what they see and touch. "At UPS it was never our intention to become a tourist attraction, but each year scores of efficiency-minded Japanese businessmen show up and ask to tour our facilities," the narrator says and then emphasizes the pun in the next line, "which is why so many Japanese find UPS the most rewarding *package* tour anywhere." The commercial ends with the company's famous tagline of that era: "We run the tightest ship in the shipping business."[31] These commercials represented a big change for UPS; it was no longer the "quiet giant" of the shipping industry but now boasted about its services and capabilities on national television.

Yet, behind this brown wall of slick advertising, UPS's growing wealth and power were based on working conditions that looked more like those of a nineteenth-century factory. The late 1970s and early 1980s were a historic turning point for the world economy, the shipping industry, and the US labor movement. Some of the notable changes of that period were the deregulation of airline, trucking, and banking industries, as well as the destruction of PATCO, the air traffic controllers' union. "Neoliberalism" became the all-encompassing term for policies of the era that continue to this very day.[32]

THE GOLDEN LINK

UPS went through several successful transformations over the decades, from its humble origins as a messenger service to its incarnations as a department store delivery service and a major player in the shipping industry. But it was during the 1970s that UPS went through its largest territorial expansion. In 1971 alone, according to *Big Brown* author Greg Niemann, "the company received ICC [Interstate Commerce Commission] authority to serve nine central and prairie states, from the Gulf of Mexico to the Dakotas."[33] Much of this territory was large, though relatively sparsely populated; however, after acquiring delivery rights in these states, UPS was able to take a big step toward uniting the eastern and western wings of its burgeoning empire. In describing this expansion, Niemann draws a rather melodramatic parallel between the railroads' conquest of the North American continent in the nineteenth century and the much slower march by UPS a century later. "Finally," writes a giddy Niemann, "in 1975, the ICC granted UPS authority to begin interstate service to and from Montana and Utah, to extend to statewide the partial service in Arizona, Idaho, and Nevada, and to connect these five states with those both to the west and the east. That made forty-eight states. The coast-to-coast Golden Link was forged![34]

Niemann's metaphorical "Golden Link," like the real golden spike that connected the Central Pacific and Union Pacific railroads and created the first transcontinental railroad in 1869, represented an engineering triumph that promised fabulous profits. UPS had crossed a threshold; now that it had conquered the US continent, it laid the groundwork over the next decade to become a global shipping giant.

In the meantime, UPS took a more aggressive bargaining position against the Teamsters. There was a historic change beginning in the mid-1970s, when working at UPS became more dangerous, when part-time work triumphed, and the union was significantly weakened. During this period, it became the company that millions who have worked for UPS in the past four decades would recognize. For UPSers whose work lives traversed the 1960s and 1970s, the change was palpable. Gerald Gallagher, who started as a full-time UPSer in 1967, became a union steward in 1973 in his hub because of the deteriorating working conditions he observed. He told historian Dan La Botz, "I can only tell you what I think happened at UPS. The company went to a more aggressive stance regarding labor-management relations. And it's my opinion that the accountants took over, and as the wages increased they started demanding increased productivity." It was then that what Gallagher called the "pusher mentality came into being at UPS."[35]

"PUSHER MENTALITY"

The "pusher mentality" was combined with a ruthless disciplining of what UPS considered underperforming workers. In 1976, UPSurge obtained an internal company document entitled "How to Get a Discharge for Low Productivity Sustained." The document charted a course for supervisors to discipline and fire long-standing employees who had been, up until then, valued and productive employees. It instructed supervisors to carefully plan ahead, since "success depends upon action taken weeks and months prior to discharge."[36] Mary Deaton, in her 1979 pamphlet *How to Beat the Big Brown Machine* vividly captured this era in the company's history. Deaton, a former UPSer in Los Angeles, quoted the company's 1976 annual report to expose the thinking behind what was happening in the hubs and at the negotiating table: "We must continue and *accelerate our efforts* to absorb as much as possible . . . rising costs by tighter controls and further improvements in our operating efficiency."[37]

What did this mean? "While more and more workers are getting injured trying to keep up with the insane velocity of work, UPS is devising more ways to make the system faster," Deaton explained. "The attack has been double edged—eliminate full-time jobs whenever possible and further increase the production of those who are working. Although part-timers had existed in isolated areas of the country for many years, the real push came in 1976."[38] These issues were openly discussed in the business and weekly news magazines of the time. Two months into the thirteen-week East Coast strike against UPS in 1976, *Newsweek* surveyed the strike and its key issues. It reported that UPS's hard drive against full-time jobs "provoked an internal fight in the International Brotherhood of Teamsters." However, the "company refused to budge from its demand to be allowed to replace all of its full-time 'inside' employees—those who sort and handle parcels in warehouses and terminals—with part-time, 'casual' workers. Teamster units in the South, Midwest, and West have already signed agreements allowing UPS to hire casuals for these jobs as the full-timers quit or retire."[39] This left the East Coast to fight alone. An exasperated federal mediator complained to *Newsweek*, "In the East, we are having difficulty with the concept of allowing part-time replacements. Unlike other regions, they have had a large number of full-time inside people for a long time."[40]

UPS's strategic goal for the 1976 contract negotiations was openly stated in *Newsweek*: "UPS wants as much uniformity as possible in this year's settlement to facilitate national bargaining in 1979."[41] The rank-and-file activists of UPSurge put winning a national contract at the top of their agenda. Their goal was to raise wage and benefit standards across the country. UPS perverted this aim by demanding a national contract in 1979 with the opposite goal in mind, to lower standards.

BIG BAG OF TRICKS

While UPS didn't get everything it wanted in the 1976 contract, it got enough and acted swiftly. Mary Deaton explained how UPS reached deep into its big bag of tricks to destroy full-time jobs:

> In the central states and East, UPS was adamant about stealing eight-hour jobs in the 1976 contract negotiations. When the contract put hoops in their way, they found ways to jump through them. In New York, full-timers were offered $9,000 [roughly $37,000 today] to quit. In Pennsylvania a new HUB was built in New Stanton and Pittsburgh and Dubois full-timers were forced on the road to make room for part-timers. Parcels were diverted from the Harrisburg HUB to Philadelphia so part-timers could be hired in Philly to work the increased volume and full-timers in Harrisburg could be laid off.[42]

This was happening all over the country. UPS was building an expanding empire on part-time work, a business model pioneered by the company and imitated around the globe for the next two decades.

Having achieved a rough uniformity during the 1976 contracts negotiations, UPS signed its first-ever national contract with the Teamsters in 1979. There were, of course, important Teamster local unions that didn't sign over their bargaining rights to the international union, including Chicago Teamster Locals 705 and 710, and New York Local 804, led by Ron Carey. In order to get local leaders to give away their bargaining rights, Teamsters General President Frank Fitzsimmons allowed nearly two dozen supplements and riders to the National Master UPS contract, which allowed for bargaining on a wide rage of issues, including pension plans, job bidding rights, and work preservation—in effect whatever wasn't covered by the national contract. All these issues were subject to member ratification. The hammer came down, however, in 1982. Despite being a profitable and growing corporation, UPS's strategic goal was to institutionalize the changing composition of its workforce from full-time to part-time. Cost-of-living adjustment (COLA) pay increases were eliminated, for example. However, the most devastating and long-lasting defeat in the 1982 contract was the permanent pay cut for part-timers. Part-time workers, who constituted roughly half of UPS's national workforce at the time and who had started at the same pay rate as full-time workers (at eleven or twelve dollars per hour) saw their pay rate cut to eight dollars per hour.

WORLD-CLASS SWINDLE

It is virtually impossible to accurately calculate the hundreds of millions, if not billions, of dollars that UPS garnered from this world-class swindle, but undoubtedly it was beneficial to the company. During the mid-1990s, UPS undertook a major expansion, hiring "an additional 46,300 workers, but more than 38,500 of them were placed in part-time jobs. Therefore, eighty-three percent of the new jobs created at UPS during this period were part-time,"[43] according to the Teamsters' research department. Today two-thirds of the 250,000 members of the Teamsters union at UPS are part-time. The "savings" in part-timers' wages was an important factor in subsidizing the company's massive expansion. It's no wonder that one of the most favored plays on UPS's name among employees is "Underpaid Slaves."

UPSurge had ceased to be a functioning and independent organization by 1982, and its members became activists in TDU. TDU did its best to defeat the proposed National Master UPS contract, but it was up against virtually the entire officialdom of the Teamsters and a full-court press from UPS to get its workers to accept what it called "a complete sellout." La Botz describes the movement organized by TDU to reject the contract: "TDU activists printed 10,000 copies of UPS bulletins, put out 1,500 buttons that said 'Vote No,' and hundreds of T-shirts with the slogan 'Harass my—, Vote No.' TDU turned out thousands of UPSers to local union meetings, and there were large votes against the contract in New York, New Jersey, San Francisco, Detroit, Pittsburgh, Cincinnati, Louisville, Philadelphia, Dallas, Toledo, and other UPS locals."[44] TDU managed to organize a 48 percent no vote, though that was not enough to defeat the contract. After surveying other major Teamster contract defeats that year, La Botz ominously concluded, "The union was slowly being destroyed."[45]

"I'D LOVE THE TEAMSTERS TO BE WORSE OFF"

This huge step backwards at UPS didn't take place in a political or economic vacuum. The soaring inflation of the 1970s provided the political cover and support for a wholesale assault on the federal regulation of major industries, including aviation, trucking, and financial services. It was the liberal Democrats who pioneered many of the neoliberal policies that had dire consequences for the trade union voting base of their party.

These figures included liberal "lions" like the late Massachusetts senator Ted Kennedy and former Georgia governor Jimmy Carter, the first Democrat elected to the presidency since the Watergate scandal and Nixon's resignation. Carter's inflation "czar," Alfred Kahn, a self-described "good liberal Democrat" and the former chairman of the Department of Economics at Cornell University, felt that unions created an unfair imbalance that disadvantaged non-union workers: "I'd love the Teamsters to be worse off. I'd love the automobile workers to be worse off," said Kahn. "I want to eliminate a situation in which certain protected workers in industries insulated from competition can increase their wages much more rapidly than the average."[46]

Carter sought to break the back of the Teamsters by deregulating the interstate trucking industry in 1980.[47] This move was followed by the Reagan administration's union-busting drive beginning with the breaking of the PATCO strike in the summer of 1981. Deregulation and outright union busting produced a dramatic shift of economic power and influence between corporate America and the working class in the United States that, despite the passage of three decades, continues to this day.[48]

In 1976 the Teamsters had peaked at just over two million members, but by the early 1990s membership had been cut nearly in half. The association had built itself into the largest union in North America in an era of when the freight industry was primarily a local or regional business. The Teamsters were simply bigger and more powerful than the companies that negotiated with them. According to Arthur Sloane, biographer of James R. Hoffa, "When Hoffa was chief bargainer for the union . . . the International Brotherhood of Teamsters (IBT) definitely held the upper hand. Indeed, it would be not going too far to say that almost no labor relations arena had historically displayed such an imbalance of power favoring the union."[49]

The largest freight company in the early 1960s was Consolidated Freightways (CF), with an operating budget of $160 million in an industry that had an annual operating budget of $7.4 billion. The next ten biggest carriers after CF collectively made barely 10 percent of the industry's revenues.[50] Compare that to the Big Three automakers, which in 1959 claimed 94 percent of all auto sales in the United States. The average trucking company was by comparison puny and dominated by the mighty Teamsters.

This dramatically changed by the late 1970s and would accelerate rapidly in the decade following deregulation. Cataclysmic restructuring of the trucking industry seismically shifted the ground underneath the Teamsters. Venerable local and regional freight companies quickly went under or consolidated and stumbled forward for a few years before collapsing.

"HALF MARINE CORPS AND HALF QUAKER"

UPS was well positioned to take advantage all the opportunities that deregulation offered to corporate cutthroats. Its nationwide network of hubs gave it a huge leg up on all the doomed freight companies. And, as the decade of the 1980s wore on and bled into the 1990s, the weight limit of packages handled by UPS kept going up, allowing it to cut into an even greater share of the traditional freight market. UPS also grew in political influence to the point that by the mid-1990s it had the largest political action committee (PAC) in Washington, DC.[51]

UPS was no longer a big kid—it was rapidly growing into a looming giant. In 1988, UPS delivered 2.3 billion packages while the US Postal Service delivered just 1.4 billion.[52] Two years later, in 1990, UPS employed nearly 190,000 workers (130,000 of them represented by the Teamsters) and operated out of 1,500 terminals across North America. Nearly 47,000 package cars rolled out on the streets every day and made deliveries for 850,000 mostly business customers in the US, Canada, Puerto Rico, and what was then West Germany. "They are such an integral part of the American landscape," *Fortune* journalist Kenneth Labich wrote in 1988, in what was the first profile of UPS by a major business magazine. Indicating the wide scope of the company's influence, the *Fortune* article was undertaken with the cooperation of the senior management team.[53]

UPS's high-profile success meant that other freight companies were running at full gallop to catch up and emulate the company's methods and labor policies. Writing in 1990, La Botz observed that UPS was "the crystal ball in which [one] can read the future."[54] What did the future show? A growing mania for productivity at the expense of workers. "UPS maintains rigid control over nearly every aspect of its operations," Labich enthusiastically observed. "Each task, from picking or delivering parcels on a route to sorting packages in a central hub, is carefully calibrated according to productivity standards. Workers know precisely what is expected, and deviations are tolerated only rarely."[55]

"Deviations are tolerated only rarely." Did this intolerance make UPS a more welcoming, healthier, or safer work place? Far from it. The working conditions inside the hubs became increasingly intolerable during the 1990s, with the bulk of the sorting and loading of packages done by an army of part-timers (nearly two-thirds of UPS's workforce by the mid-1990s), individually sorting close to 1,600 packages an hour, or about twenty-seven per minute. Supervisors relentlessly pushed and harassed their workers for greater productivity. UPS was long known for its faux military-style atmosphere, dress, and discipline. One former chairman boasted that UPS corporate culture was "half Marine Corps and half Quaker meeting."[56] The marine corps half was the one that most workers suffered under.

The inevitable result of this relentless pursuit of productivity was that UPS ranked among corporations with the highest injury rates in the freight industry. In the early 1990s, the Occupational Safety and Health Administration (OSHA) issued the company more than 1,300 citations for safety violations, and more than one-third of these cases were deemed serious. In one of the biggest OSHA cases of the decade, UPS was also fined $3 million for its failure to protect workers from hazardous materials.[57] In 1993 alone, UPS had nearly fourteen injuries for every hundred full-time workers, compared to the industry average of eight injuries for every hundred full-time workers, according to the US Bureau of Labor Statistics. In the late 1980s, UPS paid out nearly a million dollars a day in workers' compensation.[58] Things got worse in 1994 after UPS, without negotiating with the union, unilaterally raised the weight limit on individual packages from 70 to 150 pounds.

This dangerous decision contributed to a significant decline in working conditions for UPS package car drivers (93 percent of whom at the time were men) during the 1990s. The *New York Times* profiled the horrific injuries of one driver, Paul Heiman, a veteran package car driver in Kansas, whose on-the-job injuries required six operations by the end of 1995—three on his knees and three on his shoulders.[59] Heiman's experience was not uncommon. The increased weight limit resulted in package cars crammed with extremely heavy packages that used to be delivered by freight companies on pallets using power jacks or forklifts. UPS drivers were being asked to deliver these items by hand.

On top of the greater weight of packages was an increased speed of work, including the pressure to complete anywhere from 150 to 200 stops and pickups a day. Drivers' bodies were simply being worn out, and increasing stress levels were causing physical and mental illnesses among package car drivers. In 1992, the Great Lakes Center for Occupational and Environmental Safety and Health, affiliated with the University of Illinois, conducted a nationwide study involving 317 package car drivers at an "unnamed delivery company" that was obviously UPS. It reported numerous sources of stress for drivers:

> The drivers complained of a punitive attitude from front-line supervisors, daily supervisory pressure to work more hours and through lunch, stressful supervisory pressure in the trucks on their routes, and pressure on replacement drivers to outperform those on sick leave or vacation. They reported conflicting expectations emanating from differing supervisors and a disciplinary system in which they were "judged guilty, and sentenced before trial." Finally the drivers reported a stressful social environment at work fostered by a perceived lack of social support from supervisory personnel.

The researchers stated their findings clearly: "This study suggests that job stress is a psychological health hazard for these drivers."[60]

"UPSERS TURN OUT BETTER THAN MACHINES"

The slogan "tightest ship" applied to the body but also to the mind. UPS has always wanted to mold its workers' minds on the job, but in the 1990s it expanded these efforts. "In order to better control the workforce," according to La Botz, "UPS managers and supervisors are taught to use the methods of sociology to study the behavior of employees."[61] A UPS company manual called "Learning to Chart Spheres of Influences" instructed supervisors how to diagram their work area and chart the relationships between employees under their command with the goal of identifying "Informal Group Leaders." However, it wasn't enough to observe and control workers during work hours. Central to the success of the project was finding out how workers related to each other outside of work. The manual insisted, "As a manager or supervisor, listen carefully to your people to know as much as you can about their *own time* contacts."[62]

No detail was unimportant. "Supervisors are to learn if workers ride the same bus to work, attend the same church or drink in the same tavern, to find out which workers are friendly, and which antagonistic," wrote La Botz. "Most important, they are to find out who influences whom." Examples in the manual tell supervisors to "listen to employees' opinions of union elections."[63] It is unclear whether this interest in workers' political opinions was sparked by the 1989 federal court consent decree that mandated the direct election of the top officials of the Teamsters by the rank and file, but one cannot help but feel that there is a strong correlation between the two. UPS's military-style control over its workers is reminiscent of "the Borg," the drone-like collective from *Star Trek*.

However, others see this unified control as a positive attribute of UPS's corporate culture. "UPSers turn out better than machines," Niemann raved. The process by which this transformation takes place is "a kind of boot camp, indoctrinating employees with UPS's unique corporate culture and expectations. . . . By the time employees have moved a few mountains of cardboard-clad merchandise, they have either caught the UPS commitment or they haven't. If they have, that seed of UPS perseverance will spread through their systems until they too 'bleed brown blood.'"[64]

While this may seem nutty to the average person, this way of thinking does have its proponents outside of UPS. Two academic admirers, Don Cohen and Laurence Prusak, authors of *In Good Company: How Social Capital Makes Organizations Work*, sought and received the eager cooperation of UPS in the research and writing of their book. It seems clear that the two authors often just took the company at its word, rather than engaging in critical analysis of its practices. Cohen and Prusak begin their book with praise for UPS and "attribute its lasting success to elements of its persistent 'character.'"[65] While they do accurately describe the comradely feeling among drivers and the daily efforts of workers to help each other out, they veer off into company propaganda. Part of the process of UPS character building for Cohen and Prusak is storytelling. "People at UPS," they write,

> tell and retell stories of cooperation and devotion to getting the job done. . . . One story concerns an eight-months-pregnant center manager who delivered sixty packages in subzero weather when one of her drivers didn't show up. Drivers tell about making deliveries on schedule in weather that kept their competitors from FedEx off the roads. Those stories have the shape of many traditional heroic tales: the lone hero bravely facing a hostile world while lesser mortals fall by the wayside. From one perspective, comparing package deliveries to the quest for the Golden Fleece or the Holy Grail seems laughably extravagant. On the other hand, a modest but gen-

uine echo of those heroic models contributes to driver fellowship and pride in the work.[66]

This form of storytelling might seem exaggerated. However, if we take it seriously, we see an element of fanaticism to it. Beneath each exciting, motivational story is the threat of being disciplined or fired.

CHAPTER 5

AIR WAR: TAKING ON FEDEX

Like an ant colony, UPS had a collective mind.
—**Greg Niemann,** *Big Brown*[1]

In the 1980s, UPS had conquered the ground delivery market. In the 1990s, after many years of delay and inertia, it decided to take on FedEx, the company that virtually created the overnight shipping market. UPS soon made major inroads into FedEx's domination of this highly lucrative market. The decision to challenge FedEx required an enormous capital investment that led to a top-to-bottom transformation of UPS that was as great as any other in its long history. It ultimately succeeded, as it did in the ground package market, by the vast expansion and exploitation of its part-time workforce.

Originally called Federal Express, FedEx was founded in 1971 by Fred Smith. On the night of April 17, 1973, six jets arrived to FedEx's Memphis facility with 185 packages and envelopes in need of sorting. From very modest beginnings, the company evolved into one of the most recognized corporations in the United States."[2] The FedEx tagline "When it absolutely, positively has to be there overnight" contributed to the company's image as a modern, tech-savvy, and reliable corporation. By the early 1980s, FedEx had "revolutionized the airfreight business and established itself as the leading overnight delivery provider," according to historians Mike Brewster and Frederick Dalzell. "What UPS had done for ground-based consolidated delivery systems in the 1920s and 1930s, FedEx did for next-day air operations in the 1970s and early 1980s."[3]

UPS was taken by surprise "when the market that FedEx had tapped into started to become clear. Particularly at law firms, financial concerns, investment houses, and other such purveyors of important and timely information," write Brewster and Dalzell.[4] A 1988 *Wall Street Journal* profile of FedEx claimed that it collected "half the revenue in what is now more than a $6 billion industry," and, astoundingly, delivered "more than 99% of it letters and packages on time."[5]

LIKE THE RUSSIAN ARMY

UPS's decision to take on FedEx was not only motivated by the prospect of getting a profitable slice of a burgeoning market, but, in a textbook case straight from Karl Marx's *Capital*, it faced a bleak future unless it could compete with and defeat its upstart, airborne rival. "Because they were keeping their collective noses to the ground," explains Greg Niemann, UPS managers were caught totally off guard in the early 1970s as "FedEx exploded into the air business, setting itself up as an airline that delivered packages, overnight ones at that. There was UPS, only minimally in the air business, primarily a package-delivery company that used the air for second-day deliveries."[6] Brewster and Dalzell note, "Despite the fact that UPS had perfected a ground-based hub-and-spoke system years earlier, the company apparently never saw the viability of this approach applied to an air network."[7] UPS had systematically spent decades building its delivery network one city, one state, and one region at a time, and now the company faced the threat of FedEx leapfrogging over its network.

Fred Smith had learned much from the US military's worldwide logistics operation while he was a pilot during the Vietnam War, and he put that knowledge to good use when he took FedEx from an idea to a business. He also learned both positive and negative lessons from UPS: "FedEx didn't intend to start up city by city as UPS always had," notes Niemann. "The concept was hatched nationwide, with its one hub, from the very beginning. Smith designed it to work systematically, the way a clearinghouse does. It copied how UPS was using its ground hubs . . . [but] FedEx revolutionized air delivery, and when UPS leadership got serious about next-day air, they did the same thing."[8]

But even when UPS top management "got serious," it still took "eight more years" to act, notes a frustrated Niemann. FedEx's success came as a late, rude awakening to the company. "The vast delivery market that had taken UPS sixty-five years to accumulate was suddenly jarred by this upstart, Federal Express, a company no one had even heard of," notes Niemann. "Most UPSers took the ostrich approach, ignoring the new company. Some denigrated it, saying, for instance: How are they going to deliver them on the ground? Their network's too small. People don't need that much delivered overnight. Costs are too high. They'll probably go under."[9]

This ostrich-like behavior extended to the highest levels of the company. "We rarely mentioned the new competition," according to Niemann, who was part of UPS's management in the late 1960s and early 1970s in Southern California and worked as a liaison for top management. "In fact, UPS annual reports of the late 1970s and even 1980 made no mention of FedEx, still decrying the US Postal Service as the number one competitor."[10]

Meanwhile, Fred Smith, as late as 1988, took UPS's slow response as a sign of a sclerotic management. Smith lampooned his Big Brown rival as drab, regimented, unimaginative, and inflexible in a *Wall Street Journal* interview: "UPS is like—I don't mean this disrespectfully—the Politburo. And with those zillion brown trucks, like the Russian Army."[11] A Cold War audience would have readily recognized Smith's references, coming as they did shortly before the collapse of the Berlin Wall and the disintegration of the former USSR.

Niemann held a similar view of the company but with a positive twist. Whereas Smith saw drab regimentation, Niemann saw dedication and focus: "As efficient army ants, UPS managers and employees optimized procedures in one delivery location; then adapted and cloned them in new locations as brown package cars found their way across America. And like an ant colony, UPS had a collective mind—its corporate culture, which infused all individuals with incredible motivation, keeping feet on the ground, eyes focused, and noses on the trail of quality service."[12] Despite its late start, Niemann's "army" finally moved into the overnight market, "one toe at a time."[13]

STRATEGIC SHIFT

The person responsible for this strategic shift in direction was George Lamb, named chairman and CEO of UPS in May 1980.[14] Lamb's 2001 obituary in the *New York Times* captured his pivotal role at this transformative moment in UPS's history:

> Mr. Lamb oversaw the company's transformation from a loose patchwork of domestic routes to a tightly knit national network that became the springboard for sending packages overseas. . . . With a domestic network in place, Mr. Lamb then oversaw the company's first forays into the overnight delivery business, as well as its expansion overseas. Although U.P.S. began experimenting with Canadian service in 1975, and with making deliveries inside Germany a year later, it did not bridge the Atlantic and begin regular shipments to Europe until 1985.[15]

In 1982, Louisville International Airport was chosen for the site of UPS's central air hub, which was modeled on FedEx's Memphis hub. Why Louisville, Kentucky? Both Memphis and Louisville are located in an aerial geographic region referred to as Cargo Alley. "If you want a system that connects every point in the US to every other point," said founder Fred Smith, "the hub has to sit somewhere in a trapezoid between Memphis in the southwest, to Champaign, Illinois, in the northwest, over to Dayton, Ohio, and down to Chattanooga. It has to sit in that footprint."[16] From Memphis and Louisville, FedEx and UPS cargo planes can reach nearly 80 percent of the continental United States in two hours or less.

By 1985, UPS's "Next Day Air" (NDA) service was available in the continental United States, and it also began flying documents and packages between the US and six European countries. Chicago package car driver Dave Healy recalled that in the early days of NDA, the commit time, or deadline, was noon, but supervisors continually urged drivers to deliver packages earlier in their routes, until a 10:30 a.m. commit time was reached.[17] The race to deliver overnight packages earlier in the morning hours was on. During this time, however, UPS relied on commercial or chartered planes to fly its envelopes and packages. It wasn't until 1988, when the Federal Aviation Administration authorized the company to operate its own aircraft, that UPS Airlines was formed.[18] "By the end of 1989, UPS owned 110 airplanes, including seven 747s, and leased an additional 247 airplanes," wrote Niemann.[19] To build this new airline from scratch, UPS hired a host of well-paid pilots and airplane mechanics.

However, it would have been impossible for it to succeed without major and, in many cases, permanent concessions from the Teamsters. There was little to no mention of air delivery operations in Teamster contracts with UPS before 1987. The 1987 National Master UPS contract and the local contracts that followed were a major turning point. The national contract was voted down by 53 percent largely due to the campaigning of TDU. Despite the majority no vote, it was imposed on an angry membership by Teamsters General President Jackie Presser. Whole new job categories were created, including part-time air drivers, air walkers (who delivered and picked up air packages and envelopes on foot), and air hub and gateway employees. The goal was to move this work from full-time, high-wage package car drivers to part-time, low-wage workers. There were no full-time jobs created under the contract for workers in the new air hubs. UPS had won a gold rush of concessions from the Teamsters in the 1980s, and they had struck a new vein in the 1987 contract.

MORE AND MORE CONCESSIONS

What was bad for UPS Teamsters in the 1987 contract turned into a disaster in 1990. Ron Carey's predecessor, William McCarthy, negotiated the 1990 National Master UPS contract. McCarthy still had the ambition of running for Teamsters general president in the 1991 elections. Negotiations, however, were largely on the company's terms, and he put it up for vote and threatened a national strike. The TDU "UPS Contract Bulletin" warned that, among the many problems with the proposed contract, it included "virtually unlimited use of low-rate Special Air Drivers to displace union-scale work."[20] The *Chicago Tribune* outlined some of the controversial issues of the proposed contract:

> In a move that rankled union activists, the contract also established a new category of part-time workers in the company's overnight air service division. While that division accounted for only 5 percent of UPS shipments last year [1989], it's the fastest growing part of the business. UPS earned $693 million on $12.4 billion last year. Earnings have been flat over the last two years as the company invested heavily in building a 123-plane air-service fleet and in starting up an overseas operation.[21]

McCarthy miscalculated badly, and his lack of leadership produced high anxiety among the Teamster membership at UPS. And, with the rest of the union leadership hopelessly divided between competing factions focused on the upcoming election, this ensured that the Teamsters were in no position to organize a national strike. Taking no chances, UPS stepped into the void and pressed its advantage. It crafted a two-pronged contract campaign (foreshadowing even bigger efforts through the 1990s to undermine Carey's leadership) to get the proposed contract passed, one inside the hubs, and the other in the media. TDU reported: "In each area, management has designated a 'District Contract Ratification Coordinator,' who oversees the corporate effort to get us to vote yes. Supervisors are required to approach us, and to predict how each of us will vote. Their job is to get as many of us as possible to vote yes on a first offer, and they will be evaluated on how many yes votes they can generate. The lessons learned will be used to put a little flavoring on a second offer they expect us to jump at."[22]

While UPS had always worked hard to try to undermine the union activists, especially during contract votes, this appears to have been a more concerted strategy than in the recent past. The company, according to historian Michael Schiavone, mounted "'a well-organized campaign in which it held numerous work-site meetings to boost the proposed pact' in an attempt to persuade workers to accept the contract."[23]

Unfortunately, there was no second offer as the contract passed on the first round of voting. Many people in the union were shocked that it passed so easily, especially since the previous national contract had been voted down. According to McCarthy, "Many of the company's employees were frightened by management's ability to use permanent replacement workers, or scabs, in the possible event of a strike."[24] Ron Carey, who was well into his campaign for general president and who had made opposition to concessions at UPS a major campaign issue, told the *New York Times* that he was "considerably surprised" by the vote. "The company has done a good job of intimidating, saying there would be a six-week strike and people would lose their homes."[25] There is also no doubt that some of the most backward members of the old guard helped UPS. Frank Snow, a business agent for Teamsters Local 705 in Chicago, told the *Chicago Tribune*, "If there's a national walkout, we've decided to continue to work."[26]

UPS also evidently began a media campaign directed at influencing its customers by swaying the tone of news coverage of the company. A UPS press officer could have written *New York Times* reporter Nick Ravo's commentary on the 1990 contract: "United Parcel Service of America Inc., with its almost egalitarian corporate culture and its deep roots as a high-paying union employer, might seem an unlikely target for a possible nationwide strike by the International Brotherhood of Teamsters."[27] UPS was making a clear effort to develop reliable friends and allies in the mainstream media and promoted "experts" like Jeffrey Sonnenfeld as the "go-to-guy" for extensive interviews. The strategy of portraying UPS as a virtually worker-owned company and the union as a meddlesome outsider would be employed with greater effort and resources during the coming decade. UPS got what it wanted in the 1990 contract, and it went on a building spree of air hubs across the country—locations staffed primarily by low-wage, part-time employees.

THE DARLING OF THE CORPORATE COMMUNITY

UPS had grown by leaps and bounds, evolving into a mega-corporation that would have been virtually unrecognizable at its modest beginnings. It had begun to challenge Federal Express's domination of the overnight delivery market, and as the largest package delivery company in the world, it was laying the foundation to become a global behemoth.[28] In 1987 alone, UPS made over $700 million in after-tax profits on $10 billion in revenues, delivering packages to 850,000 customers in fifty states, Puerto Rico, Canada, and West Germany.[29] It was also the darling of the corporate community throughout the 1980s. Surveying the past decade and looking ahead, *Fortune* writer Kenneth Labich wrote in January 1988, "For the fourth straight year, UPS tops its industry in *Fortune*'s corporate reputations survey. . . . It is far and away the most profitable U.S. transportation company. Competitors try to emulate the reliability of its service; customers applaud the steadiness of its prices; air rates have stayed the same since the company launched its overnight service five years ago. But what makes UPS stand out is its ability to attract, develop, and keep talented people."[30]

Despite such fawning adulation in the business press, by the end of the decade, even UPS could not escape the growing public backlash against corporate greed and union busting. Oliver Stone's wildly popular 1987 film *Wall Street* is perhaps popular culture's best dramatization of this corruption. UPS tried its best to deflect the backlash by emphasizing its management style as represented by the odd and austere personality of its founder James E. Casey. The company tried to present itself as the very antithesis of the modern American corporation. As Labich described it, the "company is almost aggressively *egalitarian*. The Greenwich, Connecticut, headquarters and regional centers are located in extremely Spartan buildings; in the parking lots, executives hunt for slots along with hourly employees. Everyone is on a first-name basis, and no one, even Chairman and Chief Executive Officer John W. Rogers, 54, has a private secretary. He and other top executives share a secretarial pool, but they all do their own photocopying and make their own travel arrangements."[31] Rogers proudly told Labich, "We have no stars but many bright lights."[32] It is as if Rogers were trying to say there are no Gordon Gekkos here. Gekko, of course, is the great villain of Stone's *Wall Street* and the man who famously declares, "Greed is good!"

Carl Kaysen, then a thirteen-year UPS board member and a professor of political economy at MIT, went even further than Labich and described the company's management style, incredibly, as an experiment in "managerial socialism." Kaysen gave Labich an example of what he meant: "When we have our meetings in Greenwich, we directors troop downstairs to the cafeteria, stand in line, and pay our $2.10 for a tuna sandwich. The only difference is we sit at a reserved table so we can talk."[33]

This faux egalitarianism fooled few working UPS Teamsters. The target of such silly propaganda was the business and mainstream media, who ate it up—tuna fish sandwiches and all. But these stories do highlight just how sensitive UPS was to its public image and how willing it was to spend time and money to hide what lay behind its brown walls.

CHAPTER 6
DEMOCRACY COMES TO THE TEAMSTERS

The convention reaffirms that in the event of a U.S. Department of Justice suit against the IBT using the racketeering statutes, TDU will intervene to strongly oppose a court-appointed trusteeship, and to support a plan that will provide for a supervised one-member, one-vote election for International Union officers.
—Teamsters for a Democratic Union convention resolution, 1987[1]

Just when it seemed that UPS had the Teamsters well under its heel, an eruption of democracy threatened the whole corrupt deal. In the 1980s and early 1990s, across the Teamsters and especially at UPS, there was growing frustration—if not outright rage—at the catastrophic decline of the union during the past decade. UPS's incredible prosperity was primarily due to its commanding position in the package delivery industry. However, its profits were significantly enhanced by the impoverishment of its highly exploited and expanding part-time workforce—nearly two-thirds of its employees—and the deteriorating working conditions of its package car drivers. It had demanded and easily won major concessions from the Teamster old guard that controlled the union throughout the 1980s.[2]

The Teamsters had once been synonymous with high-paying jobs and a powerful union, but things had changed dramatically. Even the coveted package car and feeder (semi-trailers) driving jobs at UPS, while growing in number, were shrinking as a proportion of the workforce and full-time hub jobs bordered on extinction. UPS didn't just have a sweetheart deal with the Teamsters; it had a gold rush.[3] The Teamsters' old guard leadership appeared to be oblivious to the world around them. The union lost 300,000 members between 1981 and 1986.[4]

THE LAST DAYS OF THE EMPERORS

The most famous Teamster leader, James (Jimmy) R. Hoffa, went to prison in 1967 and disappeared after his release in July 1975, and was presumed murdered. His successors, Frank Fitzsimmons, Roy Williams, Jackie Presser, and William McCarthy lived opulent and garish lifestyles. Like the rich and powerful in the last days of the Roman Empire or the former USSR, the last emperors of the Teamsters got dumber and more corrupt as time went on. Hoffa's successors felt protected by their close relationship with the Republican Party, especially with President Ronald Reagan. The Teamsters had endorsed Reagan for president in 1980 and for reelection in 1984 despite his administration's virulent anti-union politics, which were destroying the US labor movement.[5]

Jackie Presser, who became an FBI informant in the early 1970s and a Teamster leader in 1981, committed crimes that were authorized by his FBI handlers. Presser hoped that Reagan's attorney general, Ed Meese, would shield him from prosecution, but Presser's offenses proved too blatant for Meese. Presser and other top Teamsters were under investigation by the Department of Labor and the Department of Justice. Then, former Teamster leader Roy Williams made explosive revelations in October 1985, divulging what everybody else in the world already knew: the Mafia controlled the Teamsters, and he personally was under the control of Kansas City Mafia boss Nick Civella.[6]

The undemocratic nature of the Teamsters had long been a public scandal and enabled Mafia control of the union, but nothing had been done to stop it. The Teamsters' top officers, for example, were "elected" by many unelected convention delegates, a system that facilitated a top-down, mobbed-up control of the union. "More than a dozen past and present officers of the department," wrote an exasperated *New York Times* columnist A. H. Raskin on the eve of the Teamsters 1986 convention, "including a former Secretary, Ray Marshall, have expressed their belief that the procedures used by the union are illegal under Landrum-Griffin."[7] The Landrum-Griffin Act guaranteed secret balloting and regular election of union officers, overseen by the US Department of Labor.

"However," a frustrated Raskin declared, "no formal finding to that effect has ever been made, and the department studiously refrained from interfering in the designation of delegates for the Teamsters' five-year convention that opens in Las Vegas today."[8] Raskin blamed "the long reach of political palsmanship into the [Labor] department," which was "most dismayingly evident in the department's do-nothing response to demands from a tiny but indomitable band of rebels in the International Brotherhood of Teamsters that the 1.7 million members of that scandal-stained union be given a direct right to vote for its president and for the convention delegates who now pick him."[9] Raskin's "indomitable band of rebels" was the Teamsters for a Democratic Union (TDU). TDU was the only organization of rank-and-file Teamsters that had the credibility to organize a campaign for the right to vote against the federal government's effort to impose a trusteeship (the government taking control of and running the union). Despite the hostility of the old guard, TDU fought on through the terrible 1980s and was making headway.

Beginning in the fall of 1985, TDU launched a right-to-vote campaign, including a petition demanding "the right to vote for IBT president and International officers on a basis of one member one vote."[10] "As a result of this campaign, TDU collected over 100,000 signatures on its petition, which it duly delivered to the Teamster convention in Las Vegas in May."[11] The 1986 Teamsters Convention—appropriately held at Caesars Palace in Las Vegas—was notorious for its garishness and arrogant display of power by Jackie Presser and his mobbed-up friends. Four bodyguards dressed as Roman legionaries, infamously carried Jackie Presser on a throne at one of the convention's more gaudy parties. Despite Presser's appearance of iron-fisted control of the delegates and tendency to rail at his enemies from the podium, the end was slowly coming for the Teamster old guard. A Presser ally, US Labor Secretary William Brock, even warned delegates at the convention to "clean house."[12]

It took another year before the Department of Justice finally acted and announced that it would file a civil Racketeer Influenced and Corrupt Organizations (RICO) suit to remove the entire general executive board of the teamsters and place the union under the control of a federal trustee. The headlines were ominous, suggesting that the entire labor movement was under threat. A *New York Times* story on June 11, 1987, had the headline "U.S. Seeks Control of Teamster Union."[13] Federal prosecutor Rudy Giuliani (future mayor of New York City) announced that his office would lead on the case and it would be tried in New York before Judge David Edelstein. According to Teamster historian Dan La Botz, it was "the first time that the federal government had attempted to take over an entire labor union."[14]

While the Teamster leadership was under siege from federal prosecutors, national and local contracts between the Teamsters and UPS came up for renewal, and UPS was fully prepared to take advantage of the situation. TDU, with its slender resources, put a major effort into defeating another concessionary contract with the very profitable UPS. Largely due to its efforts, 53 percent of UPS Teamsters voted against the National Master UPS contract proposed by the ailing Jackie Presser, but not enough to overcome the two-thirds rule to defeat it.[15] Despite the majority vote against the contract, Presser imposed it, pleasing UPS but disillusioning an already restless union membership. It was his last act of betrayal against UPS Teamsters.

Presser died one year later, on July 8, 1988, and thus avoided going to prison. That left the final surrender to the justice department to his successor William McCarthy. On March 13, 1989, the justice department reached an agreement with the IBT to settle the RICO suit. It established a court-supervised independent review board with wide-ranging investigatory powers to clean out corruption, including barring of corrupt officers from the union for life. Most importantly, it provided for the direct election of the convention delegates and international union officers in 1991.

TDU's position against government trusteeship prevailed. The *Wall Street Journal* reported, "The terms of the settlement were greatly influenced by the concerns and platform of Teamsters for a Democratic Union."[16]

RON CAREY RUNS FOR PRESIDENT

Ron Carey was well into his fifties when he embarked on the most important phase of his union career. For Carey and for TDU, the upcoming 1991 election for convention delegates and international union officers was a once-in-a-lifetime opportunity to transform the Teamsters. Few others could have carried the reform banner into the impending bare-knuckle, cross-continent campaign. Sam Theodus, the president of Local 407 in Cleveland who had challenged Presser from the floor of the tumultuous 1986 convention, could have conceivably led the effort; Detroit Teamster rebel Pete Camarata was another plausible leader. Yet, while courageous and principled in their own rights, neither Theodus nor Camarata could have provided that special appeal to UPS Teamsters that Carey possessed. Carey announced his candidacy in November 1989 before a packed house of supporters. There was much do, and the outcome was far from certain.

Carey may have been a unique figure, but it is unlikely that he would have been seen as a major threat to the Teamster establishment without many years of hard work by TDU. It was the only network of Teamsters rank-and-file reform activists throughout the United States and Canada that could challenge the old guard of the union. Eventually nine of the sixteen candidates on the Carey slate for seats on the general executive board of the Teamsters were members of TDU, including the indomitable Canadian Diana Kilmury.[17] Carey also reached outside the Teamsters for a campaign manager who could bring a fresh eye and ingenuity to his campaign. He chose Eddie Burke, an organizer with the United Mine Workers of America (UMWA), who impressed him with his organizing skills and creativity during the Pittston Coal Strike, when he led the first sit-down strike of the UMWA in fifty years.[18] It was a bold move by Carey.

Burke put Carey on the road to hit every major city and work-place where there were large concentrations of Teamsters, and when the ballots were counted in December 1991, the Carey slate won a stunning victory with 48 percent of the vote in a three-way race against two old guard slates led respectively by Walter Shea and R. V. Durham—not a majority but enough to sweep his entire slate into power. Carey notably beat his nearest competitor, Durham, by nearly 60,000 votes. The TDU imprint on the victory of the Carey slate was unmistakable. TDU, in a post-election analysis, had this to say:

> A close look at the election results shows clearly that where TDU organizing has been strongest, the Carey slate win was strongest— even in the opposing camp's backyards. But the Carey win goes be-yond that; the size and breadth of the margin of victory show that the campaign was articulating a need for change that rang true for a wide range of Teamsters. And many rank-and-file campaigners were able to tap into that desire for change because of the train-ing, experience, and commitment they had developed over years of building TDU.[19]

Carey's victory in 1991 was a vindication for the many members who had been struggling for decades to wrest control of the Team-sters from the mobbed-up old guard. Many had lost their jobs and suffered threats to their lives, as well as physical beatings. The win was also a personal triumph for Ron Carey. The *New York Times* vividly captured the moment: "Bristling with the passion of the wronged and rejoicing in his victory, Ronald Carey, the presumed new president of the International Brotherhood of Teamsters, pro-claimed Today 'It's goodbye to the mafia.' 'This union will now work in the interests of its members,' Mr. Carey said. . . . 'It's the mem-bers that will come first.'"[20]

What did UPS make of Carey's triumph? Brooding managers in their new gleaming corporate campus in the Atlanta suburb of Sandy Springs did not welcome the changes in the Teamster lead-ership. Like many of those in corporate America, they did not react favorably to democracy coming to the Teamsters. The UPS hierar-chy had believed, like many outside observers, that Carey had little chance of winning. In the end, they believed that the old guard would survive. When it didn't, confusion and resentment set in. Niemann described Carey as a "disenchanted former UPS driver" who had "taken over the Teamsters union in the nineties and vowed 'to get' UPS."[21]

THIS BUILDING BELONGS TO YOU

February 1, 1992, was a crisp, sunny Saturday in Washington, DC, when over six hundred union members and their supporters gathered on the steps of the Teamsters headquarters for the inauguration of Ron Carey. While waving pennants that proclaimed "The New Teamsters," Carey pledged, "I will use the full power of this office to rid this union of mob influence and win this battle once and for all." The imposing five-story marble building had cast a sinister shadow for many decades. Longtime TDU activist Dan Campbell remembered it as "the forbidden palace," a place off-limits to rank-and-file Teamsters, while others mocked it as the "Marble Palace," a symbol of extravagance and corruption. Carey declared that he would move quickly to get rid of the worst excesses of the old guard: "The Teamster limousine, the condominium in Puerto Rico, the luxury jets, they're all going on the market." "Clean 'em out," shouted Gary Foreman, a thirty-three–year Teamsters veteran, who with a group of fellow Teamsters from St. Louis held red-handled brooms aloft. When asked by a reporter what the brooms meant, Foreman told him, "The brooms mean we're making a clean sweep of the Teamsters, new people all the way through."[22] Carey also put forward a broader social vision for the Teamsters—a huge change from past presidents: "Our mission is to take the enormous resources of this union and give them new direction and new purpose, to win better contracts, to improve pensions, and to organize new workers, to pass national health insurance."[23] He ended his speech by inviting the crowd of supporters with a welcoming sweep of his arms: "Now I invite all of you to join me. This building belongs to you once again."[24]

The 1991 Teamster election brought to power people whom UPS viewed as the enemy within—people whom the Teamster old guard, UPS, and other major freight companies had worked hard for many years to marginalize or drive out of the union. Now the reformers held the reins of power at the highest level. The world had been turned upside down. Like UPS itself, *Big Brown* author Greg Niemann saw Ron Carey as a nightmare come to life. He voiced UPS's darkest fear that Carey's election meant a profound change had come to the Teamsters. In an effort to regain control, UPS responded with a strategy to aggressively attack the reformers on every front—from Congress to the shop floor—hoping to over-whelm and defeat them. They believed that by crippling Carey a "counterrevolution" could be fostered in the union that would oust him in the 1996 Teamster election. At times there was little doubt that UPS was winning, particularly in the battle over OSHA in Washington, and it seemed that the old guard was close to pull-ing off a political coup. However, despite their machinations, the reform Teamsters moved forward, drawing into activity thousands of members who had previously seen their union as a distant, cor-rupt machine.

CHAPTER 7

A WAR ON EVERY FRONT

*The courage of Teamster members won this agreement. No corporation
has the right to break workers' backs just to make another buck.*
— **Ron Carey, February 1994, on the national safety strike**[1]

When Ron Carey and the New Teamsters were sworn into office
in February 1992, they had less than eighteen months to prepare
for the expiration of the 1990–93 national UPS contract and the
two dozen accompanying local contracts, riders, and supplements.
It was a daunting task. With expansion of UPS operations, the
number of employees represented by the Teamsters soared to over
182,000 at over 1,500 work sites scattered across the country. This
included 67,000 package car drivers, 15,000 feeder drivers who
crisscrossed highways throughout North America and Puerto
Rico, and over 100,000 mostly part-time workers at hubs. The
part-timer ranks had recently swelled by thousands at newly built
air hubs.[2]

It was also a workforce highly stratified by years of retreat and
concessions. Labor journalists and historians Sheila Cohen and
Kim Moody write that the UPS workforce of the late 1980s and
early 1990s included "just about every level of the working class. The
drivers, although not exclusively white or even male, [were] among
the highly paid full-time workers described as 'Reagan Democrats,'
while the sorters and loaders [were] racially diverse, mostly part-
time, and fairly low paid."[3]

UPS had easily wrangled major concessions from the Teamsters during the 1980s that swiftly added hundred of millions of dollars to UPS's coffers and helped finance its vast expansion; with a new round of concessions in the 1990 contract, it had become a major player in the overnight delivery market. After decades of a compliant Teamster leadership, UPS was now in uncharted waters and didn't like it at all. The company was making profits and had no intention of giving back any of these monumental wage and benefit concessions. In fact, it wanted more.

THE NEW TEAMSTERS

Even before contract talks began, Carey and the New Teamsters began to do things differently from their old mobbed-up predecessors. While there wasn't the grand strategy toward the contract negotiations that became a defining feature of the 1997 Teamster contract campaign, there was a clear change in the posture of the union. *The Teamster* magazine was renamed *The New Teamster*, with Matt Witt as editor, and turned sharply from its old preoccupation with leadership to a new focus on the concerns of union members.

The March 1993 issue of the magazine featured a major exposé of UPS, which aimed to reveal the heavy demands placed on the average rank-and-file worker. The article, "The Tightest Ship," featured Nancy and John Youngermann, a couple who were both stewards at UPS's huge Earth City, Missouri, hub. Nancy was a part-timer who started work late at night and returned home in the early mornings. She barely had time to get her son ready for school. John was a package driver who worked long days and could hardly make it through dinner with his eyes open.

The Teamsters also conducted the first-ever national survey of UPSers in preparation for negotiations and published the results in the April–May issue of *The New Teamster*. In a four-page spread called "People Before Packages," the survey shockingly revealed: "UPS members throughout the U.S. showed that a large majority have had health problems from job stress. More than half have had problems related to diesel fumes. More than 80 percent have had job-related back problems in the past year, and almost two-thirds have suffered hand, wrist, or arm pain."[4] Workplace health issues, long ignored by the old guard, and the management policies that produced them would be at the center of upcoming negotiations. Mario Perrucci, the Teamsters' package and small parcel director, made this abundantly clear: "Like any negotiations, these will involve issues of dollars and cents. But there's an underlying issue of UPS's policy of putting packages before people. That's got to change."[5]

When Ron Carey sat down across the table from chief UPS negotiator Dave Murray for the start of the 1993 national UPS contract talks, he had Perrucci by his side. Perrucci was elected on the Ron Carey slate and was a regional vice president. He was not a TDUer but came from what labor journalist and Carey campaign chronicler Ken Crowe called "the traditional local Teamsters Union political structure."[6] He was the secretary-treasurer, or the principal officer, of Local 177 based in Hillside, New Jersey, where a majority of its eight thousand members worked at United Parcel Service. Perrucci had been a package car driver at UPS and a member of the local union since 1966. He was elected secretary-treasurer in the fall of 1977. Local 177 was for all intents and purposes the New Jersey twin of Carey's New York Local 804.

Along with Carey, Perrucci built a reputation as a militant who was not afraid to call strikes or defy judges. In 1980, he called a strike at twenty UPS centers, "disrupting the movement of more than two million packages," according to the *New York Times*, after the company fired three workers who had been on leave to serve as Local 177 business agents.[7] Two years later, he defied federal judge Clarkson Fisher who ordered 3,600 UPS strikers back to work. The *New York Times* reported that Perrucci "said the walkout had resulted from the company's announced intention of using package handlers as drivers in a new overnight air service."[8] He also led a strike against UPS over package weight limits and the handling of hazardous material.[9] "His reputation as a hard bargainer was well known," recalled long-time UPS and TDU activist Dan Campbell:

> Mario and Ron were both fighters that came from the package driver ranks at UPS. No wonder they became associates. I remember a time at a TDU Convention when Mario was addressing the attendees, and he said that he wasn't always a supporter of the re-

form movement, but he asked people not to judge him so much by where he came from but where he was now and the direction he was going. In 1993 he and Ron were the lead bargainers at UPS national negotiations. For much of the negotiations it was Mario at the head of the negotiation team for the union.[10]

Negotiations were "tense from the very beginning," recalled Perrucci over two decades later.[11] UPS was determined to test the new leadership from the outset of the contract talks. Dave Murray, UPS's chief negotiator, was especially unhappy with the participation, for the first time, of rank-and-file UPS workers on the Teamster negotiating committee. Murray made it clear to Perrucci through his words and demeanor that he didn't like having rank and filers contradicting or challenging him. But Perrucci insisted that he wanted these very people on the committee. "I was a package car driver for eight years and one year as a full-time clerk. But I wanted people on there who could immediately respond to UPS. If they [UPS] said, 'That's not happening,' we had people who could say, 'Yes it is.'"[12] The Teamster negotiating committee "wasn't the usual suspects," according to Campbell. It included Campbell, a package car driver from Michigan; Wesley Jenkins, a feeder driver from Texas; and a part-timer hub worker.[13]

Murray's arrogance was on full display, and he refused to seriously negotiate for many months. Campbell vividly recalled the many times that "Mario would regularly go off on Murray. In one particular exchange Mario told Murray he was so pissed that he couldn't even stand the sight of him, and we took an abrupt caucus."[14] Further, to the annoyance of UPS, the Teamsters "for the first time in recent memory, kept rank-and-file members involved through bulletins and meetings," reported *Labor Notes*, an independent labor magazine based in Detroit.[15] There was a transparency to negotiations like never before. Then UPS, according to the *Wall Street Journal*, introduced "more tension into already heated talks," when it revealed on June 15, 1993, that "UPS two weeks ago wrote a two-page letter to a dozen National Labor Relations Board regional offices to ask that its operations be considered under the Railway Labor Act. That would require longer periods of mediation and a waiting period before its workers would be allowed to strike."[16]

At this point, the Teamsters had not taken a strike vote, and this maneuver by UPS to change the jurisdiction that had governed the labor relations at the company for over six decades was a threat held over the head of the union. Three months of negotiations had passed without any significant progress.

BACK IN THE OLD DAYS

The Teamsters and UPS agreed to extend the national contract past the July 31 expiration date, but by the end of August it was clear that UPS wasn't budging. The Teamster national negotiating committee rejected UPS's measly wage proposal of a 35-cent-an-hour increase for each year of a company-proposed six-year contract, twice the length of previous contracts. Carey called the company's offer "insulting and ridiculous" and called for a strike vote, which probably should have happened before negotiations began.[17] *Bloomberg* reporter Aaron Bernstein described the situation this way:

> Back in the old days, contract talks between United Parcel Service Inc. and the International Brotherhood of Teamsters were predictable. Union bosses made noises about fighting valiantly for their members—and then cut deals with UPS, telling their 165,000 UPS members to swallow hard. But this time, reform-minded Teamsters President Ron Carey is leading his first go-round with the union's biggest employer. And he's having a heck of a fight getting more out of the company than his lackadaisical predecessors.[18]

A defiant Carey told the media, "UPS is faced with a union leadership that's not going to operate in the interests of corporate America."[19] While wage issues were important, safety issues were too, and, for many people in and around TDU, the creation of full-time jobs out of part-time positions was important in rebuilding the union's strength on the shop floor and strengthening the reform movement.

However, the Teamsters were not in the strongest position to organize a prolonged national strike. Strike pay had been raised from $50 a week to $200 at the contentious 1991 convention, but without any mechanism to pay for the increased benefits. There was only $30 million in the national strike fund, and the *Wall Street*

Journal happily and repeatedly told the business community that this sum "would be largely drained by a one-week nationwide strike against UPS." Carey, though, arranged a $50 million loan for the strike fund from the AFL-CIO to bolster the union's bargaining position.[20] UPS Teamsters voted 65,000 to 4,000 to authorize a national strike, but the company tried to downplay the significance of the vote as a "relatively routine bargaining strategy." Still, it clearly had an impact.[21] For historian Dan La Botz, after "sluggish negotiating, UPS got serious about a tentative contract only when the membership voted 94 percent in favor of strike authorization and the Teamsters decided to stop extending the old contract. The agreement won the use of Teamster drivers for the new three-day select service [a ground package service] and the union negotiated into the national contract an 'innocent until proven guilty' clause that was a first for a U.S. union."[22]

The Teamsters also won the creation of five hundred full-time jobs out of the existing part-time positions, a small but important reversal in the destruction of full-time jobs, and a significant wage increase of $2.25 an hour over four years for full-timers.[23] On the downside, the contract was extended by one year, and starting pay for the burgeoning part-time workforce remained at a paltry $8.00 an hour and remained virtually unchanged for the next three decades.

Labor historian Michael Schiavone pessimistically concluded, "Although the 1993 contract was an improvement on 1990, it further demonstrate[d] how difficult it was for the Teamsters to achieve a good contract. Thus, neither the 1990 nor the 1993 UPS agreements were a major success for the union."[24] Looking at the bare facts, it is hard to disagree with Schiavone, but it is also important to look at the direction of the union. In 1990, UPS Teamsters voted to accept a concessionary contract opposed by both old guard General President William McCarthy and his reform challenger Ron Carey, but three years later they voted overwhelmingly for strike action if UPS didn't budge in negotiations. The union, however, was moving haltingly forward; the expectations of its members were raised, and its a leadership was willing to take on the company.

THE 1994 SAFETY STRIKE

Just a few months later, however, UPS threw down the gauntlet in the most significant challenge to the reform leadership yet when it announced a significant increase in package weight—something negotiators had denied they were planning during the previous year's contract talks. Dan Campbell pointedly asked the UPS negotiators about their future plans: "As I remember it, it was the Safety and Health Subcommittee negotiations. I said to the company negotiators something like: 'So, do you guys have any plans to raise the package weight?' The company spokesperson replied something like: 'Maybe to 75 pounds.' Looking back, we should have read more from their nonverbal cues as well as the slight hesitation prior to the answers they gave. Clearly, they were lying."[25]

Safety issues were a top concern of union negotiators and rank-and-file UPSers. Did UPS fear that Carey would call a national strike (and have sizeable support for doing so) if doubling the weight limit came up in the contract negotiations? Already by the early 1990s UPS was one of the most dangerous companies to work for in the package industry, with an unsafe seventy-pound weight limit.

In late January 1994, UPS unilaterally announced that they would more than double the weight limit of packages from 70 pounds to 150 pounds starting on February 7, 1994. This was part of UPS's effort to gobble up more of the traditional freight market without the corresponding heavy lifting equipment traditionally used to move such weighty material. Injury rates would undoubtedly skyrocket. How would the union respond? After negotiations between the Teamsters and UPS went nowhere, Ron Carey set Monday, February 7 as a strike date.[26] UPS got a five-day injunction against the Teamsters barring any strike action, but Carey courageously defied it. The first-ever national safety strike against UPS was on. "The company," according to *Convoy Dispatch*, TDU's national newspaper, "directed supervision to call each and every Teamster, some 170,000, over the weekend prior to the strike to tell them they would be fired if they struck."[27]

It was a major test of strength between UPS and the new reform leadership, and over 90,000 UPS Teamsters responded to the strike call.[28] Local unions led by Carey supporters in major cities like New

York, Boston, and UPS's hometown of Seattle, gave the strongest support, along with locals in Wisconsin and cities including Cleveland, Columbus, Atlanta, Hartford, Pittsburgh, and Charleston, West Virginia. Bob Hasegawa, the recently elected reform president of Seattle Local 174, said, "One of my proudest moments was the safety strike. We were the only one in the western conference of Teamsters that went out."[29]

Though the strikers were only a minority of UPS's national workforce represented by the Teamsters, they were located in key choke points of the company's "hub and spokes" distribution system, thus making it very vulnerable to even selective and limited strike action. "Violating the restraining order was a bold step that forced the company to compromise," according to La Botz.[30] Within a day the company threw in the towel. The Teamsters won important concessions on the handling of these new, heavier packages. "The courage of Teamster members won this agreement. No corporation has the right to break workers' backs just to make another buck," declared a victorious Ron Carey.[31] UPS, however, filed suit for financial damages. Federal Judge Joyce Green in Atlanta, the same judge who imposed the injunction against the Teamsters before the February 7 strike, dismissed UPS's $50 million lawsuit on June 30, 1994.[32]

The suit was dismissed despite the best efforts of old guard leaders. "It's the first time I can recall the international telling the locals to be in contempt of a court order," said R. V. Durham, president of an 8,000-member Teamsters local in Greensboro, North Carolina. "Why should I expose my local to damages for an illegal strike?" Durham was Carey's major opponent in the union's 1991 election.[33] Such statement could have been extremely detrimental to the union's case in court. *Convoy Dispatch* responded by plainly stating the facts: "When asked for solidarity, these so-called unionists responded with duplicity and cowardice. They and their attorneys organized scabbing and pressured locals to scab. Then after the strike they publicly called it illegal and predicted a UPS court victory, knowing full well that UPS attorneys could turn their words to the company's advantage. No one got fired. No member got fired. No local got sued. The International beat the UPS suit."[34] Long-standing TDU national organizer Ken Paff put the safety strike in context:

The 1994 safety strike was an important piece of the history leading to the historic 1997 strike. Carey showed he was willing to take on UPS, including even striking during the life of the contract. The old guard officials directed members to work during the strike; in effect, more than half the locals actually scabbed on the strike. It was still successful in just a day, as UPS was shut down in so many big markets. Management learned to work with the old guard behind Carey's back to try to weaken the union. And Carey learned he had to go out mobilizing and educating members, to take on UPS.[35]

Convoy Dispatch reported that the safety strike also "sent a scare" through the management of big freight companies like Yellow and Roadway, which were on the eve of contract negotiations with the Teamsters over the much-battered National Master Freight Agreement. Donald Rockwell, freight industry analyst for Merrill Lynch, the giant financial services corporation, told the media, "They look pretty aggressive, don't they? I thought the Teamsters would be more willing to work with the (freight) companies. Now I'm a little more skeptical."[36] It had been a long time since a US union could scare the bosses.

NO TO "TEAM CONCEPT"

UPS continued to pursue other avenues to weaken the union and undermine the reform leadership, but it was stymied on several fronts. On August 25, 1995, UPS's petition to the National Labor Relations Board to change the jurisdiction that covers its operation to the much more employer-friendly Railway Labor Act was denied. The NLRB, after citing past cases that looked unfavorably on the company's petition, also thought it was worth citing the "long-standing history of collective bargaining between the Respondent (UPS) and the IBT under the NLRA [National Labor Relations Act] [as] an important corollary factor . . . None of the more than 100 cases referred by the Board . . . has involved an entity which, after decades of collective bargaining in accord with the rights and procedures set forth in the NLRA, essentially sought to transfer to a different system of rights and procedures under the RLA [Railway Labor Act]."[37]

The year 1995 was when UPS rolled out its "team concept" program. Also known as total quality management (TQM) or management-by-stress, depending on the industry or corporation, the program was a favorite management strategy in the US auto industry in the 1980s, implemented with the cooperation of the once powerful UAW. Team concept programs were specifically designed to weaken a union on the shop floor, both ideologically and organizationally, by promoting an identification of the already overworked union worker with the company's productivity goals, and getting workers to supervise each other. It was classic "divide and conquer" in modern dress. Most team concept programs violate the National Labor Relations Act's ban against "company unions," specifically Section8(a)(2), which prohibits employers "to dominate or interfere with the formation or administration of any labor organization or contribute financial or other support to it." [38]

Ron Carey and the new reform leadership of the Teamsters "was one of the few in the United States to explicitly reject the 'team concept' and the whole 'partnership' notion."[39] Looking back two decades, it seems obvious that UPS's goal was to weaken the Teamsters in preparation for the 1997 contract negotiations. Teamsters communications department staffers Matt Witt and Rand Wilson wrote:

> UPS announced that it was unilaterally implementing a new "Team Concept" program. Draped in the rhetoric of labor-management "cooperation" and "trust," the program would allow the company to replace the seniority system with management favoritism and to set up "team steering committees" that could bring about workplace changes without the elected union representatives. Management . . . [was] caught off guard when the union launched a full-scale membership education campaign showing the differences between the company's promises of "partnership" and the program's fine print that undermined the union contract.[40]

After an initial burst of money, time, and energy, UPS turned to high-priced consultants for team concept programs. The company lost interest in them, however, when it became clear that these costly advisors had stimulated counter-organizing by the union in many local unions under reform leadership with the help of the Carey administration. Witt and Wilson concluded, "Like the fight over package safety, the union's campaign to defend workers' rights helped build membership unity heading into the

1997 contract negotiations."[41] In Washington, UPS had the upper hand and pressed forward its advantage, using its newfound political influence to shred decades of laws that protected the American worker.

CHAPTER 8

THE CAMPAIGN TO DESTROY OSHA

Most employers would describe OSHA as the Gestapo of the federal government.

—**Representative John A. Boehner (R-OH), 1995**[1]

During the 1990s UPS became a major political force in Washington, DC. It was the single largest campaign contributor to federal candidates; it launched or financially supported major lobbying efforts; and, according to *USA Today* it multiplied its "clout by maintaining [a] private town house to host fundraisers and hold quiet talks with those it [was] seeking to influence."[2] UPS supported the "Republican Revolution" of 1994 that brought to power Newt Gingrich as the speaker of the House of Representatives, as well as a host of right-wing cranks committed to wiping out two generations of laws protecting US workers. After Gingrich and his supporters took office in January 1995, UPS poured more cash than ever into Washington lobbyists to press forward its destructive agenda. What did UPS want from this new Congress?

Big Brown had a wide-ranging agenda, but it had one specific goal in mind. It wanted to reduce OSHA, the Occupational Safety and Health Administration, to a toothless agency with only an "advisory role" to industries known for their dangerous and deadly working conditions. Not content to buy political influence in Washington alone, UPS also made a major effort to buy friends in the academic and media worlds, especially those who could offer "helpful" testimony before Congress and shape the company's image as a responsible "corporate citizen," not an OSHA violator.

WHY DID KEN MARTIN HAVE TO DIE?

By the early 1990s UPS was one of the largest private-sector employers in the country—and one of the most dangerous to work for. "Since 1972, UPS has been cited for 2,786 OSHA violations and has paid $4.6 million in fines, receiving more worker complaints than any other company," Aaron Freeman wrote in the *Multinational Monitor*, an investigative magazine devoted to the misdeeds of large corporations.[3] Mainstream media outlets also began to focus on working conditions at UPS hubs around the country. The *New York Times* ran a major exposé, "In the Productivity Push, How Much Is Too Much," that highlighted the growing number of physically devastating injuries resulting from the company's unilateral decision to raise the weight limit of packages from 70 pounds to 150 pounds in February 1994. "On the very day that change went into effect," wrote *Times* reporter Christopher Drew, UPS worker Henry Gallet "felt a sharp pain while pushing a 126-pound box of flour-shifting screens onto his truck. His doctors had to use screws and clamps to fuse a slipped vertebra back into place." Gallet was then an eleven-year veteran UPS driver based in Kansas City."[4]

Time magazine told the story of Karen Dawson, another veteran driver, who "felt her back pop as she tried to lift a package in August 1994 from the top shelf of her United Parcel Service truck in Atlanta." It was an 85-pound box that wouldn't have been there six months earlier. She underwent surgery for a ruptured disk and was disabled by the incident.[5]

The *Atlanta Journal-Constitution*, in a special investigative report on UPS's campaign contributions entitled "Delivering the Bucks," reported in 1996 that there had been 1,300 citations against the company since 1990. The company had spent $176.5 million on workers' compensation in 1994 alone.[6] Over one-third of these citations were designated "serious," which according to OSHA means that they could have led to serious physical harm or even death.[7] The *Atlanta Business Chronicle* reported, "Since 1984, UPS has averaged one on-the-job fatality per year. The fatalities do not include vehicular accidents, which are reported to the US Department of Transportation. All but one death reported to OSHA occurred at a UPS facility. Workers have been run over by vehicles driven by co-workers, squeezed between machinery, and struck in the head by falling packages."[8]

The *Chronicle* highlighted the case of Ken Martin, a sixteen-year veteran tractor-trailer driver, who was crushed to death against a loading dock at UPS's hub in Pleasantdale, Georgia. Martin had planned to go to his son's Little League game the night of his death, on August 22, 1994, but was called in to work at the last moment. A coworker driving a yard shifter (a vehicle used to move trailers) didn't see Martin and killed him while backing up. OSHA had previously cited UPS for this defect in the vehicles.[9] Looking at the numbers, it's clear that there was a direct correlation between UPS's push for greater productivity and the resulting increase in workplace injuries and even deaths starting in the mid-1970s and skyrocketing after 1990. UPS promoted itself during the 1980s as "the tightest ship in the shipping business," but this slogan had a more troubling meaning to its workers than to its customers. By the early 1990s, UPS was paying out one million dollars per day in workers' compensation for injuries received on the job.[10]

OSHA and UPS reached a Corporate-Wide Settlement Agreement (CSA) in November 1993 regarding the handling of hazardous materials and worker training. OSHA had cited UPS over these issues in Lenexa, Kansas, and other hubs around the country. However, while UPS was willing to sign an agreement on this issue, it was not willing to agree to a similar corporate-wide settlement agreement on ergonomics—designing a safe workplace—despite its atrocious track record. "While the Haz-Mat CSA had a major impact on UPS," reported the Teamsters communication department, "an ergonomic CSA would profoundly alter the entire UPS work process. Faced with this possible threat, UPS decided to mobilize an all-out effort to challenge OSHA—and in particular ergonomic standards. This became even more important after UPS secretly decided to go over 70s packages [to exceed a 70-pound package limit] sometime in mid-1993. Undoubtedly, they knew that with over-70s, lifting injuries would sky-rocket."[11]

Meanwhile, there had been a growing demand from the labor movement for action on ergonomic standards. "In 1990, 35 unions petitioned OSHA to issue emergency temporary ergonomic standards to curb workplace repetitive stress injuries," wrote journalist Aaron Freeman. "These standards, one of the agency's most ambitious worker safety initiatives in recent years, were designed to reduce cumulative trauma disorders (CTDs) . . . Specific types of CTDs include carpal tunnel syndrome, tendonitis and lower back pain."[12] The Bureau of Labor Statistics determined that CTDs accounted for 60 percent of all worker occupational injuries in 1991 and one-third of workers' compensation claims in 1988. In 1993 there were 302,000 work-related CTD cases reported across all industry lines. Keith Mestrich, of the AFL-CIO's Department of Occupational Safety and Health, correctly described CTDs as an "epidemic problem in the work place."[13]

In response, OSHA began citing and fining companies for ergonomic violations. "By 1990," according to Michael Weisskopf and David Maraniss, "eight hundred ergonomic violations were imposed by OSHA—one quarter of its general duty clause cases—costing employers more than $3 million in fines. Four UPS facilities were among those cited for unsafe package sorting and loading practices."[14] UPS faced fines of nearly $140,000. This was the tip of the iceberg at UPS. The Teamsters reported that "UPS workers suffered 10,555 lifting and lowering injuries that required more than first aid in 1992."[15] UPS, instead of using its world-class engineering department to design or redesign its workplaces or package cars to be easier on the human body, went in the opposite direction. It expected its workers to lift, sort, and deliver heavier and heavier packages, without any change to the design of the workplace or delivery vehicles.

CASS BALLENGER: UPS'S OSHA HIT MAN

While the Teamsters were able to wrangle some important concessions on the handling of these packages, the increased weight limit
stayed in place. UPS then set its sights on OSHA. The company
had a historic opportunity to weaken OSHA due to the Republican
resurgence produced by Bill Clinton's disappointing first two years as
president. Clinton had won the presidency from the hapless George
Herbert Walker Bush by promising jobs in the recession-bound economy, as well as health-care reform and a striker-replacement bill that
would ban companies from permanently hiring scabs during strikes or
lockouts.[16] Clinton's failure to deliver on all these campaign pledges
disillusioned the Democratic Party's most active supporters across the
country, while the promises he did keep—such as signing the North
American Free Trade Agreement (NAFTA)—had a similar impact.
The Republicans, led by Georgia congressman Newt Gingrich, were
emboldened by Clinton's string of failures and captured control of the
House of Representatives for the first time in forty years.

UPS's Political Action Committee (UPS PAC) was the biggest
PAC in the United States in the early to mid-1990s. *Time* reported
that "UPS poured $2.6 million into House and Senate campaigns
in 1993 and 1994."[17] While UPS hedged its bets and roughly split
its money evenly between Democrats and Republicans in the 1994
election, it moved quickly to bond with the new Republican leadership. UPS and a newly founded organization with a deceptively
concerned-sounding name, the Coalition for Occupational Safety
and Health (COSH), of which UPS was the biggest financial contributor, "lavished $3.6 million on members of the House of Rep-
resentatives."[18] The top five recipients were Republican leaders of
the new Congress: Tom DeLay, the new majority whip, received
$64,750; Newt Gingrich, the new speaker, received $44,774; Bob
Livingston, the new chair of the powerful Appropriations Committee, received $34,500; Dick Armey, the new majority leader,
received $31,000; and David McIntosh, the new chair of the House
Oversight and Reform subcommittee, received $30,137.[19]

Gingrich rushed to implement the campaign pledges outlined
in his "Contract with America" by putting the House under his
firm control. He filled key committee chairs, appointing such peo-

ple as Cass Ballenger (R-NC) to chair the House Subcommittee on Workforce Protections, which had legislative oversight over OSHA. OSHA had been subject to a slander campaign for many years by industry trade groups and lobbyists, and their right-wing hit men in Congress. One of Gingrich's most loyal lieutenants was John Boehner (R-OH), who famously declared, "Most employers would describe OSHA as the Gestapo of the federal government."[20] Lost in the whirlwind attacks and outright lies spread about OSHA was the fact that it had actually been created during the Nixon administration and was an outgrowth of militant efforts by workers in the late 1960s to bolster workplace safety.

The liberals in Congress and the labor movement saw OSHA differently. For them the agency was understaffed and underfunded.[21] The woeful state of OSHA was dramatically illustrated by the fire at the Imperial Food Products plant in Hamlet, North Carolina, that took the lives of twenty-five workers and injured fifty-four others on September 3, 1991. Most of the plant's exit doors were locked in violation of the law. During its entire history, the plant had never received a safety inspection. The fire was a massacre, and the plant owner was later sentenced to twenty years in prison.[22] Though the fire took place in Representative Ballenger's home state of North Carolina, it apparently didn't stir his conscience. Ballenger was UPS's point man for OSHA; he was also an old-fashioned southern bigot, complete with a statute of a black jockey on his front lawn.[23]

To say that Ballenger hated OSHA would be an understatement. According to the *Washington Post*, during the 1994 election, wherever "Ballenger spoke, checkbooks opened at the mention of the Occupational Safety and Health Administration." Ballenger would ask audiences, "Guess who might be chairman of the committee who'd be in charge of OSHA?" And after he told the crowds it would be him and that he needed their donations, "'*whoosh!*—I got it. This was my sales pitch: "Businessmen, wouldn't you like to have a friend overseeing OSHA?"'[24]

Ballenger was open for business, and business was good. UPS was especially rewarding to him. From 1989 through 2004, UPS contributed $45,000 to his campaigns, and the company was the top campaign contributor during his entire tenure in office.[25]

Soon after taking control of the committee chair, Ballenger openly revealed what he had planned: "OSHA's mission has become misdirected into simply finding violations of regulations and issuing penalties," he declared. His alternative? "We believe that a more effective workplace safety and health program would rely primarily on non-enforcement efforts."[26] Non-enforcement efforts? US workers faced a dangerous future if thinking like this prevailed. But UPS would need more than an eager committee chairman to get what it wanted. UPS made the biggest financial contribution to the formation of the Coalition for Occupational Safety and Health, comprised of one hundred of the Republican Party's most politically powerful allies in the corporate world on January 30, 1995. The conveners of the conference, according to Weisskopf and Maraniss, believed that "their time was at hand."[27]

To complete its team of OSHA hit men, UPS hired Dorothy "Dotty" Strunk as its chief Washington lobbyist on health and safety issues. Strunk, the former acting director of OSHA under President George H. W. Bush, was hired to work closely with Cass Ballenger in rewriting the laws governing OSHA's mandate. After leaving the first Bush administration, she worked as a legal advisor to several mining companies that also sought to weaken OSHA. Then UPS spokesperson Bob Kenney remarked that Strunk's "experience in health and safety is certainly a reason we brought her in."[28] "Dotty's draft," the 628-page revision of OSHA's rules, was dubbed "Ergo Light" by a triumphant Strunk. Not taking any chances that OSHA would issue ergonomic standards before her and Ballenger's bill was passed, "she successfully lobbied House appropriators to cut off funds for issuing ergonomic standards."[29]

The proposed legislation promoted "across-the-board deregulation" and contained "special favors for certain industries. The chemicals industry, for example, would achieve its objective of preventing state regulators from exceeding federal OSHA standards. The steel industry, for its part, would be freed of the requirement that employers keep records on work-related illnesses that do not require medical treatment. OSHA uses these records to identify which industries it should target for inspections."[30]

Ballenger proposed two bills to gut OSHA, but he was forced to withdraw them. Yet not before UPS secured one big victory. *Time* reported in January 1996, "Last month [December 1995] the company joined a coalition of 250 business and trade groups that stifled OSHA's attempts to develop a standard aimed at reducing the incidence of conditions like carpel-tunnel syndrome, an inflammatory wrist ailment triggered by repetitive motion. The victory was won even before the agency had a chance to issue the proposed standards for discussion."[31]

Joseph Dear, then assistant secretary of labor for OSHA, said, "It's special-interest lobbying at its worst. I think it's incredible overreaching to say that an agency can't collect data about one of the largest injury problems in the workplace today."[32] OSHA remained underfunded and understaffed, and enforcement dropped significantly during the Clinton years. During this period, OSHA workplace inspections dropped to a new low.[33]

The Clinton White House and labor secretary Robert Reich were more than willing to make concessions to the Gingrich Republicans and industry lobbyists. Clinton and Reich, for example, had their own corporate-friendly plans for OSHA—"Reinventing OSHA," they called it.[34] They did manage to keep ergonomics research alive. Clinton "ordered the Department of Labor to continue work ergonomics rules that would protect the American worker from strained backs, torn tendons, carpal tunnel injuries, associated with repetitive motion, and a broad range of workplace MSDs, or musculoskeletal disorders," wrote journalists Lou Dubose and Jan Reid.[35] In the waning hours of his administration, Clinton had his officials in the labor department post new ergonomic rules, only to have them opposed by a coalition of business groups, including UPS. Soon after the inauguration of President George W. Bush, Tom DeLay led the effort to overturn these regulations using an obscure congressional rule. Feeling smug and victorious, DeLay boasted to the *Washington Times*, "I can't get this grin off my face. I go to sleep and wake up with it."[36]

CHAPTER 9

LAST, BEST, AND FINAL OFFER?

All these little nobodies come to work for us, and now they think they're
somebody because they work for UPS.

—Ed Lenhart, Northern California
UPS chief negotiator, 1997[1]

The 1996 Teamsters election was a bruising contest between Ron Carey and James P. Hoffa for the leadership of the union. This was the second election for international union officers and delegates to be monitored by the federal government, and it proved more contentious than the first in many ways. Ron Carey and the reform movement had moved the union forward, eliminating many of the perks that traditional Teamster officers had embraced as entitlements and removing many corrupt officials through trusteeships.[2] The old guard overwhelmingly reacted with fury and sought revenge on Carey and his supporters. Teamster employers and their allies looked approvingly upon this burgeoning counterrevolution. "In all honesty, my client's interests are best served by a return to the old Teamsters," declared Gary Marsack, a Milwaukee-based lawyer representing Teamster employers.[3]

The old guard rallied around the lackluster James P. Hoffa, son of the infamous Teamster leader and a career lawyer. Hoffa had lacked standing as a Teamster to run for office in 1991, but five years later, he led a slate to oust Carey. "Junior Hoffa," as reformers disparagingly called him, was viewed as a political nonentity. "He's an empty suit," Ron Carey declared. "He's a front man for the mob. If he didn't have that last name, he wouldn't have a chance. He'd be back at his country club playing golf."[4] Hoffa's long association with organized crime and corrupt union officers was well documented by the Carey campaign, but he was treated with kid gloves by the media.[5] He was continually referred to as "son of the legendary Teamster leader," for example. Carey, on the hand, was subject to withering attacks and a smear campaign by the same media outlets; few of these outlets retracted the worst smears when they were proved false. William Serrin, the former labor reporter for the *New York Times*, called the media smears on Carey "one of the most egregious disinformation campaigns in modern American journalism."[6]

The *Wall Street Journal*, the leading media voice of the US business class, was salivating at the prospect of a Hoffa victory. Typical of the *Journal*'s coverage was Glenn Burkins's "Teamsters Watchers Ponder a Hoffa Win," published on the eve of the 1996 vote count: "The race to elect a Teamsters president is thought to be neck and neck, but observers already are wondering what an upset victory by James P. Hoffa might mean for the divided union and its employers."[7] The *Wall Street Journal* was the right-wing and, many times, shrill voice of corporate America, so one can safely assume that the paper's concerns lay with the interests of Teamster employers.

CONTRACT CAMPAIGN BEGINS

After taking office in February 1992, Ron Carey had initially hoped to find some common ground with the defeated and divided remnants of the old guard. But he met with little success. While a few minor old guard figures were willing to accommodate themselves to his administration, most took the approach of rule or ruin. The old guard was especially strong in Chicago, the site of the largest concentration of Teamsters in the United States and the transportation hub of the country. By the end of the 1993 national UPS negotiations, an exasperated and furious Carey declared, "For 19, 20 months, I've held out this olive branch. It's not a matter of working together anymore. It is open warfare."[8] It was clear that any successful UPS campaign for the upcoming 1997 UPS contract had to be run out of Washington, DC, though with the expectation that local unions controlled by the old guard would be actively hostile, slow to respond, or even likely to ignore any contract campaign initiatives. Fortunately for Carey, there had been a major political breakthrough in the fall of 1995 that raised the hopes of reformers nationally: Jerry Zero and the Reform Pride Movement (RPM) won the leadership of Teamsters Local 705 in Chicago after a contentious, raucous trusteeship.[9] Local 705 was one of the most important UPS locals in the Midwest, and having it in the hands of reformers strengthened the future contract campaign.

Local 705 represented overwhelmingly part-time UPS workers at the company's strategically important Chicago Area Consolidation Hub, or "CACH," located southwest of Chicago. CACH was the center of a transportation vortex for transcontinental shipping. Its huge workforce employed as many as 8,000 workers during the course of the year, and it reached its zenith each year during the Christmas "peak season." For volume of packages handled, CACH was second only to Worldport, UPS's air hub in Louisville. CACH became one of the key battlegrounds between the company and the union. However, Local 705's twin, Teamsters Local 710, also based in Chicago, remained firmly in the hands of the old guard, under the leadership of Frank Wsol. Local 705 and Local 710 had independent contracts with UPS, but they bargained concurrently with the national union.

The 1997 UPS contract shaped up to be a battle for the future of the entire union, and to win the demands that the union was putting forward, Carey knew the Teamsters would have to organize on a vastly different scale than in previous battles. "You have to have something that brings you together. When you are organized, you then create the leverage you need," recalled Carey.[10] Rand Wilson was tapped to be communications coordinator and campaign strategist for the contract campaign. Before coming to the Teamsters, Wilson had worked since the 1980s as a union organizer and led several important solidarity and labor-centered political campaigns. "Wilson started in the labor movement as a member of the

Oil, Chemical and Atomic Workers Union (OCAW). . . . In 1989 he helped coordinate solidarity efforts in Massachusetts during a successful three-month strike by 60,000 telephone workers against health care benefit cost-shifting. The strike victory helped spur the formation of Massachusetts Jobs with Justice," a coalition of labor and community organizations.[11]

With a background like that, Wilson was the right person for the job. "I volunteered on the Carey campaign in 1990–91," he recalled two decades later. "Friends who were working in DC for Carey recruited me to the national staff in 1995."[12] Planning for the UPS contract fight began during the summer of 1996. Steven Greenhouse, a labor reporter for the *New York Times*, observed Wilson in action during the fractious 1996 Teamster convention in Philadelphia:

> Tucked in a booth belonging to the union's Parcel & Small Package Division, Rand Wilson was preoccupied with another, distant battle. He was buttonholing dozens of U.P.S. shop stewards and stuffing their pockets with a booklet called "Countdown to the Contract." It contained a month-by-month calendar until the July 31 strike deadline and gave myriad tips on how to escalate pressure on the company and build a communications network to keep workers informed and involved.[13]

"The International Union began sending bulletins to every UPS member's home," later wrote Wilson and fellow communications department staffer Matt Witt. The bulletins "highlight[ed] the importance of Teamster families' involvement in the upcoming contract campaign. Nine months before the contract deadline, every member received a survey asking them to help shape the union's bargaining priorities."[14]

With Ron Carey and Teamsters Local 175 president Ken Hall (who was appointed small package director after Perrucci), Wilson crafted the membership survey, asking members how the union negotiating committee should prioritize the following: creating more full-time jobs, increasing wages, and improving pensions. But "Countdown to the Contract: UPS Teamster Bargaining Survey" was more than just a long list of questions for members to answer. "The bargaining survey was a very important part of the contract campaign," said Wilson. "Working closely with the Research Department, we put a lot of effort into how we framed issues so that the questions didn't divide full-timers from part-timers, or feeder drivers from package car drivers. The distribution and return of the surveys was just as important because that allowed the leadership to gain intelligence about which locals had the organizational capacity to get a large number filled out and returned. It signaled which were willing to actively participate."[15]

It was generally expected that UPS would continue the push for major concessions from the union, and possibly even greater ones than demanded in the past. Unsurprisingly, the survey found that, for 90 percent of members, the top priority was creating more full-time jobs.[16] The Teamsters Research Department produced a well-documented booklet in 1997 entitled *Half a Job Is Not Enough* that denounced the employment trend at UPS: "The last Teamster-UPS contract was negotiated in 1993. Since then, the part-time workforce at UPS had grown by 43 percent, while the number of full-time jobs has grown by only 10 percent. UPS has hired an additional 46,300 workers, but more than 38,500 of them have been placed in part-time jobs. Therefore, 83 percent of the new jobs at UPS have been part-time jobs."[17]

Increasingly, part-time work was being treated as the norm. According to the booklet, "one would expect part-time employment to grow as the company expands. However, the shift to part-time jobs is way out of proportion when compared with overall growth in the economy. Since 1993, the volume of packages handled by UPS grew by 8 percent. Total company revenues grew by 26 percent. But part-time jobs grew by 43 percent, much more rapidly than the company as a whole."[18]

UPS made over $4 billion in profits during the life of the 1993–97 contract.[19] It was well positioned to create more full-time jobs and close the wage gap between part-time and full-time workers, and UPS workers knew it. More than 100,000 of them signed a petition demanding that UPS stop increasing the number of part-time jobs and start creating more full-time ones.[20]

During the past two contract negotiations, the Teamsters had struggled to counter the company's daily propaganda broadcasts issued at "Pre-Work Communication Meetings" (PCMs). This time, new package director Ken Hall ensured a regular flow of information to the ranks and asked "all Teamster local unions to set up 'member-to-member' communication networks. Under these networks, each steward or other volunteer was responsible for communication with approximately twenty workers. The International Union deployed education staff and field representatives—some of them UPS rank-and-filers—to help locals get the networks established."[21]

The "member-to-member" campaign was the first and largest initiative in the union, if not the entire US labor movement, to involve 185,000 rank-and-file union members in a contract campaign.

"WE WANTED PEOPLE WE COULD COUNT ON"

The Field Services Department was to play a crucial role in the upcoming contract campaign. Carey created the department soon after taking office in his first term, and it organized contract campaigns and ran strikes for contracts negotiated by the international union in Washington. David Eckstein directed the department and worked closely with Rand Wilson to train a crew of field representatives ("field reps") to focus exclusively on the upcoming UPS contract campaign. Forty representatives were drawn from a cross section of the varied Teamster membership, including freight, car haul, warehousing, and UPS. "We wanted people we could count on," Eckstein recalled. "We wanted to create an army the company couldn't buy."[22]

The field reps were expected to work around uncooperative local officials. "We had a lot of resistance in Minnesota and Wisconsin," Eckstein remembered.[23] Carey and Eckstein held two-person meetings with local officials about the upcoming contract. Eckstein vividly remembers Carey laying it on the line: "I know some of you don't like me, but this is a national contract campaign and it is going to happen. We have two plans: Plan A is where we give you everything you need to move the campaign in your local, and Plan B is the same as Plan A but we move it in your local without you."[24]

Carey made it clear, according to Eckstein, that the full weight of the general president's office would be brought to bear on uncooperative local officials, including the possibility of trusteeship.[25]

The overlapping issues of the newly launched UPS contract campaign and the final months of Carey's reelection campaign were obvious. Carey and the reformers had to fight on two fronts simultaneously—against both UPS and Hoffa, who threatened to dismantle all the work done to move the union forward. The Carey campaign crafted its reelection efforts with flyers and pamphlets featuring questions and assurances like "Who do you trust? The choice is clear," and "Ron Carey Has Walked in Our Shoes."[26] For most UPS Teamsters, the choice *was* obvious, and, in the final vote count, Carey won with more than 52 percent of the vote, nearly four percentage points more than he had in 1991. Carey claimed victory on December 15, 1996, and in front of an audience of cheering supporters, he told Hoffa and the old guard, "We're moving out of the station. The station and the train are about reform, about cleaning up the corruption. If he [Hoffa] wants to get on that train and be supportive, then we encourage that and welcome that. If that is not his intention, then the train's moving out of the station and, we say, 'Goodbye. God bless you.'"[27]

Carey's stunning victory felt more like the triumph of a long-shot underdog rather than a sitting president. However, Carey didn't get to enjoy his success for long. Teamster election officer Barbara Zack Quindel, who had first certified Carey's election on January 10, 1997, uncertified it shortly after due to charges of fundraising violations by his campaign. These charges hung ominously over UPS contract negotiations well into the coming summer.[28]

Carey would later be forced to take a leave of absence from office and was barred from future runs for president. However, in the early months of his second term, he and the rest of the union were focused on the upcoming battle at UPS. In Chicago, on March 7, 1997, four days before national negotiations began, the Teamsters organized a national contract meeting with two representatives from each of the 206 UPS locals to outline contract goals and strategy. Three days later, UPS Teamsters rallied in ten major cities, including Atlanta, New York, Philadelphia, Chicago, Dallas/Fort Worth, Los Angeles, and Seattle. "UPS is a billion-dollar company," Carey told the media, "that can afford to provide good full-time jobs with pensions and health care."[29] On March 11, proposals were exchanged and, as predicted, the company demanded wide-ranging concessions. Sitting beside Carey at the negotiating table this time was not Mario Perrucci but Ken Hall. Perrucci's downfall on corruption charges in 1995 had opened up a big vacuum in the national leadership that was filled by the relatively unknown but ambitious Hall, a West Virginia Teamster official who had no personal background at UPS, unlike Carey or Perrucci. In 1993, he had been appointed an international representative by Carey before becoming package director.[30]

ONCE AGAIN, DAVE MURRAY

In 1997, the UPS negotiating team was once again led by labor manager Dave Murray, whose arrogant behavior was notorious during the 1993 negotiations. UPS negotiators were shocked to see public mobilization occurring so early in negotiations, a key difference from the 1993 negotiations. Baffled, one company representative asked, "What's going on?"[31] Throughout March, before the next round of contract talks, the Teamsters doubled the number of rallies. In April the union launched a campaign to document unsafe working conditions that netted 5,000 safety grievances on specially crafted "EZ Grievance Forms."[32] Once again rank and filers were prominently placed on the UPS National Negotiating Committee, including Wesley Jenkins (Dallas), Todd Hartsell (Des Moines), Dave Dethrow (St. Louis), and Mike Knear (Louisville).[33] Present also were veteran TDUers Bob Hasegawa, the recently elected president of Seattle Local 174, and Dan Campbell, a full-time business agent working for Texas Local 657.[34]

At the same time, UPS labor managers were engaged in dirty dealings behind the scenes. In early April it was discovered that UPS's Washington State labor manager, Jim Kline, and other company executives were working with old guard officials to undermine local negotiations. More reminiscent of the Three Stooges than anything else, UPS executives called Seattle Local 174's hotline to listen to the latest contract update but forgot to hang up the phone when the voice mail started to record. Seattle Local 174 President Bob Hasegawa chaired the bargaining committee for the Washington State rider of the national UPS contract. "Right now even

Bush is not giving a whole lot of attack to Hasegawa," a frustrated Jim Kline could be heard saying. Kline was referring to old guard official Doug Bush, secretary-treasurer of Local 589 based in Port Angeles, Washington. "I'm having a beer with Bush next Wednesday," jumped in division manager Mike Minor, "and we're going to have a heart-to-heart."[35] It is not known if this "heart-to-heart" meeting ever happened.

The conversation moved on to how best to use another old guard official, Rod Mendenhall. Hasegawa had defeated him for the leadership of Local 174, but he had since been hired at a nearby Teamster local based in Everett, Washington. Mendenhall already had been pushing to rid the local bargaining committee of rank-and-file members supportive of the reform movement and replace them with others who had more pro-company sympathies. One company executive on the recording didn't have a particularly high opinion of Mendenhall, fearing that the official could screw up their plans. He hoped that "Rod doesn't fuck the thing." After Mendenhall's efforts to skew the committee were revealed, he resigned from the bargaining committee.[36]

Where else was such underhanded dealing taking place? There were two dozen supplements and riders to the national contract, which created ample room for possible collaboration between UPS and the Teamster old guard to undermine the contract campaign. The truth is we may never know the extent of their efforts.

Contract negotiations were suspended from April 22 to May 13, 1997. Soon after they resumed, it became clear that UPS had no intention of moving forward. There was little doubt in the minds of Carey and many others that UPS felt bolstered by the lack of support for the contract campaign by old guard–led local unions. On May 14, Carey, in a sharply worded directive to UPS locals, declared, "It has been called to my attention that some local unions are not complying with the negotiating committee's policy and strategy." He instructed all UPS locals to "implement and carry forward the policy and plans of the Teamsters National Negotiating Committee with an emphasis on membership involvement and participation." Doing so would be "crucial to winning a successful contract."[37]

OLD GUARD SABOTAGE

Tim Buban vividly remembers the difficulties of dealing with old guard local union officials. Buban was a driver at Consolidated Freightways and a long time TDU member in Milwaukee-based Local 200 when he was asked to be a field representative for the UPS contract campaign. He was assigned a large territory stretching southeast from Minneapolis to Rockford and Chicago, an area that included UPS's Rockford air hub. Buban tried to work as cooperatively as possible with old guard local leaders like Dick Heck of Local 638 in Minneapolis and Frank Wsol of Local 710 in Chicago, but he was rebuffed, undermined, or threatened at every turn. Unlike Wsol, Heck was a member of the Teamsters national negotiating committee. "Heck was horrible," Buban recalled. "I asked him for a list of his UPS stewards and he said he would mail them to me. But when I opened the mail there were only names—no contact info or even the hubs they worked at. When I called Heck and asked why he sent me this useless info, he said he would get back to me later.[38]

After one long stay in Minneapolis, Buban informed Heck that he was going home to Milwaukee for a few days' rest. He later received a late-night phone call from one of Heck's staffers who told him, "We don't need you to come back. We have things in hand here."[39] Undeterred, Buban kept returning to Minneapolis.

Local 710 was even worse to deal with, according to Buban. Local 710 was a petty fiefdom where Frank Wsol struck a grandfatherly pose while his underlings victimized critics of his regime. Ron Carey had suspended Wsol and three other members of the local union staff, including UPS union representative Robert Falco, who failed to defend Nicholas Johnson, a Local 710 UPS driver who had been unjustly fired by the company. Wsol and Falco retaliated against Johnson after he criticized Wsol in a letter to *The New Teamster*.[40] Johnson was later put back to work with full pay and benefits by an arbitrator, and, unfortunately, Wsol later returned to power with his regime intact. Falco told Buban on their first meeting, "I know you're in TDU, and a lot of my members are fed up with TDU and may beat you up. I'm not saying *I* would or tell *them* to."[41] Buban took this as a threat but was undaunted. He worked cooperatively with many part-timers and feeder drivers at the Rockford air hub. "I never met a rank and filer in Local 710 who wasn't supportive of what we were doing," he recalled.[42]

It should also be recognized that implementing the contract campaign in many reform-led locals was a highly uneven process. A lot of the difficulty stemmed from the obvious circumstances: the old guard had controlled many locals until very recently, and some of the best reform activists had been elevated to the staff of local unions or the international union in Washington. The pioneering aspects of the member-to-member campaign ran up against many local reform leaders, who preferred to rely on the traditional union structure of union representatives (still often called business agents, or "BAs") and officially recognized, and in many cases appointed, union stewards. Days of Action were little more than the full-time staff coming down to the nearest UPS hub and handing out flyers in the morning and then going back to the office. Activist stewards, field reps, and TDU members filled the gaps in the contract campaign. Despite these shortcomings, the campaign shaped the workforce for a confrontation with UPS that was unprecedented in the history of the company.[43]

"TRYING TO WEAR OUR BARGAINERS DOWN"

Still, negotiations were going nowhere on the national level, and so the Teamsters broke off negotiations on May 15, two days after they had resumed. *Convoy Dispatch* argued that UPS was "trying to wear our bargainers down and wear the rank and file down by focusing on demands that they know will never be accepted. Their hope? That they can scare us into throwing up our hands and accepting what we've got now."[44] *Convoy Dispatch* listed the many concessions that UPS was demanding this late in negotiations:

- A complete company takeover of health, welfare, and pension funds
- A seven-year contract
- Expanding Article 40, the air operations section, to have part-timers doing all of the air work at the expense of full-time jobs

- No increase in the start pay of part-time workers
- Force UPSers to cross picket lines, even for Teamster-authorized strikes
- Water down the "innocent until proven guilty" language won in the previous contract[45]

Dave Dethrow, one of the rank-and-file members of the national negotiating committee, kept an account of negotiations that was later published in *Convoy Dispatch* and provides many fascinating insights. He was the elected chief steward of St. Louis Local 688 and a veteran TDU activist at UPS. Dethrow joined the negotiations on May 19 in Atlanta. Dethrow initially had reservations about his role on the committee and wondered, "Would I have a voice or be a token?" However, he was warmly welcomed by Ron Carey, who told him, "It's good to see an old friend." In spite of this welcome, negotiations were "frustrating" from the beginning for Dethrow, who found Dave Murray to be "arrogant and pompous." Three days into that bargaining session, the union caucus met and it was clear that UPS wasn't budging on major issues. "We needed to send them a signal," Dethrow recalled. "When the company returned to the table, Ken Hall informed them that we were leaving. They sat there dumbfounded as we walked out. I enjoyed that thoroughly."

AN ESCALATING CAMPAIGN

During the break in negotiations, the Teamsters escalated the campaign on UPS with more rallies and contract-related events. Not every rally was well attended. When Ron Carey spoke at a sparsely attended event in Atlanta at the end of May 1997, UPS officials were contemptuous: "They're trying to stage a Broadway production of 'Les Miserables,' and what we're seeing is a high school production of 'Annie Get Your Gun,'" said UPS spokesperson Mark Dickens.[46] Delighted by the small turnout, UPS drew the wrong conclusion and assumed that Carey's demands (including the demand for more full-time jobs) were mere posturing. The company kept misreading the battlefield. Meanwhile, the Teamsters drilled down on their efforts. By the beginning of June, all UPS shop stewards received a seven-minute video about the contract negotiations and stickers saying "It's Our Contract. We'll

Fight For It" were distributed in tens of thousands across the country.

The Teamsters also took the contract campaign international—an unprecedented development for a US-based union. The Teamsters approached the International Transport Workers' Federation (ITF), the oldest of the European-based trade union secretariats, which coordinates international solidarity campaigns between different unions in the transport industry. In February 1997, the ITF had held a meeting of all unions worldwide that represented or aspired to organize UPS workers in their respective countries. They met to form the World Council of UPS Trade Unions in London. Plans for a global day of action were formulated. Media coverage of the planned event had so jarred UPS that its United Kingdom general manager called then ITF general secretary David Cockcroft and asked if there was going to be a one-day worldwide strike. While no worldwide strike was planned on May 22, the world council organized in eleven countries "more than 150 job actions and demonstrations at UPS facilities worldwide."[47] One of the stickers handed out at the events read, "Around the World, United for Good Jobs at UPS: International Day of Trade Union Action." Solidarity strikes also took place in Italy and Spain, and a multinational union protest was held at UPS's European headquarters in Brussels.

The second meeting of the World Council of UPS Trade Unions was scheduled in Washington in early June 1997 to coincide with the national UPS contract negotiations. Forty representatives of UPS unions from around the globe met to discuss coordinated activity as the contract deadline approached. Ron Carey took the opportunity to introduce each representative one at a time to the company bargainers (much to the annoyance of UPS chief negotiator Dave Murray). "The clear implication was that there was going to be an international strike," said Dave Eckstein, former director of the Teamsters Field Services Department.[48] Whether Murray and other company negotiators thought this was yet another example of posturing we may never know, but the visiting members of the world council saw the efforts of the Teamsters very differently. Chris Hudson, the organizing director of the Irish Communication Workers Union (CWU), recalled, "When I visited both New York and Washington to meet with the Teamsters I was impressed at how they saw the need to organize UPS globally."[49]

Once negotiations got back into session, Dethrow recounted how Murray returned to his old tricks. There was a dreary predictability to the company negotiator's behavior: "All of the company's sinister proposals were still on the table. Management people were acting as though they were going through the motions, as if they could manipulate us like they did in the past. Murray was still insulting our members, his employees. Some of the company people acted as if they had trouble staying awake."[50]

The Teamster negotiating committee had many committed reformers and rank-and-file activists and also old guard figures that represented large areas of the country, including Dick Hec,k who represented Teamsters in Minnesota and whose cozy relationship with UPS negotiators was a source of tension. "UPS labor manager Denny Holmes," Dave Dethrow noticed, "would visit with union committee member Dick Heck almost every morning before negotiations." Holmes and Heck, in fact, jogged every morning together, according to Dan Campbell.[51] Dethrow wondered "what they talked about" and added, "I don't believe either Ron Carey or Ken Hall welcomed that sort of [fraternizing]. I know I didn't."[52]

Throughout July, across the country, nearly every Teamster local union conducted strike votes, and typically voted 90–95 percent in favor of strike authorization. Did UPS view even this as an example of posturing? While UPS presented a stony face to the Teamsters, the contract campaign was clearly having an impact inside and outside the hubs. Clearly responding to the union's campaign for higher wages, a frustrated Dave Murray told UPS supervisors in an audiotape sent out across the country soon after negotiations began in March that eight dollars an hour was not only an adequate part-time wage but in many areas of the United States it would be considered "a fine full-time wage." Murray was also angered by the transparency of the negotiations. "In the past," he said, "commitments were made to not speak to the members or the employees for whom the contract is being negotiated. The reason this was viewed as a wise position for both parties was that the communication of positions taken during negotiations often raises the expectations of those people who ultimately could be voting on the ratification of the agreement."[53]

If Murray thought that such arguments would bolster the company's position in public or stiffen the spines of frontline supervisors, he was sorely out of touch with reality. When UPS discovered that the Teamsters had gotten hold of the tape, refashioned it with responses to Murray from rank-and-file workers, and distributed it freely in July under the title "From the Horse's Mouth," Murray flipped out. An enraged and embarrassed Murray wrote to Ron Carey,

> We demand that your union provide us with a written undertaking by the close of business on Friday, July 18, 1997, that agrees to I) cease and desist from creation and distribution of your union's audiotape; II) deliver up to UPS for destruction all copies of the audiotape in its possession; III) provide us with a list of the names and addresses of the individuals to who you have distributed the infringing tape; and IV) delete any and all references to the tape in your newsletters, website and any other communications in which it appears.[54]

He was ignored.

"THEN WE'RE GOING!"

The credibility of UPS had sunk to a new low after the company announced that it couldn't afford to create large numbers of full-time jobs, even though UPS had made record profits of $1 billion in 1996 and was on track for bigger profits in 1997. It was against this background that Murray, in July 1997, declared that the company had made its "last, best, and final offer." A true insult, this offer proposed a lower wage increase than the previous contract, pledged to create only two hundred new full-time jobs nationally, increase subcontracting of union work, and demanded to take total control of the full-time pension fund.[55] Not to be outdone by Murray, Ed Lenhart, UPS's chief negotiator for the Northern California supplement, declared at the bargaining table: "All these little nobodies come to work for us and now they think they're somebody because they work for UPS."[56]

In Washington, as the midnight deadline on Thursday, July 31 approached, federal mediators asked to meet with two representatives from each side. Dave Dethrow remembered that the "tension was thick."[57] In Chicago, there was an excited atmosphere at the main gate of the Jefferson Street facility, UPS's main hub. Part-timers and feeder drivers lingered outside the security station waiting until the last moment to go into work or to walk a picket line. One part-timer showed up with a handmade poster that read: "UPS means 'Under-Paid Slaves!'"[58] When it was announced that Carey had postponed the strike, there was some disappointment, but it wasn't clear what was happening. On Sunday, August 3, Ron Carey told the media that if UPS did not address the union's key issues, "I assure you at 12:01, we'll be on strike."[59] Two hours before the new midnight deadline, Carey emerged from the mediator's office and met with his staff. Dave Eckstein remembered that Carey agonized about calling a strike. Despite all the preparation, every battle requires a leap of faith. "Are we ready to take on this company?" he asked everyone. Eckstein spoke up, "We'll have a problem if we don't." "Then we're going!" Carey replied.[60] The strike was on.

CHAPTER 10
PART-TIME AMERICA WON'T WORK

If you were to pit a large corporation against a friendly, courteous UPS driver, I'd vote for the UPS driver.

—**Jim Kelly, CEO of UPS, 1997**[1]

Holding signs declaring "On Strike," small groups of UPS workers and Teamster officials descended on hubs across the country late Sunday evening, August 3, 1997, but it wasn't until the next morning that the scale of the strike became visible to the world. Outside UPS facilities stretching from the Maine coastline to the Hawaiian Islands gathered anywhere from dozens to thousands of striking workers. Glum-faced, white-shirted supervisors stood, arms crossed, inside the fence lines and guard shacks. No workers or trucks were going in or out. The crowds of workers slowly made themselves into picket lines; most had never been on strike before. It was clear by mid-morning that 185,000 Teamsters were on strike, and 2,000 UPS pilots and hundreds of unionized mechanics joined them in the company's first truly nationwide strike.[2] Nothing was flying and nothing was getting serviced. If UPS management ever believed it was popular with its employees, that delusion was shattered on the morning of August 4, 1997.[3] Big Brown was shut down.

"WE CERTAINLY DON'T STAND
ON THE PICKET LINE LIKE GUMBY"

The Teamster's fighting slogan was "Part-Time America Won't Work," and these words were boldly printed on tens of thousands of placards carried on picket lines across the country. As the strike continued, UPS began to lose $40 million a day in business. Picket lines in Somerville, Massachusetts, and Warwick, Rhode Island, erupted into confrontations with the police as hundreds of workers tried to stop trucks driven by management scabs from crossing the picket line.[4] George Cashman, the president of Boston-area Teamsters Local 25, responded to reporters' inane questions about heckling scabs by declaring, "We certainly don't stand on the picket line like Gumby."[5] Meanwhile, packages piled up in enormous mounds, and customers were left hanging. UPS had never believed there was going to be a strike and had no Plan B.[6] Other big shipping companies, including the US Postal Service, Emery Worldwide, FedEx, Airborne Express, and DHL couldn't handle the increased volume of work. The postal service, the first option for many UPS customers, groaned under the crushing weight of hundreds of thousands of new packages flooding its system.

Murray took to the media to warn of the supposed dire consequences of the strike. "The economy is going to have 5 percent of its gross national product not moving," he announced soon after negotiations collapsed.[7] But UPS's attempts at scaremongering had little effect. It became clear that despite the inconveniences, the strike was very popular. The widespread favorable response came as a shock to UPS management and was an outcome that far exceeded anything the Teamsters could have imagined. The key issues—part-time work, low wages, unsafe working conditions, and the need for pension and health care protection—reverberated far beyond the ranks of UPS workers. "This strike is a consciousness-raising event," Daniel Yankelovich, chairman of a public opinion polling firm, told the *New York Times*. "What so often happens is that an event like this suddenly and unexpectedly focuses attention on something that is on people's minds and makes their concerns more of a political issue."[8] The strike brought to the surface the enormous anger that had been building among American workers for two decades and gave it a rallying point.

UPS scrambled with little success to replace strikers with management, and labor agencies provided scabs, but they simply could not replace the enormous numbers of workers on the picket line. A desperate UPS and its allies led by the National Association of Manufacturers lobbied President Clinton and labor secretary Alexis Herman to halt the strike under powers given to them by the Taft-Hartley Act. Clinton refused—despite a White House study that concluded that the "UPS strike will touch nearly every sector of the economy, and that the current makeshift delivery system will not survive the onslaught of packages."[9] Undoubtedly, Clinton's refusal to intervene had to do with public support for the Teamsters, as well as opinion polls revealing that 75 percent of respondents were opposed to presidential intervention.[10]

"I think that the biggest reason that the public supported the strike," said Matt Witt, the Teamsters' communications director, "was that the workers rather than the union officials did so much of the talking, and when they did, they showed how they were standing up for working people generally and not just themselves."[11]

PUBLIC HEROES

Many strikers found themselves in the unaccustomed role of public heroes. Complete strangers would bring food and drinks to the picket lines, or shake their hands and thank them for what they were doing.[12] There was constant honking of car and truck horns in support of the strikers. Approached by reporters on the first day of the strike, the strikers had been unsure of what to say, but their confidence grew by the day. Depending on the type of hub, most picket lines were a mix of part-time workers, package car drivers, and feeder drivers. To the great surprise of many reporters, many part-timers revealed that they knew more about how the economy worked than most Nobel laureates. Striker Laura Pisciotti told the *New York Times* while walking the picket line at UPS's CACH, "These companies all have a formula. They don't take you on full-time. They don't pay benefits. Then their profits go through the roof."[13] Pisciotti's work commute took an hour each way, and she worked no more than twenty-five hours a week, earning just a little over $8.00 an hour.

Other strikers echoed this idea: "'People don't even look at workers as human beings anymore," said UPS part-timer Leatha Hendricks. "To them I'm just a machine. All they care is you got strength in your back. And when your back goes out of whack, it's over. You're gone." Linda Borucki, a thirteen-year part-timer at the company, agreed: "You look around and it's hard to find real full-time work anymore. How do people expect you to make it?" Mike McCarten, a ten-year part-time UPS worker, said, "You can't feed your family on promises. You can't make house payments on promises."[14]

These and other UPS workers articulated problems that ran through the lives of millions of American workers. If the Teamsters were enjoying a public relations success, UPS was having the opposite experience. The darling of the business community and politicians, UPS and their fawning acolytes found themselves caught in the media spotlight and called out for arrogantly ignoring the strikers' demands. "We are willing to continue to discuss the matter with the Teamsters, but we must emphasize that our last, best and final offer remains unchanged," Kristen Petrella, UPS spokeswoman, told the *New York Times* three days into the strike.[15] Such statements won few friends and influenced no one. They instead reinforced UPS's image as greedy, insensitive, and out of touch with the needs of workers. Four days into the strike, Dave Murray told the *PBS NewsHour*, "There's a whole lot of part-timers who only want part-time work."[16] Apparently, UPS workers disagreed. In response to the company's repeated claims that workers were satisfied with their lot at UPS, Rand Wilson said: "All the spin doctors in the world can't compensate for what people think and feel."[17]

The perennial political melodrama of the 1990s—the conflict between the Clinton White House and the Republican-controlled House of Representatives—was blown off the front page for a few weeks.[18] *New York Times* columnist Bob Herbert called the UPS strike "a crusade against low wages."[19] Herbert, one of the leading columnists for the paper, spoke for millions when he wrote that the UPS strike "is best seen as the angry fist-waving response of the frustrated American worker, a revolt against the ruthless treatment of workers by so many powerful corporations."[20] Even right-wing *Chicago Sun-Times* columnist Dennis Byrne was compelled to write,

"Working men and women have paid dues enough; it's time to pass around some of the prosperity."[21] The UPS strike became a national referendum on the state of the economy.

CHICAGO: SHUTTING DOWN THE LOOP

During the first week of the strike, the Teamsters encouraged package car drivers in several cities to visit their customers or "run their routes" with a part-timer to explain the goals of the strike.[22] It was a clever tactic because package car drivers were overwhelmingly popular with customers, something that UPS had long recognized as an important selling point for the company's services.[23] Even Jim Kelly, CEO of UPS, admitted, "If you were to pit a large corporation against a friendly, courteous UPS driver, I'd vote for the UPS driver."[24] During the second week of the strike, the Teamsters began to employ more militant tactics in several cities. In Chicago, Teamsters Local 705 Secretary-Treasurer Jerry Zero dispatched Richard DeVries to shutdown scab deliveries in the greater Loop, the downtown business and shopping area. DeVries, a union representative for the movers division of Local 705, was well-practiced in the application of labor law to picketing and had a reputation for militancy and methodical planning.[25] He led many job actions, including strikes and organizing drives, in rebuilding Local 705's presence in the moving industry. He also knew the alleyways and receiving docks, and the unionized personnel that staffed them, better than anyone else in the Teamsters.

DeVries organized mobile picket squads that shut down scab delivery operations at such well-known landmarks as the Sears Tower and the Amoco building, drawing out all the building's janitors and other union workers.[26] After a squad of DeVries-led picketers descended on the 52-story IBM building, managers posted signage (much to the chagrin of UPS) that said, "No! UPS Deliveries Here" on the main delivery dock. When *Chicago Sun-Times* reporters checked the legality of this tactic, Chris Gangemi, of the high-powered law firm of Winston & Strawn, told them, "Under the National Labor Relations Act, unions are allowed to request that customers not do business with UPS."[27] Local 705 picketers also shut down deliveries to McCormick Place, the premiere convention center in Chicago, prompting Mayor Richard J. Daley to demand that Jerry Zero remove the picketers. Zero refused.[28] Such militant tactics didn't scare off support for the strike. Opinion polls revealed that the public supported the Teamsters two to one over UPS.[29]

Contingents of union workers began visiting the picket lines and Teamster rallies across the country. In New York, a march of 1,000 Communications Workers of America (CWA) members joined a picket line, chanting, "Big Brown, shut it down!" One CWA member told striking Teamsters, "You're fighting for all of us."[30] At a huge rally on August 6 outside the Chicago UPS Jefferson Street hub, Carey, expressing the anger of the strikers, said, "We're really fighting for America's future. I know first-hand about UPS. I spent twelve years on a truck." Carey continued, "One member of the UPS negotiating committee said publicly, 'What are people complaining about? $16,000 a year is a lot of money.' All I have to say is if that is great money let's pay *them* $16,000 and subcontract their jobs. Let's take away their pension."

John Sweeney, president of the AFL-CIO, declared that the Teamsters "have picked up the gauntlet for all American workers. Their struggle is our struggle."[31] He went on to pledge the support of thirteen million union members, representing forty million union households, until the Teamsters won.

In addition, the Independent Pilots Association, which represented all UPS pilots (who had been working without a contract with UPS since December 1996) honored Teamster picket lines, effectively grounding UPS air operations centered in Louisville.[32]

The solidarity shown by the pilots was remarkable given how badly they were represented by the Teamsters; they had even voted by 99 percent to decertify from the Teamsters and form their own independent union.[33] But the pilots were completely on board with the Teamsters' contract campaign from the very beginning. Teamsters and pilots staffed the "war room" of the national UPS strike headquarters in Washington, DC, recalled former Field Services Department director Dave Eckstein. They "helped us picket and answered calls from their members in the war room along with ours."[34] Dan Campbell, working as a union representative in Texas, said that the pilots "were great and gave the UPSers a lesson in solidarity."[35] Not one UPS pilot, many of them veterans of the first Gulf War, crossed the picket line during the strike.[36]

Solidarity meetings and rallies were held across the country. In Chicago, veterans of the labor movement—some with careers that spanned the militant 1930s Congress of Industrial Organizations (CIO), the rank-and-file rebellions of the 1970s, and the Illinois war zone labor battles of the mid-1990s—spoke in support of the Teamsters.[37] Bennie Jackson, the recording secretary of Teamsters Local 705, represented the strikers. Jackson, an African American former UPS worker who started on the loading dock at Chicago's Jefferson Street hub in the late 1960s and participated in a wildcat strike, told the audience in a hoarse voice that he remembered what it was like to be "treated like slaves." He went on: "I understand the plight of the part-timers. I know what it is like to be in a truck when it's ninety degrees to one hundred and twenty degrees. . . . We have a lot of members who were former welfare mothers, and UPS isn't offering them any medical benefits. Their children aren't being offered any medicine."

Jackson told the audience of having read a letter addressed to a group of part-timers from Christine Owens, a UPS district manager in Chicago. The letter claimed that the Teamsters had only $20 million in strike funds, and when that ran out union members would be crossing the picket line. "What is your response to Christine?" Jackson asked the group of part-timers. They said, "Hell, no! Hell, no!"[38] The rally had something of a revival feel, and there was a feeling of change in the air. Maybe a turning point in the fortunes of the long-beleaguered US labor movement had been reached.[39]

SMOKESCREEN?

A frustrated UPS, however, did not go down without a fight. The company and its allies in the academic world began a concerted campaign to undermine the strike's rationale and goals, and to smear Ron Carey's reputation. It started with the usual company complaints about a strike. Ken Sternad, a UPS spokesman, told the media that the strike was an "unnecessary and irresponsible action."[40]

The attacks escalated from there, with the *New York Times* reporting that some executives of UPS were saying that "the part-time issue [was] a smokescreen, suggesting that the union's real complaint is with a company proposal to set up a new pension plan and pull out of the existing multi-employer plan, in which United Parcel is by far the biggest contributor."[41]

A smokescreen? Hardly. The Teamsters under Ron Carey's leadership had been battling UPS's campaign through two contracts to increase the number of full-time jobs. For over a year preceding the strike, the Teamsters had been campaigning around the issue. It was one of the top issues in every membership survey, a major demand in the Teamster contract proposal, and the most talked-about issue by strikers on the picket line, as well as the issue that UPS was the most defensive about. It was not some last-minute canard but rather a demand coming from the UPS rank and file. For example, Victor Fountain, a part-time yard shifter, told the *New York Times* at the beginning of the strike, "I never would have thought I'd have been here 19 years and still working part-time. I don't understand why we can't have full-time jobs."[42] There were literally tens of thousands of Victor Fountains working for UPS across the country.

In addition to protesting the expansion of part-time work, Carey expressed his disdain for UPS's desire to take over members' pensions and offer workers a new company-controlled plan:

> They have had a pension plan for part-timers for over 25 years. There really has been no increase in that pension plan. Twenty years of no increases, and now they want to take control of this. . . . The company wants to stick their hand right into the members' pockets, families' pockets, and take away some of those benefits by not putting those investments back into the plans to provide protection and provide increased benefits.[43]

PAID MEDIA HACKS

When UPS's attempt to reframe the issues failed, the company tried to shift the discussion to the political struggle between reformers and the old guard in the union. "This strike is really due to unstable internal union politics," said Jeffrey Sonnenfeld, a professor of business administration at Emory University, a former UPS worker who was portrayed as a neutral commentator.[44] Sonnenfeld, though, wasn't the best messenger for UPS because he had a long track record of fawning adulation of the company. Even more important, according to media expert Deepa Kumar, "On August 4, the Teamsters put out a press release with information that Sonnenfeld was a consultant for UPS. The press release stated in no uncertain terms that Sonnenfeld was the director of an organization that had received $1.125 million in grants from the UPS Foundation."[45]

The Teamsters exposed Sonnenfeld as a paid UPS stooge, but he continued to be a regularly featured media commentator on the strike. Sonnenfeld tried to diminish the mandate for change given to Carey by the rank and file of the union from two international elections. But his attempt to undermine the rationale for the strike and its goals failed, resonating only with a very tiny core of anti-Carey activists and business media commentators.

When all else failed, UPS tried, of all things, to claim the moral high ground on the democratic rights of Teamster members. Dave Murray, UPS's chief negotiator, said, "We don't believe that the time was right for a strike with us having a good contract offer on the table. We believe our people should have the opportunity through the democratic processes within the Teamsters Union to vote on that contract. If (the workers) then turn it down, that's when the union should look to use their economic weapons like strikes."[46] Similarly, UPS CEO Jim Kelly, on *Face the Nation*, said, "We think the best way to get them back to work is to have them vote on a great proposal that we currently have on the table."[47] In Chicago, UPS called a press conference to announce the results of a poll of dubious value, which claimed that 80 percent of Chicago-area respondents wanted the Teamsters to allow a vote.[48]

What was UPS up to? Above all, it hoped to portray UPS workers as hostages to an undemocratic leadership. This was actually a more accurate description of the circumstances of workers under the mobbed-up old guard who used to run the international union. In addition to their expressed concern for democratic process, many UPS executives were under a delusion about the happiness of their employees. Murray and Kelly actually thought they were well-liked and popular. Company executives "were armed with internal employment satisfaction surveys showing that UPS workers were happy and loyal and that they found the terms of the company's offer to be generous," according to a post-strike assessment by the *Wall Street Journal*. This belief may have been one of the biggest miscalculations in the history of UPS.

Ken Paff also argued that the real motivation behind UPS's call for a vote "is to induce people to scab by saying, 'If you like this offer, if you like a bonus, you'll get a bonus but the union won't let you vote on it, so you should scab.'"[49] This effort to undermine the strike also failed.

A WEIRD ARMAGEDDON?

Confused by the popularity of both Ron Carey and the strike, UPS and its allies were flailing. Ten days into the strike, the *Wall Street Journal* published an editorial called "Ron Carey's Weird Strike" that perfectly captured the confusion and panic in the upper reaches of the US business class: "The UPS strike is so weird it's hard to know where to begin. Somehow we're supposed to believe that the mighty Teamsters, after signing a contract with the very same company in 1993, has suddenly decided it must paralyze the nation's parcel-distribution system to have it out over mostly voluntary part-timers and various pension arcana. These matters may be worth an argument, but Armageddon?"[50]

It's hard to tell if the editorial was one last attempt to marshal management's wavering troops or a sad, incoherent rant—or both. "UPS must feel it's fallen down the rabbit hole," the editorial continued, sounding concerned for the company. "Here's a company that's about as close as it gets to being a model corporate citizen." But it was actually the paper's editorial writers who had fallen down a rabbit hole and emerged into a new world where a union fought for its members and where striking workers had a huge, supportive audience.

While the corporate class sympathized with UPS, Carey's opponent, Jim Hoffa, and his staff pledged support against UPS and refrained from any criticism of Carey's leadership for the duration of the strike. On the surface, at least. It would have been political suicide for them to express opposition, considering the popularity of the strike and the looming possibility of a rerun of the international union elections. "Internal politics stops at the picket line," Richard Leebove, a Hoffa spokesman, disingenuously declared.[51] Just beneath the surface the struggle between reform and old guard forces continued to brew, with some Hoffa supporters during the strike echoing many of the company's arguments.[52] In one important case, their perspective wasn't hidden at all. Chicago's Local 710, led by Frank Wsol, the biggest old guard UPS local in the Midwest, extended its contract with UPS and didn't go out on strike with the rest of the country. Wsol said that his local union would honor picket lines set up by striking Teamsters.[53] This drained away valuable time and resources from other areas. Tim Buban, the upper Midwest contract campaign field representative, remembered spending nineteen hours a day maintaining a picket line outside UPS's air hub in Rockford, Illinois. Buban actually got a lot of help from the Rockford-based Teamsters Local 325, which didn't have any UPS members. Though old guard supporters controlled Local 325, Buban recalled, "to their credit they helped staff picket lines and organized rallies."[54]

For the officers and staff of Local 710, collaboration with the worst practices of the company ran deep in their bones. Buban vividly remembers a few days after the strike began being approached by a Local 710 business agent on the picket line with a proposition that he knew was a scam. By this time, Buban had had many run-ins with the Local 710 staff. The business agent said to Buban, "The company needs to make a few deliveries with trucks that were loaded before the picket line went up. What's going to happen is a management guy is going to drive the truck through the picket line and outside a 710 driver would get in the truck, and make the deliveries."[55] Buban was shocked by this blatant attempt at collaborating with scabbing. Weary from long hours of picketing, he paused for a moment to give his best response, but at that moment a Local 325 member jumped in and said, "Where's he [the 710 UPS driver] going to punch in?" Obviously, the driver would have to cross a picket line somewhere to punch in. Buban immediately replied, "Wherever there is a time clock that's UPS, and we will have a picket line around it." Buban remembers that the Local 710 business agent, who thought he was so clever, was caught out and left, sulking.[56]

"IMPORTING MISERY FROM AMERICA"

Meanwhile, in Europe, transport unions rallied to support the Teamsters. The International Transport Workers Federation (ITF) "turned its London-based headquarters into a global command center for strike activities . . . issuing daily updates to unions, the public, and the business media," according to John Russo and Andy Banks.[57] The ITF leaflet "UPS: Importing Misery from America" was translated into five languages and distributed across Europe. German UPS workers, the largest concentration of European UPS workers, were represented by the Public Service and Transportation Workers Union, known by its German acronym ÖTV.[58] The ÖTV "coordinated strike support throughout Germany," including in Cologne, the location of UPS's air hub for European operations. "When reports that the unions in the Netherlands voted to support coordinated Europe-wide sympathy strikes reached the ÖTV union in Germany, its executive voted to endorse a strike action regardless of its legality."[59] On August 18, the French transport workers' federation put forward a plan to shut down Orly Airport, near Paris. Outside of Europe, railroad workers in India refused to transport UPS packages, while in the Philippines, workers from the Civil Aviation Union "organized a motorcade of 100 cars that surrounded the UPS subcontractor in Manila, preventing the transportation of packages for a day."[60] However, plans for Europe-wide strike action were called off when a deal was struck between the Teamsters and UPS three days into the strike.

Feeling completely isolated, UPS threw in the towel and reached a tentative agreement with the Teamsters on August 20, 1997, fifteen days after the strike began.[61] UPS agreed to the union's main demands and approved the creation of ten thousand full-time jobs out of low-wage, part-time positions; the largest wage increases in UPS history; and protection against subcontracting of union jobs. The company also backed off its plan to hijack the full-timers' pension funds.[62] According to the *New York Times*, "Carey hailed the agreement as 'historic turning point for working people in this country. American workers have shown they can stand up to corporate greed,' he said."[63] It was the biggest labor victory in a generation.

The success of the strike led many people to believe that the US labor movement was finally poised for a dramatic comeback. Historian Nelson Lichtenstein wrote that the strike ended "the PATCO syndrome, a sixteen-year period in which a strike was synonymous with defeat and demoralization."[64] Many believed that the Teamster victory would propel organizing in some non-union areas of the economy, including within the ranks of UPS's chief non-union rival, Federal Express. However, even in the atmosphere of celebration, dark clouds were on the horizon.

CHAPTER 11

THE "GET CAREY" CAMPAIGN

I am convinced that if this subcommittee had not acted, Ron Carey would still be president of the Teamsters.
                                                        —Pete Hoekstra (R-MI), March 2000[1]

Enraged by its defeat, UPS sought to inflict a heavy blow on Ron Carey and the Teamsters. Carey recalled:

> [There was] an incident which occurred in the last hours of those strike negotiations which illustrates the level of animosity the corporate community felt for me: One of the negotiators for UPS said, in the presence of then-Secretary of Labor Alexis Herman, "Okay Carey, we agree on the union's outstanding issues," and he proceeded to leave the conference room. As he was leaving, he leaned over the conference table and said to me, "You're dead, Carey, and you will pay for this, you s.o.b." I looked at Ms. Herman, and asked, "Did you hear that?" She responded, "I heard nothing."[2]

OPPORTUNITY FOR REVENGE

The opportunity for revenge presented itself two days after the strike when Barbara Zack Quindel, the Teamster election officer, voided the results of the 1996 election in which Carey narrowly but clearly triumphed over James P. Hoffa Quindel, a liberal labor lawyer based in Milwaukee, had been under enormous pressure all spring and summer to rule on the validity of the 1996 election after three people connected with Carey's 1996 reelection campaign, including Carey's campaign manager Jere Nash (a former consultant to the Clinton-Gore campaign), were indicted for campaign fundraising violations. A rerun election was to be held by the end of the year pending federal court approval. In her ruling, according to the *New York Times*, "Ms. Quindel did not find Mr. Carey to have been personally involved in violations."[3] The key players in the fundraising scandal were former community organizer Michael Ansara, liberal fundraiser Michael Davis, and Jere Nash. Together, they came to be known as the "Gang of Three." Despite Nash's claim that Carey knowingly conspired with fundraisers Davis and Ansara in conducting illicit fundraising activities, Quindel cleared Carey to run for reelection—a rematch with Hoffa.[4]

What were these fundraising violations? Veteran labor journalist Steve Early explained that Davis "devised various ways of leveraging and transforming union expenditures into Carey's campaign revenue through 'contribution swaps.' His partners in this enterprise—unwitting or otherwise—included institutions and individuals ineligible to donate money to Carey because they were union vendors, employers or relatives of either."[5] The contribution swaps included deals with such long-standing liberal lobbying groups as Citizen Action, major figures in the AFL-CIO like former Mine Workers leader Richard Trumka, and liberal Democratic donors like Barbara Arnold. The Teamster contributions to the various lobbying groups came to around $850,000 in return for nearly $220,000 in illegal contributions to the Carey reelection campaign. Carey denied any knowledge of these illegal activities and proclaimed his innocence. When word of the swaps came to light, he returned the disputed donations and ordered his staff to cooperate with federal investigators.[6]

What else did the "Gang of Three" get up to? They "conspired to finance a costly 'air war' on Carey's behalf that was viewed as a safe political substitute for fighting it out on the ground," writes Early. "Their crowning achievement was a panic mailing of 1.7 million fliers sent out during a one-week period so late in the campaign that many Teamsters didn't get them until after they'd already voted while others received as many as five different Carey leaflets on the same day."[7] This costly air war, a gigantic waste of time and money, had little to no effect on the vote. Writing in *The Nation*, journalist Alexander Cockburn explains:

> To suggest that Carey's narrow victory over Hoffa last December came courtesy of this last-minute slush is silly. As Quindel ponders whether to certify that December ballot she should remember the oldest law of elections, which is that as the ballot approached there are fewer and fewer undecided voters to appeal to, and these are usually cross-pressured, unlikely to vote and not receptive to last-minute mailings, which is what the above-mentioned was paying for (though the mail shot reached many Teamsters after they'd voted).[8]

Nevertheless, the swaps and the air war did damage Carey's personal reputation for honesty and integrity. They also breached a wall in his administration, allowing his enemies and the long-standing enemies of the Teamster reform movement to pour through.[9]

OLD GUARD EMBOLDENED

Quindel's ruling overnight emboldened the Hoffa forces that had been marginalized by the media focus on Ron Carey during the recent UPS strike. Shortly after the ruling, Hoffa appeared on three Sunday news programs, including the right-wing, anti-union *Fox News Sunday,* where he said, "Carey should step aside—be removed and disqualified from the race because this is a burgeoning scandal, and right now he is an illegitimate person in the position of president. He has not been elected by the members. The election has been thrown out. His term is over."

Carey responded to Hoffa on *Meet the Press,* declaring that Hoffa is "a real pro in terms of smear and distortion." Hoffa, Carey added, has "never negotiated a contract, he has never walked a picket line, he's never been elected to any position in this union." Carey responded to the charges of illegal activities by his campaign aides, saying, "You have people you trust, and in every organization you have those that step over the line."[10]

In spite of the fallout from Quindel's ruling, Carey's personal popularity was at an all-time high after the UPS strike, and he was emerging as a nationally recognized spokesperson for a revitalized labor movement. Dan Clawson, a professor of labor relations at the University of Massachusetts, told the *New York Times*, "If [Quindel's] decision had been made two months before the UPS strike, it would have been extremely serious for him. But it's a different thing after the strike." Hoffa's name recognition—with its appeal to a nostalgic era of Teamster power—had been his only personal asset during the 1996 election, but this couldn't compete with a real, live leader of a revitalized union. Carey was expected to easily triumph in the 1998 rerun election.[11]

The Hoffa forces, however, sought and received crucial help from UPS's Republican allies in Congress to oust Carey. Quindel's ruling inflamed UPS when it was revealed that she postponed her decision until the UPS strike was over. The company began to attack her, claiming in a letter to David Edelstein, a federal judge who oversaw union activities, that she wrongly chose sides "in a momentous labor-management dispute." UPS spokeswoman Gina Ellrich said that the company was not seeking any specific action from the court. Rather, they wanted it put on the record that the delay in Quindel's announcement "contributed to the length of the Teamsters strike."

Quindel responded directly to UPS: "UPS seems to misunderstand. The election officer's duty as a court officer is to run the election process for the benefit of the members. The members of the union can't have faith in the consent decree if they see it as interfering with their economic livelihood." The Teamsters' reply to Quindel now had more punch to it: "It's not surprising that UPS management is unhappy with the Teamsters' general president after our members' historic victory. UPS has no business attempting to meddle in internal union affairs. [The letter] they sent to Judge Edelstein has no legal significance."[12]

It may have had no legal significance, but the letter acted as a clarion call to anti-Carey political forces inside and outside the Teamsters. An informal "Get Carey" network had existed since the early days of his administration, and its public voices were the *Wall Street*

Journal and other media outlets and so-called "investigative reporters." The network had pumped out one lie, distortion, or smear after another through the years—each of which was exposed as false and dismissed. The independent review board (IRB) famously investigated Carey in the early days of his administration and declared in July 1994, "An investigation . . . into a variety of allegations made against General President Ronald Carey of wrongful association with organized crime members and associates, of improper receipt of payments from employers, and other miscellaneous allegations was carried out. For reasons detailed below, the evidence uncovered in this investigation does not support recommending a charge based on any allegation against Carey."[13]

The IRB's eighty-five page report declared at least sixteen times that there is "no evidence to support this allegation."[14] Frustrated to the point of despair, the "Get Carey" campaign was given a new lease on life because of the real crimes committed by non-Teamsters on Carey's campaign staff. The IRB also opened its own investigation into allegations against Jere Nash on August 28, 1997.

FROM HERO TO THE HUNTED

Meanwhile, as his enemies plotted against him, Ron Carey launched his second bid for reelection as Teamster president outside the 43rd Street UPS hub in Manhattan on September 11, 1997. "Carey again!" shouted about three hundred union members rallying before their morning shift.[15] He told the assembled drivers that UPS was suffering from "sour grapes" and had retaliated against Teamsters across the country for frivolous violations of company rules, including not having their shoes shined. "They don't know how to lose professionally," Carey said. He also threatened, "If the retaliation continues, we'll be back out on the streets."[16]

However, later that morning, potentially devastating news arrived that Barbara Zack Quindel had changed her mind, according to the *Boston Globe*, and was "now reconsidering whether Carey should get another crack at the job."[17] Carey's reelection campaign was thrown into disarray. "Since issuing the decision, certain information has been presented to me by a party to the appeal," Quindel wrote to Kenneth Conboy, a former federal judge who handled the election appeals under the consent decree. This alleged new information included notes written by Carey's personal scheduler, Coleen Dougher. "The notes were sent to Quindel last week by a lawyer for the Hoffa campaign who contends that a Hoffa supporter received them anonymously."[18] As soon as the opportunity presented itself to drive a stake into the heart of the old guard, it just as quickly vanished.

The next two months were one of the most stressful times in the lives of Ron Carey and Teamster reformers. It was open season on Carey. "I believe he will be removed or disqualified or indicted," crowed Richard Leebove, Hoffa's communications director and a former follower of neo-fascist cult leader Lyndon LaRouche.[19] On September 19, Nash, Davis, and Ansara pleaded guilty in federal court.[20]

Four days later, Quindel resigned as the federal court's election officer because of "the appearance of a conflict of interest."[21] What was the conflict? It came to light that William Hamilton, the Teamsters' political director based in Washington, DC, had arranged for a $5,000 campaign contribution to the New Party, a small liberal-and labor-supported party in Wisconsin, of which Quindel's husband was a leader.[22] Judge David Edelstein then assigned Conboy "for the sole purpose of investigating and deciding the issue of the disqualification of Ronald Carey from the rerun election."[23] In less than a month, the whole political atmosphere around Carey had been radically transformed. He had gone from hero to the hunted.

Hamilton resigned in late July 1997 and called the federal investigation into the 1996 Teamster election a "circus."[24] Hamilton was, for Steve Early, one of the "Beltway insiders preoccupied with Democratic Party deal-making, White House invitations and congressional 'access.'"[25] Hamilton was later revealed to be the fourth man in the Nash-Davis-Ansara network, and while it is hard to feel any sympathy for him in retrospect, much of what he said about the suffocating pressure of the time period was undoubtedly true. Hamilton described, in his resignation letter, the "turmoil created by the prolonged investigation by the US Attorney in New York, the delay in certification of the union election results and the calculated external distribution of documents held by Federal investigators." He complained that "documents voluntarily handed over" to federal investigators somehow found their way into "the hands of Hoffa operatives who then spun them to the press."[26]

One of these operatives was Gregory Mullenholz, a mid-level administrator who had worked for the Teamsters under Mr. Hoffa's father.[27] At the behest of veteran Chicago Teamsters organizer Danny Moussette, Mullenholz began sending notes, documents, and computer discs "containing, among other things, copies of memos from William W. Hamilton Jr., head of the Teamsters' government-affairs department. He later also received personal notes of Mr. Carey's scheduling secretary. Everything was passed on to Mr. Leebove," who directed Hoffa's communication team.[28] Leebove then passed all of this material on to sympathetic journalists and Republican congressional staffers. Many of these very same moles would testify before Congress as hostile witnesses against the Carey administration.

The circus moved from New York grand jury rooms to congressional hearings in Washington when Michigan Republican Representative Pete Hoekstra announced that his oversight subcommittee would conduct hearings into the Teamsters.[29] Hoekstra was not part of the old Republican Party–Teamster political alliance like fellow Republican US Senator Orrin Hatch, who had spoken at Jackie Presser's funeral. Hoekstra was born in the Netherlands and came to the US when he was three years old with his family and settled in Holland, Michigan. Holland was part of Michigan's second congressional district, the largest concentration of Dutch Americans in the country and a solidly Republican voting district. Hoekstra won an upset election against nineteen-term Republican Guy Vander Jagt by presenting a modest image, including campaigning by bicycle, against a comfortable, perk-loving incumbent. He came to Congress within a year of Ron Carey coming into office, at a time when the Teamster reformers began rebuilding their beleaguered union. Hoekstra cultivated connections with freight companies like UPS and with Detroit's old guard Teamsters (led by Lawrence "Larry" Brennan, James P. Hoffa's mentor), and others who had an interest in stopping Teamster reform.

HOEKSTRA'S WITCH HUNT

In January 1994, soon after the Republican landslide election, the new speaker of the House, Newt Gingrich, appointed Hoekstra as chair of the House Committee on Education and Workforce with its powerful Subcommittee on Oversight and Investigations.[30] Hoekstra's new role gave him the power and position to launch various legislative initiatives against the labor movement and Ron Carey's Teamsters. For example, he wanted to alter the basic labor laws that governed working conditions in the country. Tom Leedham, Carey's warehouse director, remembered Hoekstra as "a congressman who tried to eliminate the forty-hour workweek, gut overtime and job safety laws."[31]

Soon after, the Teamsters launched a corporate campaign directed at the car haul industry and Hoekstra appeared on *The Washington Review,* a TV news series sponsored by the American Trucking Association. He threatened, "We'll have a whole series of hearings to get to the bottom of this corporate campaign issue."[32] Hoekstra appeared soon afterwards, according to Carey, at a "news conference with the American Trucking Association, [and] with the US Chamber of Commerce to outlaw strategies [corporate campaigns] by the Teamsters."[33] Not to let the smallest issue slip by that could favor unions, Hoekstra also proposed, reported the *New York Times,* "a bill that would protect companies [retail department stores and malls] who grant access to charities from union claims of discrimination."[34]

With an anti-union track record like that it wasn't difficult to see Hoekstra's political agenda when he scheduled hearings into the Teamsters 1996 election after Quindel overturned Carey's victory. This was the political opportunity of a lifetime, and he seized it with both hands. He promised the hearings would show that the Teamsters under Carey had been taken over by a "pattern of coercion that exists from top to bottom."[35] One week before the scheduled first day of hearings, Carey received a letter from Hoekstra. It was a shameless effort to put Carey on the defensive. Hoekstra pleaded with Carey not to "retaliate" against any witnesses testifying at the upcoming hearings.

Carey rightly sensed that these "hearings" were likely to be a political show trial. After he declared that the Teamsters "would not retaliate against any witness participating in a governmental investigation," Carey moved on to the heart of the matter: "It may well be true that a handful of political partisans are eager to dress up testimony by a dramatic claim that they fear 'retaliation.' If these people say that they fear retaliation, they are not telling the truth—and it calls into question the reliability of any information they could give your subcommittee."[36]

Carey's prediction turned out to be prescient, and the hearings did far greater damage to his public image than he could have imagined. While his candidacy hung dangerously in the air, Hoekstra's hearings created a political atmosphere that made it possible for Carey to be disqualified from the rerun election.

Pete Hoekstra opened the first day of hearings on October 14, 1997, by speaking to his fellow subcommittee members with a serious, if not sanctimonious, tone. Many of those present, including Republican Representative Charlie Norwood and Cass Ballenger, were also veterans of UPS's war on OSHA. Hoekstra said, "I am also sure that by the end of the day you will agree that there is little you could have done that would have been more important than being here today. Amid all this high drama surrounding the money trail, an important fact is being overlooked. At the center of this controversy are real lives—the lives of individual Teamsters that suffered significant injustices during the 1996 Teamsters election."[37]

Who were these victims of injustice? Dane Passo, a member of Teamsters Local 705 in Chicago, led a parade of witnesses who testified under oath to have been victims of political persecution, discrimination, and violence reminiscent of the days of the Mafia-controlled Teamsters. The testimonies cast Ron Carey in the mold of past generations of presidents, suggesting that he didn't deserve the reputation of a reformer.

The *Wall Street Journal* and the *Chicago Tribune* highlighted the testimony of Passo, calling it "some of the strongest testimony" heard by Hoekstra's subcommittee.[38] In a prepared statement, Passo told a frightening story:

> On February 14, 1996, I and several other Hoffa supporters were peacefully leafleting the Local 705 meeting hall on behalf of the Hoffa campaign prior to the regular stewards' meeting. Zero,

standing at the head of fifty of his supporters, ordered me to leave the hall. I told him that the election rules permitted me to be there and that I had confirmed my understanding with the local elections officer, Julie Hamos. I offered to show him the election rules, but he refused, saying, "I don't give a fuck about the election officer or the rules—you're leaving." He then struck me in the head and kneed me in the groin, knocking me down four stairs to the ground floor. Several others of the people with him, which included three officers and several business representatives of Local 705, proceeded to kick me while I was on the floor. As I lay there, Zero told me to get up and leave. I told him I was unable to stand, at which point he grabbed me by the hair and dragged me about ten feet to the curb. Zero is 6 feet tall and weighs over 300 pounds. I was taken by ambulance to a nearby hospital where it was determined that I had suffered a lacerated kidney and contusions to the face.[39]

Passo's account is vivid and terrifying, and there is little doubt that a serious physical altercation took place. Cooler heads should have prevailed that night. However, the idea that a single episode could serve as proof of a reign of terror against Hoffa supporters was more than just inaccurate—it was pure sensational exaggeration.

"NO MATTER WHAT IT TAKES"

Who was Dane Passo? He was the leading figure of the anti-Carey forces in Chicago's Local 705 and had previously served as a steward, an organizer, and a business agent under Dan Ligurotis, the mobbed-up former secretary-treasurer of Local 705. Ligurotis gained notoriety for shooting his son to death in the basement of Teamster City, the office complex where many Teamster local union offices and Chicago-area Joint Council 25 are located.[40] As a loyal Ligurotis supporter, Passo supported his bid for international union office in 1991. Ligurotis, however, was removed from office on corruption charges and a trusteeship was imposed on Local 705 in 1993. Carey appointed his former campaign manager Eddie Burke as trustee, along with longtime Local 705 reformers Jerry Zero and John McCormick as assistant trustees, in an attempt to clean up the notoriously corrupt and violent local union. Passo declared war on the trusteeship, according to Bob Bruno, a professor of labor and industrial relations at the University of Illinois, who later extensively interviewed Passo for his 2003 book *Reforming the Chicago Teamsters: The Story of Local 705.*

Passo told Bruno that from the moment Burke arrived at Teamster City, he was consumed with one goal: "destroy these guys, no matter what it takes." And he meant it. At the first general membership meeting called to explain the trusteeship, Passo went into action. "We threw pop cans, coffee, fruit, and stuff at Burke and raised so much hell that he had to adjourn the meeting," he boasted to Bruno. "I spoke out big-time against the trusteeship and accused Zero and the rest of being TDU pieces of shit."[41] Passo was an enthusiastic provocateur, but he also had something of a self-destructive streak. He organized a slate of Hoffa supporters to challenge Zero and McCormick for office in the first local elections to be held after the trusteeship in 1995. Passo organized the Real Teamster Slate (RTS) made up of former staffers and stewards, like him, from the Ligurotis era, as well as some new faces. Zero and many others in the local union thought Passo would likely win the election. However, Passo couldn't resist engaging in the kind of disruptive behavior at union meetings that made him a name throughout the local. He found himself suspended from membership during a crucial moment in the campaign. His suspension was upheld by Ron Carey. The RTS lost the election, according to Zero, because of Passo's "knucklehead behavior."[42]

Soon afterwards, Passo supporters pulled off a surprise victory in the Local 705 delegate race for the upcoming 1996 convention when they won all eighteen delegates.[43] It was during the election campaign for convention delegates that Passo provoked a physical confrontation with Jerry Zero that later resulted in Zero's suspension from union office for one year.[44] This triumph seriously weakened the Carey forces at the 1996 convention where the Hoffa forces repeatedly disrupted the convention.[45] The following year, while testifying before the Hoekstra subcommittee, the "United Slate," led by Dane Passo, ran a vigorous, well-funded campaign for local union office. After the votes were tallied in December, Passo came within 250 votes of defeating Zero for secretary-treasurer.[46]

This is hardly a picture of a besieged, terrorized opposition. James P. Hoffa, after he was elected general president of the Teamsters, rewarded Passo for his years of service by appointing him "special assistant" to the general president, a role that gave him virtually a free run of the union. Within a few years, Dane Passo and former Hoffa running mate Bill Hogan were both barred for life from the union by the independent review board for their role in a scheme to drive down wages and benefits for Las Vegas Teamsters to benefit a company that one of Hogan's family members had a stake in.[47]

For many hours, Passo—along with Washington-based Teamster organizers Vince Hickman, Barbara Dusina, Bob Kreuzer, and Texas Teamster Wesley Coleman—regaled Hoekstra and other committee members with stories of being "pressured to give more than $1,000 each last year to the Carey campaign or face possible loss of their jobs." Colemen, a former TDU member, claimed "he saw a half-dozen staff organizers doing campaign work for Mr. Carey during their regular work hours."[48] This "testimony" not only went largely unchallenged but was egged on by the Republican committee members. On top of this, the committee then heard four and a half hours of testimony from Gregory Mullenholz, a former supervisor in the Teamsters political action committee in Washington. Disappointingly, for Hoekstra, Mullenholz couldn't provide "any solid proof" that Carey knew or had cooperated with the illegal fundraising schemes by Nash, Davis, Ansara, and Hamilton.[49] However, Mullenholz did reveal, in what should have been the bombshell of the day, that he had been secretly sending internal Teamster documents to Robert Baptiste, a prominent lawyer for the Teamsters under then-president Jackie Presser and, at the time, for James P. Hoffa. The media chose not to look deeper into the story until the *Wall Street Journal* ran a story about Hoffa's "moles" in late December.[50]

"A CIRCUS FOR ANTI-LABOR REPUBLICANS"

Nancy Coleman, a Teamsters spokesperson, called the Hoekstra hearings "a circus for anti-labor Republicans." She felt there was "an unfounded understanding by these people that if they didn't give money, they'd be retaliated against. That's ridiculous, because none of these people have been retaliated against."[51] TDU national organizer Ken Paff, in a press release, called on the House Committee

on Standards of Official Conduct to investigate possible misconduct by Hoekstra. "It appears that Congressman Hoekstra is using
his office, and taxpayer money, to further the campaign of James
Hoffa Junior," Paff argued. He further charged, "These so-called
hearings have no legitimate purpose and are designed to showcase
one candidate in the Teamster election, in hopes of gaining millions of Teamster dollars for the Republicans."[52] Dave Eckstein, the
Field Services Department director under Carey, knew many of the
accusers very well and believed there was no merit to their claims,
as did the new Teamster elections officer:

> These folks all worked for us and were encouraged by the Hoffa
> campaign to make false allegations—in my opinion—to get jobs
> if Hoffa won. This matter was taken up by the elections office of
> IRB and there was no wrongdoing found. In fact, they accused me
> of telling them they had to give. We held a non-mandatory after
> work–hours meeting in Washington, DC, and [I] said if anybody
> was interested in donations and or working on the campaign after
> hours it was OK under election rules. Nobody was forced or led to
> believe they had to. In fact, most of these people were notorious for
> supporting Hoffa; that was their right. Carey never asked anyone
> to help that was not interested. I testified at the elections office, and
> the investigation found no merit in their accusations.[53]

There may have been no merit in their accusations, but they provided good copy for the press. "Teamsters' Reform Image Tested,"
with a large photo of Passo and other Carey accusers, was prominently featured in the *Chicago Tribune*, while the *New York Times*
ran a story with the headline "Teamsters' Union Staff Members Cite
Pressure for Donations."[54] The Hoekstra hearings also provided the
Wall Street Journal with the opportunity for a little red-baiting in
one of its editorials:

> One watches the proceedings and comes away with the impression
> of a U.S. labor movement and its leadership simply drifting left-
> ward and away from the mainstream of the country's life, even as
> its own members settle in the center. The New Party is the brain-
> child of Joel Rogers, a University of Wisconsin professor who now
> serves as national party chair. A believer that "property rights are
> unequally distributed under capitalism," he has joined with unions

to promote super-minimum wage initiatives in various cities. The New Party's national organizer was a longtime activist in the radical Teamsters for a Democratic Union, and many party members are active Teamster supporters of Mr. Carey.[55]

Speaking before the National Press Club on October 20, 1997, while he waited for Conboy's decision on his candidacy, Ron Carey pointed to the financial backing of members of Hoekstra's oversight subcommittee to suggest that the hearings were not without bias:

> UPS gave campaign contributions to House Speaker Newt Gingrich, Representative Pete Hoekstra of Michigan, and, at least four other Republicans on the Hoekstra House subcommittee. Republican members of that subcommittee received more than a quarter of a million dollars in campaign contributions from corporate special interests. Their contributors included UPS, FedEx, the American Trucking Association, Northwest Airlines, [and] Americans for Free International Trade.[56]

"THAT'S THE PRICE YOU PAY"

During the question-and-answer period, Carey reflected on the slander campaign against him and strongly hinted at his eventual fate:

> I guess one of the reasons I've always been in trouble is because I'm very outspoken and I say what I feel and believe very strongly in what I feel. My reputation, as I've said from day one, is not in my hands. It is not under my control. And every time I say something, as I tell you Today that probably sometime in the next week, we'll hear more stuff. That's the price you pay. And I'm going to continue to pay that price, because it's what I truly believe in, what I have fought and what I will continue to fight for.[57]

Meanwhile UPS kept up its campaign against Carey inside the hubs. Soon after striking Teamsters returned to work, UPS managers across the country posted anti-Carey material on bulletin boards. When confronted, the managers admitted to it, but, incredibly, they also claimed that posting such materials didn't constitute interference in the election. Don Black, a UPS spokesperson, self-righteously declared, "We don't take sides in union elections, never have, never will."[58] Such a statement was hard to take seriously. Kenneth Conboy directed UPS in early November to stop meddling in upcoming Teamster elections. "The largest Teamster employer was caught campaigning for Hoffa," according to TDU national organizer Ken Paff. "They admitted they distributed [Hoffa campaign material] nationwide with a directive—and this is a military outfit—to share it with all employees, to 200,000 Teamsters."[59]

UPS's intervention into the Teamsters election paled in comparison with Conboy's. He completed his investigation into Ron Carey's candidacy and announced on November 17, 1997, the feared ruling disqualifying Carey from being a candidate in the upcoming rerun election. Carey appeared before reporters in Washington, DC, to declare his innocence and denounce what he called "an unbelievable wrong decision. My answer to all of this is very simple. I have done nothing wrong, and I will fight this decision until it is overturned."[60]

Conboy had discovered what he called "significant electoral misconduct," and Carey had to be disqualified because, "failure to disqualify in this case would constitute a damaging precedent that would undermine the deterrent effect of the election rules."[61] Radical journalist Alexander Cockburn declared, "Labor's foes everywhere surely see this as a happy hour." Cockburn went on to challenge Conboy's reasoning: "The prime imperative of election rules is that the will of the electorate prevails, and Conboy lost track of this central point. Who can doubt that, in the wake of the successful strike against United Parcel Service, Carey would have swept to victory over Hoffa? Just who is being protected by the rules invoked by Conboy? Teamster members? Or are they protecting the trucking companies from Teamster power?"[62]

By contrast, the editorial board of the *New York Times* roundly supported Conboy's ruling: "A Federal election monitor made the right decision yesterday in disqualifying the Teamsters' president, Ron Carey, from a court-ordered rerun of the union's 1996 elections."[63] The right decision? For whom? One week after Conboy's ruling, Carey took a leave of absence from the presidency of the Teamsters and his New York Local 804, and appealed the decision in the federal courts.[64]

Carey gave his last public speech at the 1997 TDU Convention in Cleveland, the same venue he had used to launch his first national campaign for the Teamster presidency in 1989. When he walked into the ballroom, filled with over 600 people, the room exploded in cheers and chants of "Carey, Carey," and "fight, fight." He was given a standing ovation and was visibly moved by the reception. He had endured months of abuse and character assassination. With a wry smile on his face, he told the audience, "This guy ain't gone." Carey tried his best to put a brave face on a very difficult situation. "There will be a strong reform slate in the next election," he told the crowd. "Whether it's me at the top of it or if it's someone else, the reform slate will win." He spoke from his heart about the decision to disqualify him. "I want to look around this room and look in everyone's eyes and tell you that that decision was dead wrong," he said. "I've spent the last forty years with many of you, fighting arm in arm against wrongdoing."[65]

However, six weeks later Carey lost the appeal on his disqualification.[66] Meanwhile the IRB's investigation of him ground on with no end in sight. Six months later, on July 16, 1998, taking advantage of Carey's downfall, UPS declared "null and void" the jobs provision of the first year of the new contract to create two thousand full-time jobs—despite the company making nearly $1 billion in profits.[67] One week later, the IRB announced another dreaded ruling: Carey was banned for life from the Teamsters.[68] It was one of the lowest points for the US labor movement in modern history.

Not everyone saw it that way, however. One year after the swearing in of James P. Hoffa as Teamsters general president, a triumphant representative Pete Hoekstra held hearings to review the past several years of work by his subcommittee and boasted, "I am convinced that if this subcommittee had not acted, Ron Carey would still be president of the Teamsters."[69] He said this with Hoffa and Teamsters General Counsel Patrick J. Szymanski in attendance. Three years later, the federal government, evidently feeling that it had not humiliated Carey enough, charged him with perjury related to criminal activities of his former campaign manager Jere Nash and Nash's co-conspirators.[70] The main prosecution witness against Carey was Nash. To the shock of prosecutors and Hoffa supporters alike, the federal jury found Carey innocent of all charges in early October 2001—one month after the 9-11 attacks. Despite being vindicated by a federal court, Carey remained barred from the Teamsters.[71]

Taking to the pages of *Verdict* magazine in January 2003, Ron Carey tried to make sense of what had happened to him and the Teamsters:

> Five years ago, the labor movement was resurgent. The success of the UPS strike made it seem as though the tide had turned, that workers were no longer on the defensive, that labor was no longer dominated by business unionism. What happened in the intervening years? First, I am sad to say that the corporate establishment and power brokers were out "gunning for me," and the failure of my campaign manager and consultants gave them the opening they needed. Our reform administration played an important part in the revitalization of the labor movement, and my removal from office no doubt weakened that resurgence.[72]

Carey's frustration and disappointment are understandable. He knew better than anyone the toll his departure had taken.

"IN LOVE WITH HOFFA"

For UPS, the election of James P. Hoffa to the general presidency of the Teamsters in 1998, and his three successive terms in office, proved a boon far beyond their wildest expectations. John Schultz, a reporter for *Traffic World*, one of the freight industry's leading publications, wrote, in a notorious May 2000 article called "In Love with Hoffa," "United Parcel Service, the nation's largest transportation company, feels that it has taken part in one of the great trades of all time in labor: James P. 'Jimmy' Hoffa for Ron Carey as president of the Teamsters union."[73]

UPS had so thoroughly embraced Hoffa that during the 2006 election for international union officers, it was willing to flout campaign rules. According to an election protest filed by reformer Tom Leedham, who was challenging Hoffa for the general presidency, the labor manager at UPS's Worldport air hub in Louisville drove Hoffa and his entourage "around the ground and air district areas [and] Hoffa addressed assembled employees and instructed them to vote and to 'make sure their vote counted.'" This violation was so egregious that the election officer ruled that UPS had to grant Leedham equal access and time at Worldport.[74]

The following year, an ailing Ron Carey surveyed the proposed 2007 National Master UPS contract and scathingly denounced it:

> The proposed contract is a complete sellout. It gives back to UPS monumental gains that the members sacrificed for and won in 1997. In 1997 we stopped UPS from taking control of the Teamster pension plans, and we provided record increases. We made it clear that "Part-Time America Just Won't Work." We forced the company to create 10,000 full-time jobs by combining 20,000 part-time jobs. That achievement provided for part-timers a sense of connection, a sense of belonging to something. It gave them an opportunity for a good full-time job. And it dispelled the feeling that they were second-class citizens. That translates into a stronger union, when it's working for all the members. This contract eliminates new full-time jobs. And it makes new, part-time jobs a disaster by freezing starting wages and cutting benefits.[75]

Ron Carey died too young, in December 2008, but was saved from witnessing further historic and unnecessary concessions to UPS. Ken Paff, TDU national organizer, summarized the Hoffa years:

> Hoffa's record at UPS has been one of go-along and get-along with corporate management. In 2007 he settled early and short. He gave in to management and let them pull out from the Central States Pension Fund, crippling it; the trade-off in that deal allowed UPS freight to be Teamster organized but under a weaker stand-alone contract. In 2013 to 2014 he gave them health care concessions, and a record eighteen supplements were rejected, some up to three times. Then he overruled the vote to impose the final supplements. Hoffa has shown how to cut deals with management—and weaken the union in the process.[76]

While the Teamsters have given away billions in concessions, UPS has continued to ruthlessly pursue its goal of being the most important transportation company in the world, or, more specifically, the most important *logistics* company in the world. But what does the reshaping of the company around logistics mean for the potential power of UPS workers? Are they stronger or weaker today because of it?

CHAPTER 12
WE LOVE LOGISTICS

Amateurs study strategy, but professionals study logistics.
       —General Omar Bradley, US Army[1]

How does a bicycle messenger service become the world's largest shipping company? A similar question could be asked of FedEx and DHL. How did FedEx, a small but highly capitalized nationwide overnight air delivery service, or DHL, a small courier service shuttling legal papers on commercial airliners between San Francisco and Los Angeles and Honolulu, become global shipping giants?[2] They began as businesses providing mutually exclusive services, almost niche markets, in different eras, but all have moved far beyond their origins. In their decades-long battles for control of the global delivery market, they have practically become identical triplets. Except for the color of their uniforms or the size and shape of their trucks, you really can't tell the three companies apart; each provides the same service—from the initial pickup to the end delivery of packages.

What explains this uniformity? The rise of modern logistics, the force reshaping global capitalism. UPS emerged as one of the global leaders in the logistics industry in the two decades following the 1997 strike, although the foundation for this success was laid years before. In 1995, nearly two decades after UPS became a nationwide company and only a few years after it began its air operations, UPS Logistics Group was formed. Most people know the word "logistics" from UPS's own ubiquitous advertising campaign "We ♥ Logistics."[3] For sociologists Edna Bonacich and Khaleelah Hardie, "logistics" has two interrelated meanings. The older and still popular meaning is "the nuts-and-bolts distribution functions that a firm must undertake, namely, transportation and warehousing." However, over the last four decades the term has come to mean something else: "The management of the supply chain, including the relations between retailers, their producers/suppliers, and their carrier/transportation providers. The latter meaning has become more important with the creation of flexible and dispersed production systems, including offshore production, requiring high levels of coordination to bring products to the market in an accurate and timely fashion."[4]

Modern logistics has proven to be one of the most important stages in the development of industrial production and distribution in history. This radical transformation did not come about all at once; there was no big bang. It was a cumulative process following World War II that gathered speed and importance over the decades. Coinciding with the advancement of neoliberal economic policies, logistics has created a new global manufacturing division of labor, elevated transportation (air, land, and sea) to an even greater importance in the economy and weakened many, though not all, of the previously powerful industrial unions throughout North America and Western Europe.

What does the dominance of logistics in the world economy mean for the power of workers at UPS and other major logistics corporations like FedEx? Was the 1997 UPS strike the last successful battle of an old era, now gone? Or did it foreshadow the potential power of workers in the new global supply chain? If so, where is that power located today?

THE OLD SUPPLY CHAIN

The production of capital goods (machines and tools for manufacturing) and consumer goods has been and will continue to be central to the capitalist system. Every generation or so, however, capital reorganizes its methods of production and circulation—what economists call distribution—and in the process remakes the composition of the industrial working class. These changes can be gut-wrenching and disorienting, and it can take a significant amount of time for socialists and other working-class activists to reorient themselves. These changes include modernization of production techniques (the means of production), the organization of production and labor management, the methods of transporting goods to the market, and the means by which goods are sold to the consumer.

Getting capital and consumer goods to the paying customer has been surprisingly fraught with difficulties at times. The reorganization of capital is rarely as smooth or modernized as is sometimes thought, and parts of the system can advance quite quickly while others lag significantly behind. The rise of large-scale, modern manufacturing in the late nineteenth and early twentieth centuries was not accompanied by a revolution in retail, even though this era saw the invention of the department store. Historian Vicki Howard writes that the impact of the new-fangled department store was limited and "nothing on the scale of mass retailing today. With few exceptions, these early departmentalized emporia were single-unit independents that could not command a national or even a regional market."[5] In 1910, for example, inventor and capitalist Thomas Edison complained that "selling and distribution are simply machines for getting products to consumers. And like all machines, they can be improved with great resulting economy. But it is the plain truth that these machines for distribution have made the least progress of all machines. They are the same in many instances that they were forty of fifty years ago."[6]

Let's be clear about Edison's complaint. He was saying that the retail industry of 1910 was essentially the same as it was in 1870 or 1860. Howard confirms this, writing that in the first decades of the twentieth century, most US retail trade "still took place in financially precarious mom-and-pop businesses and in the general stores that continued to serve rural areas."[7]

The rise of the railroad in the nineteenth century was the most visible and revolutionary development for the delivery of capital and consumer goods. Innovations such as the refrigerated boxcar enabled packinghouse giants like Swift, Armour, and Hormel to send meat products across the country. Rail transport, manufacturing, and warehousing became (and still are) concentrated around the greater Chicago area. Railroad workers were the most militant, even insurrectionary, of US workers, clearly demonstrated by the 1877 railroad strikes and the 1894 Pullman Strike.[8] However, despite the revolution in rail transport, the horse and wagon in many parts of the country were still primarily responsible for the delivery of goods from the railroads to the consumer market, and this remained true well into the auto age.

The development of motorized transport, or trucking, exploded in size and scope in the decades following World War I, significantly changing the delivery of capital and consumer goods. Freight drivers, whether long haul or local (work still referred to by the nineteenth-century terms "cartage" or "drayage"), were assuming an increasingly larger share of the market as they made their pickups from manufacturers and warehouses, including the waterfront.[9] These workers played key roles in the emergence of the CIO and the Teamsters, affiliated with the AFL, in the 1930s.[10]

THE LOGISTICS REVOLUTION

In the years that followed World War II, the development of containerization and air cargo revolutionized the transport of goods around the world. The container was a transport innovation of historic importance. Mind-bogglingly simple in design, containers were essentially giant metal boxes with doors, uniform in dimension and easily stackable in large numbers. The advent of the container led to a massive restructuring of ocean transport, ports around the globe, the trucking industry, and railroads.

This restructuring of the global transportation system made transport cheaper and faster, and allowed a sizable chuck of industrial production to be moved to the Far East.[11] The North American continent, especially the US half, became a gigantic "land bridge," according to Stan Weir, where shippers—to avoid using the expensive Panama Canal—dropped their loads at West Coast ports onto rail cars and had them transported to ports along the East and Gulf Coasts, and finally loaded back onto ships bound for Europe.[12]

This is a quick sketch of the "old" supply chain and how it began to morph into the beginnings of the "new" supply chain that we are familiar with today. Where does the development of logistics fit into this story, and how has it transformed industrial production and circulation in the world today?

Looking back at the transportation landscape and economic organization of the United States after World War II, we see glaring differences from today's world: There was no federally funded interstate highway system. Many of the nation's ports were relics of the nineteenth century. Trucking companies were tiny and local, as were retailers. UPS specialized in department store deliveries, and there was no FedEx and Walmart. International shipping wasn't done by containerization. Computers were in their experimental infancy, and innovations like satellite communication, GPS, and universal bar codes were nonexistent. Finally, economic life was highly regulated by the federal government.

At this time, the term "logistics" had very little to do with business and was reserved for military art or skill. According to Deborah Cowen, professor of geography at University of Toronto, logistics have been used to enable military strategy for millennia, but this military art was elevated with the introduction of modern industrialized warfare in World War I. Global imperialist wars required a mobilization of industry, resources, and troops on a scale never before seen in human history. The successful implementation of a war strategy required a different level of logistical thinking and support and actually impacted strategic thinking itself. "Amateurs study strategy, professionals study logistics," declared US Army General Omar Bradley, who rose to prominence during World War II.[13]

Cowen explains that the complexity of modern warfare means that "the success or failure of campaigns came to rely on logistics. Over the course of the twentieth century, a reversal of sorts took place, and logistics began to lead strategy rather then serve it."[14] The close relationship between industry and the military, which created the US war machine that won World War II, also meant that logistics was soon "adopted into the corporate world of management."[15] Long before the ubiquitous advertising campaigns of UPS, a logistical revolution took place in management.

Modern logistics can be defined in Bonacich and Hardie's latter meaning of the word, as the management of supply chains.

How is that approach different from older methods of organizing manufacturing, warehousing, and distribution? For the bulk of the nineteenth and twentieth centuries, manufacturers dominated the retailers that sold their goods, especially retailers of consumer products (which grew exponentially in the years after World War II). The retail industry was dominated by the seasonal production schedules of the manufacturers. For the most part, manufacturers told the retailers what would be sold and at roughly what prices. Massive warehouses, meanwhile, stockpiled huge amounts of goods. This imbalance between manufacturers and retailers continued well into the later twentieth century.

Retail was also considered a backwater of US capitalism, despite the emergence of big downtown department stores in the late nineteenth century and the creation of popular chain stores that dotted the landscape beginning in the twentieth century, such as Woolworth and Sears. Fifty years after Edison complained of the sad state of retail in the country, management guru Peter Drucker made a similar observation. Writing in 1960, Drucker said that distribution "is one of the most sadly neglected, most promising areas of American business."[16] The new retail giants filled this "promising area." Starting in the late 1970s and early 1980s, the balance of power began shifting from manufacturers to retailers in many parts of the economy, which had profound consequences for the organization of capitalist production—and the composition and power of the industrial working class.

The rise of corporate retailers brought about punishing approaches to labor. In its early days, in the 1960s, mammoth retailer and leading logistics company Walmart (then called Wal-Mart) "cut out a raft of salesman, jobbers, and other supply chain middlemen" from its world headquarters in Bentonville, Arkansas, and "squeezed the manufacturers by shifting every imaginable cost, risk, and penalty onto their books and taught the entire retail world how the bar code and data warehouse could finally put real money on the bottom line," writes historian Nelson Lichtenstein in *The Retail Revolution*.[17] Lichtenstein argues that by the 1990s the connections of major retailers like Walmart and Nike to global manufacturing networks "were practically incestuous. They might not own the Asian or Central American factories from which they sourced all those big-box consumables but their 'vendors' were linked to them by a 'supply chain' that evoked the iron shackles subordinating slave to master."[18]

The logistics corporation is not only a new stage in the evolution of the modern corporation but has changed our understanding of the historic distinction between manufacturing, transportation, and retail. The modern logistics corporation—with the significant help of the capitalist states—has massively reorganized the global manufacturing network, the shipping and transportation systems, and the final delivery of goods. As Cowen explains, "With the rise of global supply chains, even the simplest purchase relies on the calibration of an astonishing cast of characters, multiple circulations of capital, and complex movements across great distances."[19]

This reorganization has changed the manufacturing of goods—not just the delivery of the finished products. "It is misleading to think about a singular site of production. Commodities today are manufactured across logistics space rather than in a singular place," according to Cowen.[20] While some industries, like automotive, have always relied upon outside suppliers for parts for their products, this is the norm today for all manufacturers. Cowen concludes, "the point is highlighted if we account for 'inbound logistics'—the production process of component parts that make the manufacture of a commodity possible—and if we recognize transportation as an element of production rather than merely a service that follows production."[21]

If we see transportation as a key element of modern production, then the new distribution centers of the "new supply chain" devised by the logistics giants are also an important historic development. Lichtenstein contrasts modern distribution centers with "icons of the twentieth-century industrial age":

> Unlike . . . Ford's sprawling River Rouge complex celebrated in Diego Rivera's heroic murals, or the vast Boeing Assembly building in Renton, Washington, the Wal-Mart Distribution Centers build nothing. They are neither inspiring nor grim, merely a functional set of docks and locks from one place and are destined for sale and consumption somewhere else, hundreds of miles downstream. Yet these Distribution Centers and similar facilities operated by Home Depot, Target, UPS, and Federal Express, stand at the center of

the production and consumption network that girdles the planet.[22]

More recently, the new supply chain includes Amazon "fulfillment centers." All these centers are part of the "seamless supply chain" that companies so desire. Yet the same workers who facilitate these seamless systems also have the power to undermine them. Workers now have the potential to regain the muscle lost by a generation of industrial workers in this country over the last three decades. The questions now are how workers will deploy this potential power and how corporations will respond to it.[23]

What makes this system even more vulnerable to the potential power of the workers in these new distribution centers are the "just-in-time" or "lean production" methods that have come to dominate the global manufacturing system since the early 1980s. Kim Moody made this point in *Workers in a Lean World* nearly two decades ago, though he was primarily focused on developments in the auto industry. Citing MIT's long-standing International Motor Vehicle Program, the program's researchers feared that the lean production system was "fragile." It had to be a "humane" system or, as Moody saw it, "the fragility of the system becomes a weapon of resistance."[24] We can now extend Moody's analysis of the potential for resistance to the entire supply chain.

While there are many distribution centers throughout the United States, there are three cities and related industrial complexes that are especially important for the future power of logistics workers.[25] These are FedEx's "SuperHub" in Memphis, UPS's Worldport in Louisville, and Chicago's vast complex of warehouse and rail and trucking links, starting with UPS's Chicago Area Consolidation Hub (CACH) and extending forty miles southwest to the area surrounding the old Joliet Arsenal, a military facility that can rightly be considered the original logistics hub of the United States.

CARGO ALLEY

The logistics industry is a vast and growing part of the US economy. In 2018, the nation's gross domestic product (GDP) was $20.5 trillion, according to the World Bank.[26] Spending on the logistics and transportation industry, according to some sources, totaled around

8 percent of the annual GDP.[27] A system of this magnitude can seem impersonal or even inhuman, yet despite its great reliance on satellite technology and computers, "the last mile" of the supply chain is a delivery person who ensures that the goods reach their destination. Without these people, the system would grind to a stop. This growing industry has been plagued by a shortage of drivers for decades, and the problem is expected to get worse, according to a 2014 *Boston Globe* article, which projects there will be 100,000 openings for driver positions over the next decade.[28]

The deregulation of interstate commerce had a transformative impact on the evolution of the logistics industry in the late 1970s and early 1980s. Major sections of the freight industry that had been bastions of union power collapsed within a few years or were reorganized on a non-union basis. The evolution of logistics in the delivery business was intimately tied up with the neoliberal era, and in some ways pioneered distinctive neoliberal economic policies. For example, trucking on the waterfront became the province of "independent contracts" and UPS pioneered part-time wages and work.

The big three US-based international delivery companies that emerged out of this transformative era—FedEx, UPS, and DHL—operate globally with enormous workforces that rival or exceed the size of some of the largest standing armies in the world. UPS, for example, has a worldwide workforce of 481,000 employees. DHL follows with a worldwide workforce of 550,000 and FedEx with 420,000. In contrast, the combined standing and reserve force of the British army is 81,500. The size of these workforces testifies to the importance of these corporations in national and international trade. Deutsche Post owns DHL, but it started out as a US corporation and remains the major competitor to UPS and FedEx internationally,[29] even though its spectacular failure in ground delivery forced it to withdraw from the US ground delivery market in the 2000s.[30]

UPS and FedEx air operations, based in Memphis and Louisville, are the pumping hearts of both companies. "Louisville and Memphis both languished until they deliberately embraced the overnight carriers calling each one home," write Kasarda and Lindsay in their fascinating book *Aerotropolis: The Way We'll Live Next.* "Two cities rooted in the steamboat era have been refashioned into the most important hubs of our era."[31] Looking up at the nighttime sky, you can practically see the duel between both hubs in the form of enormous air traffic congestion over both cities. The aerial overcrowding rivals that of Chicago, Los Angeles, and New York: "The midnight sky over both cities are filled with stars bearing down on you. Wait on the tarmac long enough and they gradually come into focus—727s, 747s, 767s, 777s, A-300s and MD-11s, blinking steadily as they approach in parallel, landing every ninety seconds on each airport's twin runways. They line up single file, bunched as tightly as pearls on a necklace, at least from the controllers' point of view."[32]

FEDEX'S SUPERHUB

The heart of FedEx's operations, the SuperHub in Memphis, captures on a massive scale "the evolution from warehousing to distribution to logistics," write Kasarda and Lindsay.[33] Fred Smith chose Memphis, Tennessee, for the location of FedEx's central air hub because it was on the western fringe of "cargo alley." By the time FedEx set up shop in Memphis, much of the city's industry had moved out, or was planning on heading out of the region; Memphis was known mostly as the city that killed Martin Luther King Jr.[34] In the nineteenth century, Memphis's economy was infamously based on the selling of enslaved people and on the cotton trade. The Memphis Cotton Exchange overlooking the Mississippi River was the center of business. Beginning in the 1970s, business began moving to East Memphis where, write Kasarda and Lindsay, "the airport, highways, and rail yards had given birth to an entire forest of white, multi-story warehouses adorned with the stubs of truck-loading docks."[35]

FedEx's first sort at the facility that would later come to be known as the SuperHub took place on the night of April 17, 1973, when six French-built Falcon jets brought back a total of 185 packages and envelopes. These days, three hundred planes nose up to its gates nightly, and 3.3 million packages pass through its labyrinth of belts on any given day. The SuperHub "measures four by four miles. Some 30,000 people are needed to run it."[36]

The facility is an amazing feat of engineering. "Every weekday night at the SuperHub, FedEx lands, unloads (in just half an hour, even for a super-jumbo 777), reloads, and flies out 150 to 200 jets. This all happens between 11 p.m. and 4 a.m. Central Time. The SuperHub processes between 1.2 million and 1.6 million packages a night."[37] The site is also a virtual company town, with "a hospital, a fire station, a meteorology unit, and a private security force; it has branches of US Customs and Homeland Security, plus anti-terror operations no one will talk about. It has 20 electric power generators as backup to keep it running if the power grid goes down."[38]

The presence of the FedEx SuperHub has reshaped Memphis International Airport. Memphis International has been the "busiest cargo airport in the world for eighteen years running—since the rankings began—and 95 percent of its title is due to FedEx," write Kasarda and Lindsay. [39] The Memphis airport held that title until 2009 when it dropped to number two, behind Hong Kong International Airport, where it has remained.[40]

FedEx's impact on Memphis's identity has also been revolutionary. Kasarda and Lindsay are right to call Memphis "the Pittsburgh or Detroit of the Instant Age."[41] The company is the largest private employer in a metropolitan area of a region of more than a million people, and it sits at the center of an ecosystem of warehouses, trucking firms, factories, and office parks."[42] This ecosystem includes "more than a hundred foreign companies that have set up shop around the hub." Memphis is also the final stop of the "Chicago Express" along the Burlington Northern Santa Fe (BNSF) freight line, which runs to the port of Prince Rupert in British Columbia, where goods arriving from Asia are unloaded.[43]

Excluding the FedEx pilots who are unionized, the SuperHub is one of the great non-union industrial complexes in the United States. It took from 1973 to 1989 for FedEx to become a $4.6 billion company; in 2014 alone its revenues were $45 billion. Its wealth has been built from the same source as its chief rival, UPS, namely from the labor of part-time workers.[44] Back in 1992, Kevin Coyle, in his superb book *A Day in the Night of America*, wrote a vivid description of "The Sort" at the SuperHub:

> The roads leading to the airport filled with the commuting cars and the crosswalks streamed with brigades of workers, almost 4,500 strong, in blue uniforms and steel-toed boots, marching out of the

night and into [the] Federal Express complex, through the long, wide, sci-fi white corridor and toward their stage marks for the nightly one-act drama called The Sort—three-hours-or-so sprint wherein the delivery cycle reached its busiest peak. More than three-quarters of them are college students, the moonlighting, part-time backbone of the sorting process. For a few hours, at an average wage of nine dollars an hours, they would work at a pace few could sustain over a full eight-hour shift, human cogs in the din of a vast Letter Sorting Machine."[45]

Today far more people work at the SuperHub and, similar to UPS, the proportion of college students as short-term workers has drastically fallen because of the declining incomes of American workers who seek additional part-time jobs to make up for falling wages, or who work two or even three part-time jobs for "a living." The potential power of this new generation of SuperHub workers is vast and untapped, and unionization would be a huge battle, but it would have a transformative impact on the working class as a whole because of how important these workers are to the US economy.

WORLDPORT

Worldport, UPS's *Star Trek*–sounding mammoth air hub in Louisville, Kentucky, is another engineering marvel. It is currently 5,200,000 square feet, or the size of 90 football fields, with 115 miles of conveyor belts capable of sorting 416,000 packages per hour.[46] It is the largest UPS facility in the country, employing over 20,000 workers, most of whom are members of Teamsters Local 89. It has 70 aircraft docks and delivers daily to more than 220 countries and territories around the world. UPS has spent billions of dollars over the last two decades turning the Louisville air hub, Worldport, into its showcase facility.

In April 2005, a *New Yorker* article by veteran writer John McPhee captured something of the overwhelmingly quality of Worldport for the first-time visitor: "The building is about seventy-five feet high, and essentially windowless. Its vast interior spaces are supported by forests of columns. It could bring to mind, among other things, the seemingly endless interior colonnades of the Great

Mosque of Cordoba, but the Great Mosque of UPS is fifteen times the size of the Great Mosque of Cordoba."[47]

FedEx pioneered the overnight package delivery business in the early 1970s. UPS, on the other hand, was founded as a messenger service in 1907 and went through many transformations through the decades before air delivery became central to its operations. It did some air service in its early decades of business but focused primarily on small package delivery that made it the king of the small parcel industry. UPS planned very methodically before it decided to take on FedEx in the overnight delivery business. "Nine years after the first FedEx sort, UPS landed in the opposite corner of the trapezoid with its own hub at Louisville," according to Kasarda and Lindsay. "In the intervening years, they [the US government] had deregulated American aviation, allowing any airline (passenger and cargo alike) to fly wherever it wanted whenever it wanted, using whatever aircraft it liked."[48] UPS initiated Next Day Air service in September 1982, seventy-five years after the founding of the company.[49]

UPS initially outsourced its early air transport operation, but then "it went on a spending spree, acquiring several hundred planes, including a dozen of its very own 747s. By the 1990s, UPS put the 'International' in Louisville International Airport with its nightly sorties to Europe. Even more than Memphis depends on FedEx, Louisville and its airport depend on UPS. So does Kentucky—UPS is the state's largest private employer, with more than twenty thousand workers."[50] UPS owns 251 jet aircraft and charters 298 others to deliver packages to 400 domestic airports and 415 international airports on a daily basis. It is one of the largest private airlines in the world.[51]

The packages are transported in U-Haul truck–size aluminum cans cut to fit the interior of the airplanes. These "cans" can weigh up to two tons, and they are moved about thanks "to miles of inverted casters and ball bearings studded in Worldport's floor and at its gates. The cans need only a solid push to glide across them into the hub or onto the caravans of waiting tugs."[52] Workers unload the cans and sort the individual packages. Only two sets of hands are supposed to touch the packages, while the rest of the time they are transported and guided across the miles of conveyor belts by smart labels that contain zip codes and tracking numbers. UPS has spent hundreds of millions of dollars on advanced computer software to make Worldport work. Most of this software "resides at Worldport itself, making twice as many calculations in an hour as the New York Stock Exchange does in a heavy day of trading."[53]

Highly automated and reliant on the most advanced computer technology and engineering available, Worldport still needs humans to keep running. Twenty thousand part-time workers (union and non-union) work during the crucial hours of 11:00 p.m. to 4:00 a.m. Teamsters Local 89 in Louisville has over 16,361 members, overwhelmingly UPS workers, and because of the continued expansion of Worldport, it is likely to be the largest Teamsters local union in North America in the near future.[54] Worldport, like many UPS hubs across the country, is plagued by a shortage of part-time workers, despite the Great Recession and chronic unemployment in minority communities. The reasons for the high turnover rate at the facility are frustratingly familiar: notoriously low wages and miserable work conditions.

Attempting to stabilize its workforce at Worldport, UPS has leaned on local and state governments to allow workers to take courses at Metropolitan College, in a special program created by a joint venture of the University of Louisville and the Jefferson Community and Technical College. Metro College has several locations throughout Louisville, including at Worldport. The "college" was designed "to fit the needs of UPS," *Time* reported in 1998. The student-workers "will experience a daily schedule that will essentially reverse their internal clocks. Class schedules, social activities and sleep patterns will revolve around the hours of the night shift at UPS."[55] UPS has also recruited large groups of refugees, including Somali Bantus, to meet its needs.[56]

Like its FedEx twin, the SuperHub, Worldport stands at the center of the production and consumption network of the modern logistics economy. Located two miles south of the vast runways and conveyor belts of Worldport, UPS Supply Chain Solutions (SCS), the logistics arm of the company, "burrows deep inside and straightens out kinks in the customer's operations."[57] UPS official Carl Norris explained to writer John McPhee the rationale for SCS: "A company that is concentrating on marketing and sales doesn't have a lot of time to worry about distributing problems. That's where we come in. We become a partner with the companies. We run these businesses like they're our own."[58]

Of course, UPS is paid very well for these services, which have morphed beyond just providing "distribution know-how." For example, if "your Toshiba laptop needs repair, UPS technicians are the ones standing by to fix it. The same goes for your missing Master-Card—its replacement will be printed here and rushed overnight," write Kasarda and Lindsay.[59] While such services are desirable, proximity to Worldport is what matters most to the seventy or so major companies that have set up shop near the airport, or close by in Elizabethtown and Shepherdsville, Kentucky. UPS alone has about 4.4 million square feet of "logistics space" in the greater Louisville area.[60] Its SCS division has eight secluded, heavily guarded warehouses that cater to the company's most prized customers, including Merck, Toshiba, Bentley, and Rolls-Royce (both Bentley and Rolls-Royce stock engines in nearby Elizabethtown). "Bentley's are for coupes and Rolls's are for jet engines," write Kasarda and Lindsay.[61]

As Worldport relentlessly expands its power, the workers at the facility are taking steps to assert their own. The real capacity of Worldport workers and pilots was demonstrated vividly during the 1997 national strike against UPS. Planes didn't fly and packages weren't sorted. The Great Mosque of UPS was a ghost town. Since then, the power of these workers has been continually muted or undermined, though there is clearly a growing restlessness among them. When faced with an inadequate offer from UPS, Local 89 members rejected the local agreement (called a rider) by a 90 percent no vote in March 2014.[62]

CHICAGO: THE GREAT INLAND PORT

Chicago has been at the heart of US transportation, manufacturing, and warehousing networks since the Civil War. The logistics revolution, though, has raised Chicago's status in the US and global economies to Olympian heights. With the construction over the last twenty-five years of UPS's gigantic Chicago Area Consolidation

Hub ("CACH") and several "logistics parks" on the grounds of the former Joliet Arsenal, the Chicago area has been transformed into, in the words of the Warehouse Workers for Justice, "the third-largest container port in the world after Hong Kong and Singapore."[63]

The CACH is the largest ground package facility in the world, as well as one of the most important distribution centers for the US economy and one of the important hubs in the UPS system. During peak season (the two months leading up to Christmas), the CACH employs up to 8,000 people who load and unload trailers and move as many as 2.1 million packages through the facility daily.[64] The site has twenty-five intermodal facilities (locations where large cranes move containers between rail cars, trucks, and warehouses), making it the "number one intermodal container handler in the Western Hemisphere."[65]

Unlike SuperHub and Worldport, which remain focused on air transport, the CACH has its feet firmly planted on the ground. It was built on the former grounds of a General Motors' truck and bus manufacturing facility. There are major benefits to Chicago's geographic location and transportation infrastructure that can't be reproduced on the same scale anywhere in the United States, or even the Western Hemisphere. Over 219 million people are a two-day truck drive from the city, and the six largest North American railroads meet in Chicago. UPS decided to build the CACH in Willow Springs/Hodgkins precisely because the location is at the vortex of state and interstate highways. The BNSF rail yard, located adjacent to the CACH, is one of the busiest rail yards in North America and "every 80 seconds a trailer is lifted on or off a flatcar" and moved to one of CACH's 170 bays to be unloaded. "In 2005, Willow Springs was BNSF's second-busiest intermodal yard, performing 770,000 lifts," according to the magazine *Trains*.[66]

UPS's decision to build the CACH in the Chicago suburbs foreshadowed even greater logistics developments down the road. Running southwest from the CACH on I-55 to the former grounds of the US Army's Joliet Arsenal and beyond to neighboring Elwood are massive intermodal facilities and warehouses that have been operating since 2002. Jacque Engle, a spokeswoman for Center-Point properties, the logistics management company in Joliet/

Elwood, recently told the *Chicago Tribune*, that CenterPoint has "spent nearly $2 billion, building 12 million square feet of industrial warehouse space and 1,600 acres of other development in Joliet and Elwood. Nine million square feet of warehouse space was built in Elwood alone." Will County, where Joliet and Elwood are located, is home to more than 300 warehouses. Walmart alone has 3.4 million square feet of warehousing space located there.

Joining this cluster of strategically located warehouses is Amazon. "Amazon invested about $13.9 billion from 2010 to 2012 to build 50 new warehouses, more than it had spent since its 1994 founding," notes the *Chicago Tribune*.[67] Today the company operates some seventy-five "fulfillment centers" in North America, as well as many others overseas.[68] During high-volume periods, some of the warehouses ship as many as a million items per day. Clearly, Amazon is attempting to remake the distribution system in the United States, if not the world.

When it comes to the future of work, what's true at Worldport and SuperHub is true at the CACH. The warehouse workers, drivers, and crane operations that make the CACH possible are an incredible concentration of potential power. During the 1997 strike, the CACH, like Worldport, was completely shut down and became a magnet for national media coverage of the UPS strike. Turnover among the part-time workforce at the facility remains high, and since the strike, the potential impact of these union workers has been muted. But there is every reason to think that this will change in coming years.

CONCLUSION

WHO WILL MOVE
THE WORLD?

We've really turned from a trucking company with technology to a
technology company with trucks.
　　　　　—Jack Levis, UPS Director of Process Management[1]

Data is just a proxy for control.
　　　　　—Sam Dwyer, former UPS worker, May 2015[2]

Has history come full circle for UPS? The Package King built the
foundation of its shipping empire by delivering packages for department stores from the 1910s through the 1950s. More recently,
the company took up the task of delivering packages for one very
important department store: Amazon. But after UPS's Christmas
fiasco of 2013, Amazon began laying the groundwork to do its own
deliveries, including building up its transportation network. Recent
research shows that Amazon is now shipping nearly half of its own
packages.[3] The online retail giant is even actively expanding its
drone delivery capabilities, appealing to the inner fourteen year old
of people everywhere.[4]

Today Amazon's valuation exceeds Walmart, and the speed
of its growth is increasing by the day. There is no doubt that the
expansion of Jeff Bezos's empire across North America and Europe

is dramatically reorganizing the global logistics industry. While Amazon is currently dominating the market, UPS, FedEx, and even the US Postal Service aren't sitting back quietly. In 2015, UPS purchased Chicago-based Coyote Logistics for $1.8 billion. Coyote is the new model of freight forwarding, involving no vehicles or warehousing. It is a logistics provider for 12,000 shippers, with a network of 35,000 local, regional, and national carriers. "We will provide our combined customer base with a portfolio of seamless supply chain solutions from multimodal freight shipments to small-package delivery," said David Abney, CEO of UPS.[5] Today UPS is further modernizing its capabilities, including exploring the possibility of using self-driving trucks and drones.[6]

Not to be outdone, FedEx has gone on its own impressive building spree across the United States and snatched a prized asset right from underneath the nose of UPS in Europe. FedEx bought the Dutch carrier TNT in the spring of 2015 for $4.8 billion, much to the annoyance of UPS, which had made a failed bid for the company two years earlier for $6.8 billion. *Bloomberg* reported that European regulators "formally blocked UPS's TNT bid because the Atlanta-based company failed to find a suitable buyer for parts of TNT to ensure that competition for delivery services wouldn't be squelched."[7] FedEx will now have access to TNT's extensive European-wide road network, enhancing its ability to compete with UPS and DHL. FedEx ground also announced plans to build large facilities in Middleton, Connecticut; Ocala, Florida; and, Hamburg, New York, south of Buffalo.[8] Few weeks or months go by without an announcement of a major building project by one division of FedEx or another.

Meanwhile, DHL is reinvesting substantially in its US operations. It poured $108 million into its Cincinnati air hub that processes about 46 million international shipments each year. Though it is smaller than UPS's Worldport and FedEx's SuperHub, DHL's air hub primarily focuses on international shipments from Asia and Europe, rather than domestic shipments. According to one logistics expert quoted in the *Wall Street Journal*, "If DHL is making investments in infrastructure expansion in Cincinnati, that means they're very confident that they're going to continue to grow their intercontinental network. They're likely going to add more routes and increase the size of some their parking spaces, which means they are probably upgrading the size of some of their aircraft."[9]

In other developments, DHL Global Forwarding signed an agreement with a Kazakhstan-based express company to speed the transit of rail-based freight across the Eurasian continent as an alternative to traditional sea and airfreight.[10] DHL has also invested heavily in Sub-Saharan Africa as part of its expansion into emerging markets.[11] The company additionally unveiled its Strategy 2025, an initiative focusing on digitalization and other areas that impact logistics.[12]

Not to be left out of the scramble, the USPS has emerged as a major player in the logistics industry. In 2013, USPS spent $200 million to furnish its delivery vehicles with 270,000 handheld scanners to provide real-time package tracking and plans to replace its fleet of 163,000 delivery trucks, most of which were designed to hold letters—an upgrade that could cost as much as $4.5 billion.[13] The *Federal Times* reported, "the once-in-generation vehicle procurement will allow the Postal Service to rethink how it delivers the mail—with everything on the table including technology, fuel economy and the overall shape of the vehicle."[14] In 2015, *Bloomberg* called USPS "an extension of Amazon," and Bernstein Research, which tracks the shipping industry, estimated that the postal service shipped and delivered 40 percent of Amazon's volume, or almost 150 million items, followed by UPS with 20–25 percent, and FedEx with 15–20 percent.[15] However, Amazon's reliance on USPS has recently declined as the e-commerce giant has established its own in-house delivery service; in August 2019, the postal service reported its first quarterly volume decline in package shipments in nine years.[16]

"THE FUTURE OF WORK LOOKS LIKE A UPS TRUCK"

New technology is being rapidly deployed throughout the logistics industry. "We've really turned from a trucking company with technology to a technology company with trucks," declared Jack Levis, UPS's director of process management. How this technology affects the daily lives of workers is another story. Greg Niemann once boasted that UPS workers "turn out better than machines," but UPS seems determined to turn its rank-and-file employees into cogs in a remote and ever-changing machinery. The intertwining forces of new technology and scientific management are shaping the modern workplace for maximum profit, as Harry Braverman argued in his classic study, *Labor and Monopoly Capital: The Degradation of Work in the Twentieth Century*. Braverman focused on the modern factory, but his approach applies to the daily grind of package car drivers today: "The physical processes of production are now carried out more or less blindly, not only by the workers who perform them, but often by lower ranks of supervisory employees as well. The production units operate like a hand, watched, corrected, and controlled by a distant brain."[17]

Could there be a better description of ORION, UPS's routing program? ORION "uses expansive fleet telematics and advanced algorithms to gather and calculate countless amounts of data to provide UPS drivers with optimized routes."[18] Drivers who were once valued for their "route knowledge" are reduced to implementing a software program on the 55,000 daily package car delivery routes they make across the United States. The *Wall Street Journal* summed up the new situation best with its pithy headline "At UPS, the Algorithm Is the Driver." The algorithm for ORION is one thousand pages long and was designed by fifty UPS engineers.[19]

Telematics, once understood as the application of computerization to fleet management, has now morphed into something far-reaching in the drive for big data. As journalist Jessica Bruder reports, this has made the average driver's life hell: "Now drivers were called to account for a litany of small sins. They were asked to justify bathroom breaks and any other deviations—'stealing time' in corporate-speak—that could chip away at their SPORH (pronounced "spoor") count, or Stops Per On-Road Hour."

One driver Bruder interviewed told her, "I have no problem doing a heavy, hard job. . . . But now, after you do the job, you have to look back every day and say, 'Did I do this? Did I do that?' They have a report that tells them everything that you did wrong. For instance, if you turned the truck on before you put on your seat belt, that's wasting gas." Sam Dwyer, a former driver who did a six-month stint as a package car driver, told Bruder, "Data is just a proxy for control."[20]

Many workers are straining under UPS's metrics-based system of control. Bruder includes the story of another driver, Domenick DeDomenico, who was hit by a car while making his deliveries. DeDomenico spent ten days in a coma and underwent surgery and physical therapy. When he finally returned to work, tracking data showed that he had "dipped below his pre-accident delivery rate of 13.23 packages per hour," and his mangers threatened to fire him.[21]

What part will logistics workers play in shaping the world in the twenty-first century? As I have argued in previous chapters, logistic workers have enormous economic and political power. That power has been on display on a few occasions, and each time, it has created an amazing disruption of the smooth flow of goods so valued in today's global economy. For example, in May 2015, the contract expired between the International Longshore and Warehouse Union (ILWU) and the Pacific Maritime Association (PMA), the organization representing employers of the Pacific coast shipping industry. Over the next nine months a back-and-forth battle took place between the union and the employers association.[22] The *Los Angeles Times* captured the unique power of the dockers:

> The dispute that has snarled West Coast shipping revolves around a rarity in American business—a small but mighty union. The International Longshore and Warehouse Union represents 20,000 dockworkers, a fraction of the organized ranks of teachers, truck drivers or healthcare workers. But the port workers—who still queue up at hiring halls daily for work and spend years earning full membership—stand guard over a crucial chokepoint in the global economy.[23]

The small ILWU was mighty enough to take action and cost the US economy billions of dollars by backing up the supply chain for months. However, the final agreement reached between ILWU and PMA involved serious concessions by the union.[24] What happened? The enormous power of the dockers is being slowly eaten away by the massive non-union economy that surrounds the waterfront. The west coast dockers may "stand guard over a crucial chokepoint," but once you pass through it you discover that vast swaths of the logistics industry are non-union.

ONE UNION IN THE LOGISTICS INDUSTRY

While it may be too soon to speak of having one union represent all logistics workers in North America, this unified picture should be the goal of any revived organizing in this sprawling industry. Amalgamation—the traditional demand of labor militants and socialists for small, sometimes, craft unions to combine their strengths and organize the unorganized into one industrial union representing a particular industry—is as relevant today as it ever was. Industrial unionism is not a relic of the distant past but a crucial part of the future of the logistics industry. Major sectors of the logistics world are already unionized (including UPS, DHL, and USPS, as well as FedEx pilots, dockers, and many railroad workers), and these coalitions should be the springboards for organizing the rest of the industry. The Teamsters are especially well positioned to be at the center of future logistics organizing. For example, the presence of 60,000 UPS package car drivers on the street five days a week should be an invaluable resource and inspiration for organizing FedEx, but this potential army of organizers has not been mobilized and remains untapped.

Amazon's chain of warehouses across North America should be the obvious target for a major organizing campaign. The Teamsters and the ILWU have organized and represented warehouse workers for more than eighty years, and it's high time for employees at Amazon's facilities to be included in that process.[25] Amazon has mastered the art of winning major tax credit incentives from local and state governments to build their most coveted warehouses. In Kenosha, Wisconsin, alone, Amazon received $10.3 million.[26] The working conditions in Amazon's warehouses are notoriously bad in the United States and abroad, and one big question that any organizing effort should ask is, why are taxpayers subsidizing such working conditions? The *Morning Call* in Allentown, Pennsylvania, conducted a 2011 investigation into Amazon's working conditions in its Breinigsville, Pennsylvania, warehouses. After interviewing twenty current employees, the newspaper described the conditions inside the facilities:

> Workers said they were forced to endure brutal heat inside the sprawling warehouse and were pushed to work at a pace many could

not sustain. Employees were frequently reprimanded regarding their productivity and threatened with termination, workers said. The consequences of not meeting work expectations were regularly on display, as employees lost their jobs and got escorted out of the warehouse. Such sights encouraged some workers to conceal pain and push through injury lest they get fired as well, workers said.[27]

Such nineteenth-century "workhouse" conditions cry out for action. While many Amazon warehouse workers are employed by third-party labor services that have been historically difficult to organize, a late August 2015 ruling by the National Labor Relations Board made it easier to organize workers from fast food chains to warehouse employees who work under exploitative arrangements.[28] Meanwhile, 2,000 German Amazon warehouse workers went on strike ten days before Christmas in 2014 to press demands for better pay and working conditions.[29]

Teamsters General President James P. Hoffa, at the 2002 Teamster convention, declared, "Today we stand at the threshold: Will we rest on our accomplishments? Or will we take what we've learned and earned and reinvest in our future?"[30] The course that Hoffa set has been largely concessionary with existing contracts, and his "organizing," in notable cases, hasn't offered any helpful models for future campaigns. In 2011, one of the largest groups of workers to join the Teamsters in recent memory was a cohort of 20,000 correctional, probation, and parole officers with the Florida Department of Corrections (FDOC). "This is a great day for Teamsters," Hoffa boasted.[31] But it wasn't as if the 20,000 new members had previously lacked organization. The Police Benevolent Association had represented Florida's prison guards and probation officers for more than three decades.[32] The form of organizing that Hoffa was celebrating failed to strengthen the core industries of transportation, warehousing, and logistics. Meanwhile, the small local efforts carried out by Teamster local unions at FedEx Freight have been few in numbers and a mixed bag of victories and defeats. The Teamsters need a better plan to challenge the logistics giants: Grizzly bears can't be beaten with squirt guns.

However, the recent living history of the Teamsters does provide us with a better possible course. The 1997 Teamster UPS contract campaign and strike remain the model for organizing, educating, mobilizing, and leading an enormous nationwide workforce into battle against a wealthy and politically connected logistics giant. It is a good prototype for contract campaigns with existing employers and organizing non-union logistic companies across the country.

The success of this model also may explain why there has been such a great effort to erase it from public memory. Two major US autobiographies, Bill Clinton's *My Life* and Hillary Clinton's *Living History*, make no mention of the UPS strike or Ron Carey or the Teamsters, for that matter, despite the prominence of all three in the politics of the late 1990s. This deliberate political amnesia extends to the current Teamster leadership who, when taking time to commemorate the 1997 strike, fail to mention Ron Carey, who led it.

Nonetheless, the contract campaign and strike live on in other surprising ways. Looking back, it is not difficult to see that those decisive events were the inspiration for today's vibrant "Fight for $15" movement and other bold campaigns for social justice up and down the logistics supply chain. It's time for this generation to bring those struggles back to UPS.

APPENDIX 1

DO BLACK LIVES MATTER TO BIG BROWN?

By Joe Allen

Originally published in Socialist Worker, *September 14, 2016*

Earlier this year, United Parcel Service (UPS) boasted that it was "recognized as a World's Most Ethical Company for the 10th consecutive year by the Ethisphere Institute, a global leader in defining and advancing the standards of ethical business practices."

UPS is one of the world's most recognizable corporate brands, known for many decades by its nickname "Big Brown" because of its familiar brown package delivery trucks. It has a global workforce of 440,000 and is one of the top ten employers in the United States.

Why has UPS been described as an ethical company? In a press release, Big Brown stressed that "the World's Most Ethical Companies designation recognizes those companies that align principle with action, [and] work tirelessly to make trust part of their corporate DNA."

But there's something else engrained deep in UPS's "corporate DNA": racism. Across the United States, UPS has singled out and systematically harassed African American workers, leading to civil rights lawsuits, protests by the NAACP and, in one case, a picket against racism by a local Teamsters union.

Here are some examples of the experiences endured by people of color working for UPS:

Riviera Beach, Florida: Marvin Merritt, who has worked for UPS for three years, told a local television station about the constant abuse he endured from a former supervisor. "He's walking right behind me, over my shoulder, harassing me. . . . He shook his head, and he just called me a lazy n***** and walked away, which was so wrong."

In March of this year, 70 of Merritt's coworkers and fellow Teamsters rallied outside the UPS hub, protesting what they called a pattern of discrimination at the Riviera Beach hub. The offending supervisor was removed from the building but not fired from the company.

Lexington, Kentucky: In April, a jury found UPS liable for creating a hostile workplace environment, for explicitly discriminating against one Black employee, and for retaliating against three others. "The jury awarded damages of $1.5 million to one man, $1 million to a second, and between $100,000 and $810,000 for six others, for a total of $5.3 million," reported the *Lexington Herald-Leader.*

During the trial, the paper reported, "[t]estimony was heard and evidence was introduced . . . that an effigy of a black UPS driver was hung from a ceiling for four days."

Nooses, of course, are historically identified with the lynching of Black men, most commonly in southern states. UPS's defense of its supervisors' actions was that it was a safety demonstration.

Chapel Hill, North Carolina: The *Raleigh News and Observer* interviewed UPS workers in Raleigh, Durham, and Chapel Hill and found that "Black and Hispanic workers are common targets of abusive language and over-supervision. One longtime worker said multiple supervisors would follow him as he made his rounds, looking for violations. Another worker produced certified letters sent over a two-year period informing the worker of several discharges."

One 28-year employee, Dianne Edwards, said she had been discharged 33 times!

In all of these cases UPS's actions violate not only various anti-discrimination laws but the company's national contract with the International Brotherhood of Teamsters, which represents nearly 250,000 workers at UPS across the United States.

The National Master United Parcel Service Agreement specifically prohibits discrimination "against any individual with respect to hiring, compensation, terms or conditions of employment because of such individual's race, color, religion, sex, sexual orientation, national origin, physical disability, veteran status or age in violation of any federal or state law." It also clearly states, "The Employer will treat employees with dignity and respect at all times."

Yet in the midst of this epidemic of racism, UPS CEO David Abney chose last month to express pride in his "Mississippi heritage" in an interview with the BBC.

Whatever that may mean for Abney, for many of us, Mississippi's heritage is one of bigotry, racism, and extreme inequality, backed up by state violence and state-sponsored vigilante violence.

UPS is one of the largest employers of African Americans in the United States, especially in the big metropolitan areas. The company's most visible Black workers are the package car or air drivers who deliver or pick up packages at homes and businesses, followed by the tractor-trailer drivers—called "feeder drivers" in the company lingo—on the highways.

However, the largest contingent of Black workers at UPS is among the hidden army of part-timers working all hours of the day and night in sorting facilities or hubs across the country.

The largest of these sorting facilities is the "CACH"—the Chicago Area Consolidation Hub—that straddles Chicago's southwestern suburbs of Hodgkins and Willow Springs. During the end-of-year holiday season, it can employ up to 8,000 workers. Thousands of African Americans drive or ride public transportation from Chicago's South Side or the predominately Black southern suburbs every day.

According to UPS's 2015 Corporate Sustainability Report, 23 percent of the company's US employees are African American, nearly double their percentage in the US population. Some 14 percent of its US workforce is Latino. UPS's figures don't give a breakdown according to job categories, but the vast majority of African Americans work in non-supervisory positions.

UPS wasn't always a large or even a small employer of African Americans. In the mid-1960s, at the peak of the civil rights movement, UPS had an overwhelmingly white male workforce. Greg Niemann, a former UPS manager-turned-company historian, wrote in his otherwise fawning history, *Big Brown*: "By a long-standing tradition many companies did not hire minorities, and UPS was one of them. UPS found it easier to go along with the majority of white America, and its managers indulged in stereotyping minorities rather than hiring them."

A big motivating factor in changing UPS's hiring policies was a fear of expensive lawsuits. The Equal Employment Opportunity Commission (EEOC), led by its chair, William H. Brown, a well-known Black attorney from Philadelphia, won a landmark case against corporate goliath AT&T in 1973, leading to "a very expensive consent decree," Niemann wrote. "It was a wake-up call to American industry."

UPS tried to put a more progressive face on the company, moving several men with reputations for being "liberal" into executive positions. Brown, the former EEOC chair, became the first African American to serve on the UPS Board of Directors, in 1982.

These changes from above clearly had an impact on UPS's hiring policies. However, many of them occurred during the 1970s, when the company was massively expanding its national workforce and would have been forced to hire outside of its traditional pool of white men in any event.

While UPS today can claim to have a racially diverse workforce, that clearly hasn't meant an end to racism on the job. Today's examples of racist abuse and retaliation are remarkably similar to events 20 years ago in Oakland, California. Black UPS drivers at that time went to the local NAACP to ask it to investigate their complaints of bigotry and harassment.

Some 500 people, mostly UPS workers, attended a public forum where Black drivers testified for four hours that they were routinely assigned to the most dangerous routes without protection, leading to one driver being killed and four others robbed; called "boys" and "monkeys" when they returned undelivered packages; overlooked for promotions; and ignored when they bid on safer routes, despite having seniority.

Timothy Mapfumo, a 14-year UPS employee, testified that a supervisor told him that "white drivers can relate to people in the

[Oakland] hills better and that Black drivers can relate to people in the ghetto."

A class action lawsuit was later filed against UPS on May 1, 1997, on behalf of African American drivers and part-timers from Oakland and beyond, as far away as San Bernardino. "Racial discrimination in this company is like humidity," William Lewis, a driver and 23-year UPS veteran, told the media. "You can't see it but you can feel it."

UPS lost the suit—and while it didn't admit guilt, it did agree to a wide-ranging settlement to be monitored by the federal court for three years. The agreement included a large monetary award for all African American part-timers who worked for UPS in the Northwest and Pacific regions from January 1996 to February 1999, as well as new procedures for posting the availability of jobs, job locations, monitoring of promotions and driver training.

The company paid more than $3 million in fees and costs to the plaintiffs' attorneys and another $150,000 for future costs of monitoring the settlement. Such a humiliating defeat and the stiff price tag should have been deterrents to racist behavior. But have they been?

If William Lewis was right that racism at UPS 20 years ago was like "humidity," then the effigy of a Black driver that hung from a ceiling for four days recently in Lexington is a bad sign that racism has grown more open instead.

This isn't to say that UPS doesn't have prominent African Americans in its management hierarchy. For example, Noel Massie, who is Black, is president for UPS's Southern California district, which includes Hawaii and part of Nevada, where over 20,000 UPS employees work for him.

But having Black faces in high places at UPS has meant very little for the working conditions of Black drivers and hub workers.

This isn't the exception but the rule at US companies. The last four decades have seen both a growing inequality and militarization of US society and an increasingly totalitarian workplace—they are two sides of the same coin. Thus, Black communities have suffered frightening police violence while Black workers are among those—undocumented workers are another—who face the brunt of management's wrath, scorn, and abuse on the job.

This process has created worsening conditions for all workers, expressed at times in mental health issues, suicides, and periodic explosions of violence. That was the case for Joe Tesney, a white UPS package car driver who shot and killed two supervisors and himself in September 2014. Tesney, a veteran at UPS, told his minister that he had been "troubled" over work. He was fired after a long period of harassment and was facing economic ruin.

Unlike most workplaces, UPS has been unionized for more than eight decades, and its workers are overwhelmingly represented by the Teamsters. Twenty years ago, during the struggle in Oakland, UPS driver Daniel Dugar declared, "If the union had done their damn job, we wouldn't be here now."

So where have the Teamsters been on these issues? The sad answer is, missing in action.

For the past 17 years, the Teamsters have been led by James P. Hoffa, son of the infamous Teamster leader Jimmy Hoffa who disappeared and was presumed murdered by his former Mafia friends in 1975. Hoffa Junior has shown no interest in confronting racism—or much of anything at all—at UPS, even though it is the largest employer of Teamsters in the country.

That's no surprise given Hoffa's inaction at other Teamster-represented companies.

For example, in 2010 and 2012, it was the Equal Employment Opportunity Commission (EEOC), not the Teamsters, that challenged workplace racism at freight giant YRC, the corporation created in the merger of Roadway and Yellow Freight in 2008. The EEOC charged that YRC and its predecessor Yellow had created a racially hostile workplace at its former Chicago Ridge and current Chicago Heights facilities.

Had the case gone to trial, the EEOC reported, the proceedings would have revealed "evidence that Black employees were subjected to multiple incidents of hangman's nooses and racist graffiti, comments and cartoons. The EEOC also would have presented evidence that Yellow and YRC subjected Black employees to harsher discipline and scrutiny than their white counterparts and gave them more difficult and time-consuming work assignments."

The Teamsters were absent in another case where racism took a deadly toll. In one of the most controversial mass shootings of the past decade, Omar Thornton, a Black driver and Teamster at Hartford Distributors in Manchester, Connecticut, shot and killed eight coworkers before killing himself. Thornton was accused of theft and was offered the choice of resignation. As he was leaving the building, he went on a killing spree. All his victims were white.

Thornton told the 911 operator that the massacre was motivated by racism at the workplace. Thornton's girlfriend claimed that she saw pictures, presumably taken by Thornton, of a hangman's noose and racist graffiti on bathroom walls.

"This all could have been avoided," Thornton's uncle, Will Holliday, told the media. "He went to the union a couple of times with issues concerning what was going on, and it was not dealt with appropriately."

UPS has succeeded General Motors as the largest private-sector, unionized employer in the United States. What happens at UPS and at other large unionized employers like YRC sets the standards not only for wages and benefits, but for dignity and respect on the job for all workers.

In a time of a growing awareness about the depths of racism in US society, the Teamsters, the fourth-largest union in the country and one of the largest union representatives of African American workers—nearly 450,000 men and women, or one-third of the union, are Black—should be in the lead in confronting employer racism, especially at UPS. This would require a more aggressive stance on a broad range of issues, from support for the Fight for $15 campaign to greater challenges on pension and health care concessions.

It's hard to see that happening without a change in the national leadership of the Teamsters.

A radical change is necessary in the organization of Black workers inside the Teamsters. The long-standing Teamsters National Black Caucus (TNBC) acts more like a social club than a militant advocate for one-third of the membership.

Founded in 1971, the TNBC was a pre-emptive action taken by a handful of Black officials, with the connivance of then-Teamsters General President Frank Fitzsimmons, to stop the formation of something more independent and militant, like, for example, the League of Revolutionary Black Workers in the United Auto Workers. The TNBC's founding conference wasn't even held until four years later, after Fitzsimmons, a longtime associate of Jimmy Hoffa and organized crime, appointed an ally to be its chair.

The TNBC has always been a useless creature of the Teamster Old Guard. A new Black Lives Matter–oriented caucus is long overdue in the Teamsters union.

Having a strong union means confronting and defeating the racism that employers use against Black and Latino workers and to divide the whole workforce. It also means confronting racism among members.

We have to say to UPS and to all employers: Black Lives Matter and Union Lives Matter.

APPENDIX 2

HOFFA'S NUMBERED DAYS

By Joe Allen

Originally published in Jacobin, *December 2, 2016*

Hoffa was challenged for general president by Fred Zuckerman and the Teamsters United reform slate. Along with his running mate, Tim Sylvester, the former president of New York Local 804, Zuckerman spent the last two years crisscrossing the country meeting with thousands of rank-and-file Teamsters infuriated by sellout contracts, bankrupt pensions, and cascading corruption scandals.

Besides narrowly losing the election in the United States to Zuckerman by 709 votes, Hoffa lost his "home local," Local 614 in Pontiac, Michigan, and Detroit Local 299, led for decades by his father Jimmy Hoffa Sr. Hoffa eked out a win by a mere six thousand votes out of 213,000 cast in the United States and Canada in the closest election in Teamsters history.

Back in 1996, Teamsters reformer Ron Carey, the first rank-and-file elected leader of the union who battled and defeated Hoffa and his supporters across the country in a bruising reelection campaign, denounced Hoffa as "an empty suit and a front for the mob."

Today he seems not to be wearing any clothes at all. The election results have torn to shreds the foundation of his political machine and may reduce him to a mere figurehead in the union.

"JUNIOR HOFFA"

Hoffa was never a popular or personally admired leader. He was always more bluff and bluster than substance, aided by slick advertising funded by millions in rank-and-file workers' campaign contributions and the union's treasury.

He relied heavily on his iconic father's place in Teamsters history. Various attempts to create a new Hoffa cult—embarrassingly on display at this year's Teamsters convention in Las Vegas—were embraced by the paid staff and his supporters among the many local union officers but largely ignored by the membership and even some of the officialdom.

In a sometimes revealing 1998 profile, Jeffrey Goldberg captured what many Hoffa admirers in the media and Hollywood failed to see for years: "Various commentators have, in one fashion or another, characterized him as dim, but what that may reflect is that he is wary, and often inarticulate. When he strays from his stump speech, he is not a convincing talker, and he is unskilled at grappling with policy issues."

Long derided by his critics as "Hoffa Junior" for being part of the long—and very much alive—tradition of many Teamsters officials passing positions of power to their children, James P. Hoffa has been general president of the Teamsters for seventeen years, making him the second-longest–serving top officer of the union in its history.

While he didn't directly inherit his office from his father, his last name gave him great prestige (even if it was tainted with gangsterism). If his last name had been Smith or Jones, he would never have had a labor career.

Hoffa was sworn in as general president in March 1999 after winning the special December 1998 election, called after the federal government–sponsored witch hunt against Ron Carey, the first directly elected rank-and-file reform leader of the Teamsters. Carey earned the wrath of both the Teamster old guard—corrupt and in many cases mobbed-up officers—and corporate America for his leadership of the historic 1997 national strike against United Parcel Service (UPS).

If the Carey years were a break from the Teamsters' previous pattern of collaboration with the major employers, Hoffa was a return to the old days.

BUILD TEAMSTER POWER?

Hoffa pledged that he would "build Teamster power," as in the glory days of his father's union in the 1950s and 1960s. But incompetence and concessions to major Teamster employers were visible in his administration from the start.

For example, in October 1999, after barely seven months in office, Hoffa called an ill-advised national strike against Overnite Transportation, one of the largest non-union freight companies in the United States. Organizing at Overnite began under Carey and some serious progress had been made, but the Teamsters were not in a position to launch a national strike.

The strike quickly turned into a disaster. It was stillborn, but Hoffa refused to change course, and the strike sputtered onto an inglorious defeat two and half years later. In calling the strike, Hoffa was most likely trying to "out-Carey" Carey because of his weak position in the union. After Carey was ousted from the union, nearly 46 percent of the Teamster membership voted for reform candidate Tom Leedham and a third candidate in the special December 1998 election.

The strike laid bare to anyone who had doubts about Hoffa in corporate America the fact that he was no Ron Carey. Carey had methodically and strategically planned for the 1997 national UPS strike and won a historic victory for the labor movement after two and half decades of demoralizing defeats. Hoffa recklessly gambled with the livelihoods of thousands of strikers and lost. It was an inauspicious beginning to the Hoffa era.

Hoffa largely consolidated his position in the early days of his administration by building a political machine easily recognizable to anyone familiar with big-city Democratic Party outfits like Chicago's. During his first year in office, Hoffa added 137 multiple salaries—where an officer can collect several salaries for performing little work—to the Teamster payroll.

While Hoffa and the old guard were hostile to democracy in the union, the 1989 consent decree forced them to build a well-funded campaign machine, running for reelection every five years and winning every one since 1998.

IN LOVE WITH HOFFA

For UPS, the largest Teamster employer in the United States, Hoffa has been the gift that keeps on giving. John Schultz, a reporter for *Traffic World*, one of the freight industry's leading publications, wrote in May 2000, in an article called "In Love with Hoffa," "United Parcel Service, the nation's largest transportation company, feels that it has taken part in one of the great trades of all time in labor: James P. 'Jimmy' Hoffa for Ron Carey as president of the Teamsters union."

UPS so thoroughly embraced Hoffa that it has been willing to flaunt Teamster election campaign rules. According to a 2006 election protest filed at UPS's giant Worldport air hub in Louisville, "The UPS Air District Labor Manager at the facility drove [Hoffa and his entourage] around the ground and air district areas . . . [and] Hoffa addressed assembled employees and instructed them to vote and to 'make sure their vote counted.' This violation was so egregious that the election officer ruled that UPS had to grant Leedham [Hoffa's challenger] equal access and time at Worldport."

The following year an ailing Ron Carey surveyed the proposed 2007 national master UPS contract and scathingly denounced it:

> The proposed contract is a complete sellout. It gives back to UPS monumental gains that the members sacrificed for and won in 1997. In 1997 we stopped UPS from taking control of the Teamster pension plans, and we provided record increases. We made it clear that "Part-Time America Just Won't Work." We forced the company to create 10,000 full-time jobs by combining 20,000 part-time jobs.

Carey continued:

> That achievement provided for part-timers a sense of connection, a sense of belonging to something. It gave them an opportunity for a good full-time job. And it dispelled the feeling that they were second-class citizens. That translates into a stronger union, when it's working for all the members. This contract eliminates new full-time jobs. And it makes new, part-time jobs a disaster by freezing starting wages and cutting benefits.

Carey's fears about what a Hoffa takeover of the union would produce had come true. (Shortly thereafter, in December 2008, Carey died of cancer.)

According to Ken Paff, national organizer for the Teamsters reform group Teamsters for a Democratic Union (TDU), Hoffa was a disaster at UPS: "Hoffa's record at UPS has been one of go-along and get-along with corporate management. In 2007 he settled early and short. He gave in to management and let them pull out from the Central States Pension Fund, crippling it; the trade-off in that deal allowed UPS freight to be Teamster organized, but under a weaker stand-alone contract."

Hoffa and Ken Hall, the Teamsters' general secretary-treasurer and chief UPS negotiator, thought they were clever with their deal for a card-check organizing agreement. But Teamsters retirees and spouses and UPS freight workers got the worst of both worlds: a bankrupt pension fund and terrible, substandard contracts.

2011 ELECTION

In 2011 there were signs that the political situation within the union was changing.

Sandy Pope was a founding member of the TDU and the president of a small Teamster local in New York when she decided to challenge Hoffa in the 2011 election. She was the first woman to run for general president of the Teamsters.

Wisconsin Teamsters leader Fred Gegare also challenged Hoffa for the leadership, but he was a very different rival than Pope. A previous ally of Hoffa's, Gegare's campaign represented an important break among Hoffa supporters in the Midwest that included Columbus, Ohio, leader Tony Jones and Fred Zuckerman, president of Louisville, Kentucky's Local 89, one of the largest Teamster locals in the country and the home base of UPS's global air operations, Worldport.

Gegare was an old guard figure and a longtime opponent of TDU. A coalition between the two opposing anti-Hoffa campaigns wasn't possible in 2011. The Pope and Gegare campaigns together won nearly 40 percent of the vote. Hoffa easily won the election.

Pope ran a solo campaign against Hoffa. She had no running mate or slate, but her results were revealing. TDU targeted thirteen local unions in New York and New Jersey. Pope campaigned and won a plurality. She also got the most votes in the seven Tennessee locals and, surprisingly, narrowly won the state.

Pope did her best in national bargaining units like UPS and freight. In spite of the still overwhelmingly male composition and macho culture of national bargaining units like UPS, Sandy Pope made an impressive showing. For example, in Teamsters Local 705 in Chicago she won nearly one-third of the vote—something that most observers would have thought impossible.

Hoffa hoped to humiliate his opponents in the election and pushed for the Teamster membership to vote for him in record numbers. Yet his vote fell by forty thousand votes from the 2006 election. He also lost badly in many freight locals in the Midwest.

While they won the election, Hoffa and Hall didn't seem to notice that sands were shifting under their feet. They saw the declining number of Teamsters voting as a sign that the members were happy—not that those who voted against them were enraged at their destructive leadership. Some of Hoffa's allies even began to talk of revising the union constitution to abolish rank-and-file elections, completing the old guard counterrevolution that began when Hoffa was first elected in December 1998.

VOTE NO

Under Hoffa and Hall, UPS won big. Despite the 2008 Great Recession, UPS has made record profits each year. Yet the Teamsters national bargaining committee made fewer and fewer demands on the global logistics giant.

There were also fewer numbers of full-time jobs created in each contract, and part-time wages remained incredibly low; meanwhile, UPS got one of the biggest concessions in bargaining history when Hoffa-Hall allowed them to pull out of the Central States Pension Fund—a big step towards the company's complete control of the fund and with it much lower benefits, something that reformers in the union had long fought.

UPS wanted more, and Hoffa and Hall gave it to them: Team-Care, the new inferior health care plan for UPS Teamsters. It was sold by the Teamster leadership as a purely administrative change, not a change in coverage. But it was soon discovered that coverage levels decreased for many, and wage increases and pension contributions had to be diverted to maintain previous levels.

The national contract passed by a slim majority. The battle then moved to the national contract's local supplements (mini-contracts over local working conditions), where the battle over TeamCare and issues such as the lack of substantial numbers of full-time jobs in the contract would be fought out.

There are two dozen supplements to the national UPS contract. Mark Timlin, a UPS package car driver in New Jersey and member of Local 177, was one of many veteran UPS Teamsters who had supported reform candidates in past Teamster elections but felt a great urgency to become active in opposing the TeamCare concessions. Timlin told me, "I started the Vote No Facebook page in May 2012 out of pure frustration when I saw the agreement. It was going to affect my health care when I planned to retire. In late June I went to the contract vote count. At the vote count I meet some of the union representatives from Fred Zuckerman's Local 89. I was invited to the TDU convention in the fall of 2013 where I met Sandy Pope."

Because of the activism of Teamsters like Timlin across the country, says Ken Paff, "A record eighteen supplements were rejected by rank-and-file Teamster voters, some up to three times."

Hoffa's response? He used a little-known and rarely used power granted to him by the Teamster constitution to overrule the vote and unilaterally impose the contract and supplements. Hoffa specifically chose to impose the national contract and all supplements after Fred Zuckerman's Local 89 voted it down by a 95 percent "no" vote.

Hoffa's arrogant display of power may have pleased UPS, but it enraged a sizeable section of the Teamster membership.

At the same time, Fred Zuckerman emerged as a national leader of a movement against concessions among UPS Teamsters, car haulers, and freight Teamsters. He also won the admiration of Teamster retirees in temporarily halting the devastating cuts to their pension benefits.

For Teamster rank-and-filers like Timlin, it made perfect sense to move from campaigning for a "no" vote to then trying to unseat Hoffa: "The wheels were in motion anyway. I was asked to chair the first 'Take Back Our Union' meetings in Edison, New Jersey; Philadelphia; and Pittsburgh in June 2014." The 2016 campaign to unseat James P. Hoffa had begun.

THE NEAR REVOLUTION

Looking from outside, in early 2016 it seemed foolhardy to believe a relatively small group of mostly Midwestern-based local Teamsters with little name recognition and allied with the long-standing reformers of TDU would be capable of mounting a serious challenge to Hoffa's entrenched leadership.

However, for over two years prior to the vote count in November 2016, the future members of the Teamsters United slate—Fred Zuckerman, Tim Sylvester, Sandy Pope, Tony Jones, and others—toured the country meeting with thousands of Teamsters concerned about the declining state of their union. They laid the foundation of a national campaign and produced incredible results.

"Fred called it," Ken Paff told me about Zuckerman's strategy. "If we can split the eastern region, win the South and Midwest overwhelmingly, and hold them off on the West Coast and Canada—we can win." It nearly happened.

The Midwest was key. It was here that the massive concessions in the freight industry and the impending bankruptcy of the Central States Pension Fund—where four hundred thousand retired Teamsters and their spouses will see projected 50 to 70 percent cuts in their monthly benefits—hit Hoffa the hardest. Zuckerman defeated Hoffa by over 10,700 votes in the Teamsters central region, and 2,500 votes in the South removed all of Hoffa's six vice presidents in those regions.

Chicago Joint Council 25—known for decades for the entrenched mob presence in the Teamsters that provided many of Hoffa's key personnel and campaign fundraisers—voted for Zuckerman and Teamsters United. Hoffa's most powerful midwestern vice president, John Coli, one of Chicago mayor Rahm

Emanuel's most reliable supporters in the labor movement, was tossed out of office.

Teamsters Local 705, which represents UPS workers at the company's mammoth Chicago Area Consolidation Hub (CACH) voted overwhelmingly for Teamsters United. Teamsters Local 710, long identified with some of the worst old-guard corruption and stretching across three states, voted for Teamsters United. One of the new Teamsters United vice presidents will be UPS feeder driver and Teamsters Local 710 member Bob Kopystynsky, the first rank-and-file worker elected to the general executive board of the Teamsters since Ron Carey's historic victory in 1991.

Zuckerman and Teamsters United won every state in the Midwest except Michigan, where Zuckerman got 49 percent of the vote. Hoffa suffered crushing defeats in Ohio, Indiana, and Missouri. Teamsters United won Texas. Tyson Johnson, Hoffa's freight division director, lost reelection for regional vice president and his local union vote to Zuckerman. Teamsters United candidates John Palmer of Texas and Kim Schultz of Florida won.

Reformers didn't carry the day everywhere, of course. Many local old-guard leaders like Sean O'Brien of Boston and Dan Kane of New York delivered the vote for Hoffa. The continued decline in the number of Teamsters members meant the lowest turnout in the closest election in Teamster history with a mere six thousand votes separating the winning and losing candidates.

Still, the election results raise an obvious question: what does the Teamsters' future look like?

BERNIE'S TEAMSTERS

The Teamsters are the most important transportation union in North America, with 1.3 million members and located in key strategic nodes in the American economy. It is one of the three most important industrial unions, along with the UAW and the Steelworkers.

The heart and guts of the Teamsters are in continental transportation networks: rail, freight, and especially UPS, the largest logistics company and unionized private-sector employer in the United States, with 250,000 union members.

While Hoffa has kept the overall membership numbers steady during his seventeen years in office, his long list of betrayals, unnecessary concessions, and general neglect of the old core of the union—freight, UPS, car haul—and lack of new organizing in the burgeoning logistics industry (notably Amazon) have significantly impacted the future of the Teamsters. It shouldn't be a surprise, then, that all of this has finally begun to catch up with him.

Yet he still holds the reins of power on the union's general executive board with a comfortable majority. We will know in the coming months if Zuckerman's election protest will force a new union election, but the executive board composition will remain in Hoffa's favor.

In the meantime, the election results show clearly that Teamsters want a dramatic change in the course of their union.

For the broader labor movement and the Left in the United States, the Teamsters' elections should counter some of the impact of Trump's victory and with it much inane discussion of the American working class. A befuddled Paul Krugman wrote in his most recent column, "To be honest, I don't fully understand this resentment [that elected Trump]." Yet the states that gave Trump the presidency also voted overwhelmingly to toss out Hoffa.

"We were sort of like the Bernie campaign inside the Teamsters," Ken Paff told me soon after the election. "Teamsters United brought together African American part-timers with Latino sanitation workers in California with freight drivers in the Midwest, the South, and across the country."

There is a whiff of illegitimacy to Hoffa's reelection. Zuckerman is pursuing election protests through the Teamsters election supervisor's office, and if need be, into federal court, focusing on the Hoffa slate's use of union resources in their campaign to cover up a corruption scandal—a major election rules violation that raises the possibility of a rerun election.

For the moment, according to the *Journal of Commerce*, one of the major mouthpieces for the shipping industry, "Employers that have dealt with Hoffa in contract negotiations are likely relieved." But the *National Law Review* added a cautionary note to their mostly corporate readership: "Some observers believe that the closeness of the vote could mean less willingness on the part of the Teamsters to grant concessions in collective bargaining."

James P. Hoffa told the delegates at the 2002 Teamster convention, "We will set the course of our union into the twenty-first century." While they may not have been enough to oust him from office this year, the results of the 2016 election demonstrate that many Teamsters want a future without him. Those "many" may soon become "most."

LOGISTICS' TWO FRONTS

By Joe Allen

Originally published in Jacobin, *March 28, 2017*

The modern economy revolves around the sprawling logistics indus-try. Nothing demonstrates this more clearly than the current situ-ation at Amazon and UPS. If Amazon makes good on its recent pledge, it will add another 100,000 workers to its US workforce by 2018, making it one of the country's largest—and one of the largest non-union—employers.

The US labor movement faces several existential threats right now, but Amazon's is a special kind. The company's breakneck expansion has revolutionized the logistics industry. Its impact is most deeply felt at United Parcel Service (UPS), the country's larg-est private-sector, unionized employer, with nearly 250,000 of its workers represented by the Teamsters.

UPS already lashes the Teamsters with the threat of Amazon undercutting the union's gains to justify the miserable wages paid to part-timers, impossible productivity demands, and the subcontract-ing of union work to non-union contractors. It will no doubt use the competition from Amazon to demand further concessions from the Teamsters during the next round of contract negotiations.

Teamsters United (TU), the reform challengers in last year's union election that nearly toppled the scandal-ridden and unpopu-lar incumbent Teamsters General President James P. Hoffa, recently announced the launch of a new UPS contract campaign. Fred Zuckerman, TU's candidate for general president, told supporters, we "are going to have to fight for ourselves."

Such a campaign has the potential to take on the package giant, but it can also serve as a beacon for future activists among Amazon's rapidly expanding workforce. And if socialists in the United States can develop an industrial organizing strategy, we can play an important role in helping to organize some of the most powerful workers in this country.

SEATTLE ORIGINS

UPS was founded as a bicycle messenger service in 1907 by James E. Casey. Casey, known for his taciturn personality, did few interviews during his long tenure as the company head.

Forbes magazine in 1970 dubbed UPS the "Quiet Giant" because of the stealthy way it snuck up on and overwhelmed its rivals. The company did little to no advertising. *Forbes* reported that UPS "officials believed only one parcel shipping company could exist in the United States, and it hoped that keeping a low profile would prevent anyone from copying its methods."

Keeping that low profile would quickly prove impossible. The company soon became known as "Big Brown" and developed into a global behemoth.

Today UPS employs 440,000 people worldwide—a workforce nearly as large as the United States' standing army of 460,000. It has one of the largest commercial airline fleets in the world and delivers 2.7 million packages and messages in the United States and 2.8 million to 220 other countries daily. UPS boasts, "We're a company that every day moves 6 percent of US GDP and 2 percent of global GDP through our system."

UPS is densely unionized, unlike its almost entirely non-union twin, FedEx. Both are the darlings of the business media. Along with 250,000 members of the Teamsters—mostly drivers and hub workers—UPS pilots are represented by the Independent Pilots Association (IPA), and some of its mechanics are members of the International Association of Machinists (IAM).

UPS Freight, formerly Overnite Transportation, has around

13,000 Teamsters based in the traditional heavy-duty bulk freight industry and working under local union contracts. The package delivery wing with which most people are familiar (with their ubiquitous brown delivery trucks) has over 230,000 members.

A majority—somewhere around 55 percent, according to organizers' independent estimates—of these UPS Teamsters are part-timers whose starting pay is an abysmally low $10 to $11 per hour. For three decades, starting pay for part-timers was a miserable $8 to $8.50 per hour. Part-timer poverty, along with brutally high productivity, subsidized UPS's massive expansion in the 1980s and 1990s.

Yet, despite all the logistic services that UPS offers—and the declaration of Jack Levis, UPS's senior director of process management, that, "We've really turned from a trucking company with technology to a technology company with trucks"—it is still primarily a package delivery company. UPS doesn't manufacture any goods, nor is it a retailer.

Amazon's inspiration lies elsewhere.

SAM WALTON'S HEIR

Unlike UPS's early attempts at flying under the radar, Amazon's rise has been anything but quiet. Founded in Seattle in 1994, it has become one of the most visible brands in the world and an intimate part of the daily lives of tens of millions of people.

Amazon founder Jeff Bezos is the fifth-richest person in the world, worth nearly $72 billion and treated by some with a cult-like reverence similar to that of late Apple founder Steve Jobs.

Unlike the taciturn Casey, who lived and died in a cloistered world of UPS, Bezos is a highly visible public figure. He recently purchased one of the most important newspapers in the country, the *Washington Post*. *Billboard* actually asked him if he had any plans to run for president. (He said no.) He even made a cameo appearance in *Star Trek Beyond*.

His flair for public relations is well known. Amazon's promotion of drone deliveries has captured the attention of the general public. The company also was granted a patent for Jules Verne–like floating warehouses.

Much of Bezos's business model has been influenced by Sam Walton's Walmart. In the last chapter of Walton's autobiography, *Made in America*, published around the time of his death, in 1992, he mused on whether another company could match or surpass Walmart's success: "My answer is of course it could happen again. It's all a matter of attitude and the capacity to constantly study and question the management of business." He added, if "I were a young man or woman starting out today with the same talents and energies and aspirations that I had fifty years ago, what would I do? . . . Probably some of kind of specialty retail, something to do with computers, maybe."

Walton's musings strongly hint at the possibility of an Amazon-like company as his successor. But what did Bezos learn from Walmart? "Bezos had imbibed Walton's book thoroughly and wove the Walmart founder's credo about frugality and a 'bias for action' into the cultural fabric of Amazon," according to business reporter Brad Stone in his book *The Everything Store*. Bezos was especially taken by Walton's willingness to use "the best ideas of his competitors."

Bezos was so enamored by Walmart that he poached a large number of its executives in the late 1990s. Walmart sued in response, arguing that Amazon was stealing its "trade secrets"; Walmart ultimately lost the suit.

One of the ideas Bezos borrowed from Walton was working his employees past the point of exhaustion. An early Amazon executive, for example, suggested to Bezos that because parking was so expensive near Amazon's first headquarters and warehouse in Seattle, the company should subsidize bus passes for its workers. Bezos apparently "scoffed" at the suggestion. "He didn't want employees to leave and catch the bus," the executive said. "He wanted them to have their cars there so there was never any pressure to go home."

Amazon's working conditions worsened through the first two decades of the twenty-first century as it rapidly expanded its warehouses or distribution centers ("fulfillment centers" in Amazonese) across the country.

The Allentown *Morning Call* conducted an investigation into Amazon's working conditions in its Breinigsville, Pennsylvania, warehouses. After interviewing twenty current employees in 2011, the *Morning Call* reported:

Workers said they were forced to endure brutal heat inside the sprawling warehouse and were pushed to work at a pace many could not sustain. Employees were frequently reprimanded regarding their productivity and threatened with termination, workers said. The consequences of not meeting work expectations were regularly on display, as employees lost their jobs and got escorted out of the warehouse. Such sights encouraged some workers to conceal pain and push through injury lest they get fired as well, workers said.

In 2015, working conditions for Amazon's staff at its Seattle campus were exposed by the *New York Times* to be just as horrendous:

Workers are encouraged to tear apart one another's ideas in meetings, toil long and late (emails arrive past midnight, followed by text messages asking why they were not answered), and held to standards that the company boasts are "unreasonably high." The internal phone directory instructs colleagues on how to send secret feedback to one another's bosses. Employees say it is frequently used to sabotage others. (The tool offers sample texts, including this: "I felt concerned about his inflexibility and openly complaining about minor tasks.")

The white-collar staff are told to be guided by the company's leadership principles, "14 rules inscribed on handy laminated cards." One of those rules: "Leaders are right a lot. They have strong judgment and good instincts."

Amazon's success is due to its massive online retail operation, honed to achieve customer satisfaction and reach a level of sales on a mind-boggling array of products that few other traditional brick-and-mortar retailers—notably the venerable and declining Sears, which Walmart surpassed in sales in 1989—or other online retailers have been able to compete with.

So the announcement in July 2015 that Amazon was valued more than Walmart shouldn't have come as a total surprise. While Walmart is still the world's biggest retailer in terms of revenue, Amazon's evolution from a start-up in a modest office building to a retail juggernaut employing more than 97,000 employees [in 2015] has changed the shape of the retail industry.

Walmart pioneered the creation of the modern logistics corporation with the management of entire supply chains, from the manufacture of consumer goods to their placement on the stores' shelves. Amazon is attempting to do the same thing—without, until recently, the construction of retail stores—but with one addition: controlling customer delivery through its own fleet of drivers.

OPERATION DRAGON BOAT

If Amazon is able to build its own delivery fleet, its impact on the logistics industry could be the greatest on the warehousing and delivery business since the deregulation of the US freight and aviation industries in the late 1970s and early 1980s.

Amazon has launched its own air transport network, an ocean freight forwarding company, direct delivery operations, and the myriad small, barely "independent" subcontractors servicing the final customer delivery of packages. Not since UPS's frantic efforts to build an air delivery operation to catch up with overnight pioneer FedEx or FedEx's construction of a freight operation to match its Big Brown rival has a logistics company in so short a time built such a formidable operation.

According to documents obtained by *Bloomberg*, "Amazon intend[ed] to create a revolutionary system that will automate the entire international supply chain." Furthermore, according to *Bloomberg*,

> a 2013 report to Amazon's senior management team proposed an aggressive global expansion of the company's Fulfillment By Amazon service, which provides storage, packing, and shipping for independent merchants selling products on the company's website. The report envisioned a global delivery network that controls the flow of goods from factories in China and India to customer doorsteps in Atlanta, New York, and London. The project, called Dragon Boat, is proceeding, according to a person familiar with the initiative, who asked not to be identified because the information isn't public.

Four years later, according to *Business Insider*, Amazon has 214 logistics facilities across the United States, including fulfillment-center warehouses; sortation centers, where packages get presorted for shipping; Amazon Pantry and Amazon Fresh, which deliver groceries; and Amazon Prime Now hub, a separate building to store one-hour delivery items. Twenty-eight more distribution centers are expected to be built this year.

Amazon recently announced that it will invest $1.5 billion to build a massive air hub based in the Cincinnati/Northern Kentucky International Airport (CVG). "The project will bring up to 2,700 jobs and forty Boeing 767s to CVG, according to officials, with six hundred full-time jobs coming initially," according to the *Cincinnati Business Courier*. The air hub is squarely within the region known as Cargo Alley, where planes can reach nearly 80 percent of the continental United States within two hours.

"We believe Amazon may be the only company with the fulfillment/distribution density and scale to compete effectively with global UPS/FedEx/DHL," declared a report by Baird Equity Research, a leading financial consulting firm.

Walmart consciously built its distribution centers in remote, conservative regions of the country to avoid the threat of unionization. "Amazon, on the other hand," Mark Meinster, the director of Warehouse Workers for Justice, told me, "builds in or close to major cities. At their Kenosha [Wisconsin] facility (and nobody had built warehouses in Kenosha before Amazon) the workforce is more diverse. Amazon builds in bigger labor markets [like] Chicago, [where] they have fulfillment centers on Goose Island, 28th and Western, Lisle, Joliet, and Morton Grove [both inside the city and in several surrounding suburbs]. Amazon has reversed the model of warehousing pioneered by Walmart."

This offers an opportunity to organize Amazon workers, since its drivers interact often with Teamsters drivers.

SOCIALISTS AND THE WORKPLACE STRUGGLES AHEAD

Ken Paff, national organizer of the Teamsters for a Democratic Union, says the lessons of past contract battles at UPS will be important for future organizing during the upcoming contract battle at UPS and for future organizing at Amazon.

"When the Teamsters decisively defeated UPS during the 1997 strike, under the banner of 'Part-Time America Won't Work,' John Sweeney, the then-head of the AFL-CIO, said that 'the successful

1997 UPS strike was worth a million house calls,'" Paff said, refer-ring to the organizing tactic of visiting workers at home that is central to any organizing campaign. "He was right. Amazon workers—just like all workers—will want to join a union that knows how to win."

When the Teamsters won their battle against UPS in 1997, expectations were raised throughout the entire labor movement. Immediately following the strike, activists began talking about organizing FedEx (a campaign that has yet to be successful).

A fighting union is the best advertisement for organizing new, non-union workers. A big contract win at UPS in 2018 will help draw sympathetic union supporters from Amazon to the Teamsters.

Kim Moody, one of the founders of *Labor Notes*, wrote last year:

> Eighty-five percent of the nearly three-and-a-half million work-ers employed in logistics in the United States are located in large metropolitan areas—inadvertently recreating huge concentrations of workers in many of those areas that were supposed to be "emp-tied" of industrial workers. There are about sixty such "clusters" in the United States, but it is the major sites in Los Angeles, Chicago, and New York-New Jersey, each of which employs at least 100,000 workers, and others such as UPS's Louisville "Worldport" and FedEx's Memphis cluster, that exemplify the trend.

The organizing opportunities this presents—at both companies—should be clear to the Left.

When I spoke to Mark Meinster last year about the many chal-lenges facing organizers in the non-union logistics industry, he thought we needed a spark to ignite organizing efforts. "We need something big like the 1997 UPS strike or the 2006 immigrant rights marches." Do we have that now with millions marching against Trump?

The widespread interest in socialist ideas and the explosive growth of the Democratic Socialists of America (DSA) shows that there is a generation willing to fight for greater political change. If socialists are able to channel that willingness into an industrial strat-egy, a plan to head to the shop floor and organize one's coworkers, we could shake the foundations of the twenty-first-century Ameri-can economy.

This August is the twentieth anniversary of the 1997 UPS strike, a strike that defeated one of the most powerful corporations in the world. Now that much more of the US economy revolves around the logistics industry, the 1997 contract campaign and strike looked like the strike of the future. Let's seize the opportunity.

JAMES HOFFA'S ANTI-DEMOCRATIC UPS CATASTROPHE

By Joe Allen

Originally published in Jacobin, *October 12, 2018*

Rank-and-file reaction to the October 5 vote count on the two proposed national contracts between the Teamsters and United Parcel Service (UPS) quickly went from elation to confusion to raw fury in a few minutes.

The vote count was carried live on a nationwide conference call and online. It was presided over by Ed Hartfield, the Teamsters' election supervisor, and Denis Taylor, the Teamsters' chief negotiator for UPS.

In a ceremony reminiscent of a state lottery, the results showed that the UPS National Master Agreement, the larger of the two, covering 260,000 workers, was rejected by 55 percent of the members who voted, while the UPS Freight contract, covering about twenty thousand workers, was rejected by an even greater number, 63 percent. (Slightly less than half of all UPS Teamsters voted.)

Reaction to the vote was quick, especially from those who had been campaigning for its defeat in one of the most contentious contract battles in many years. Joan-Elaine Miller, a veteran UPS package car driver in Philadelphia, posted on the popular Vote No on UPS Contract Facebook page:

"We fucking did it !!! We voted down the national and forced Taylor back to the table !!! I am crying tears of joy right now!!!!WE FUCKING DID IT!!!!!!"

It was an important victory. It's hard to carry out any kind of "vote no" campaign like this one on a national scale; it is even more difficult at an enormous, far-flung corporation like UPS that runs a twenty-four-hour-a-day operation with myriad work classifications and a high turnover rate among part-timers, which is as high as 90 percent per annum in most locations.

Local supplements were also defeated. In New York City, the agreement of Teamsters Local 804, the old home local union of the late Ron Carey, the leader of the historic 1997 national UPS strike, was rejected by a whopping 95 percent of the membership.

What made the victory even sweeter was that "vote no" campaigners led by Teamsters for a Democratic Union (TDU) and Teamsters United fought the combined forces of the company and the union. Both UPS and the bulk of the Teamsters leadership led by James P. Hoffa campaigned together to get a quick ratification of both contracts, which were loaded with unnecessary and unpopular concessions.

They also hoped to avoid the thicket of problems that ensnared them five years ago, when UPS Teamsters repeatedly voted down regional and local supplements (mini-contracts that cover certain workers and geographic areas) that prevented the implementation of the national contract for ten months.

Five years ago, the major flashpoint of the contract battle was health-care concessions. This time around, it's the controversial proposal to create a new category of "hybrid-drivers," who would make less than full-time package cars drivers and work weekends without overtime pay.

This proposal ironically came from the Teamsters themselves, who tried to sell it as a way of combating the burdensome overtime that falls on package car drivers across the country.

It was a devious ploy. UPS had dreamed for years of breaking up the high-paying package jobs, and getting the union to make the proposal instead of them was seen as a way of making a debilitating concession look like a gift. It didn't work, but it revealed that Hoffa and Taylor were willing to do the worst biddings of the company.

At the same time, a lot of opposition to the contract proposals both at UPS and UPS Freight came from a general anxiety at the continued decline of the union—and with it, the working conditions that have led to two mass shootings at UPS in the last three years.

Insult was added to injury in the final days of voting when Amazon CEO Jeff Bezos, the richest man in the world, announced that he would raise the minimum wage for new and current Amazon employees to $15 an hour. The current Teamsters-negotiated contract with UPS starts part-time employees at $13.

Confusion, however, set in after the rejection votes were announced when Denis Taylor—not the most articulate of men in the best times—muttered that the contracts were "ratified." As one of the many thousands who listened in and watched online, I thought to myself, "Did I hear that right?"

It wasn't a mistake—and it wasn't completely unexpected either. At a Teamsters-UPS national grievance panel meeting in San Diego several days before the vote count, Taylor threatened to impose the proposed contract even if a majority rejected it.

Hoffa and Taylor rely on the dubious interpretation of the Teamsters Constitution that grants the Teamsters general president the power to implement a contract if less than 50 percent of the members vote on a contract that then requires two-thirds "no" vote to reject. But this is only the case in a final offer, and, anyway, the general president can also return to negotiations if he wishes.

Hoffa and Taylor have chosen to deliberately ignore the wishes of UPS Teamsters and side with the company against their own members, despite significant portions of the UPS Teamsters who want to take the fight to the company. In June, 90 percent of UPS and UPS Freight Teamsters voted to authorize a strike, and now a majority of UPSers have voted down both Teamsters contracts. Hoffa and Taylor don't care.

Such treachery is not new to Hoffa. When he was a labor lawyer in the late 1980s and early 1990s, he was the attorney for Teamsters Local 283. Local 283 was led by an old corrupt official, George Vitale.

Vitale wanted to keep the local's members from seeing their contract and the financial records of the local union hidden from the members. Hoffa represented Vitale in federal court. The judge who presided over these cases lambasted Hoffa: "The people you represent work hard. They do physical labor for a livelihood. They are not lawyers, and most of them have no hope of ever becoming a lawyer. They hope, in fact, through their membership in a union such as this to be able to educate their children as your parents were able to, to spare them the back-breaking work they are undergoing. Their dues in this organization are paid to advance their lives, not to set off your ego."

Sounds familiar.

Right now, petitions are circulating to demand Hoffa honor the wishes of the membership. Members have made calls for an emergency meeting of the Teamsters General Executive Board to override Hoffa and Taylor. They have ignored these appeals so far.

Hoffa's sabotage at UPS is not only a catastrophe for UPS Teamsters—it is a gift to anti-union forces in the Janus era. If a boss wanted to make up a story to defeat a fledgling union drive—with indifferent union leaders who collect members' dues, negotiate a contract with a lower starting pay than non-union Amazon, and then flagrantly ignore those workers' clearly and democratically stated objections to that contract—they couldn't come up with one as good as what's just played out between UPS and the Teamsters.

James Hoffa is a gift that keeps on giving to the bosses. It's up to the rank-and-file UPS workers to decide what happens next.

ACKNOWLEDGMENTS

There are many people to thank for helping me complete this book. Alan Maass and Bhaskar Sunkara—editors of *Socialist Worker* and *Jacobin*, respectively—allowed me to take up a lot of space on their websites to explore the history of UPS and the modern logistics industry. Dan Campbell, Ken Paff, Rand Wilson, Dave Eckstein, and Anne Mackie contributed important parts of the history of UPS and the Teamsters, ranging from the UPSurge years to the Carey administration—episodes they personally witnessed and participated in. Former Teamsters 705 Secretary-Treasurer Jerry Zero, union representative Richard DeVries, and UPS driver Dave Healy helped fill in the gaps about the 1997 UPS strike in Chicago. Bill Roberts of Haymarket Books kindly edited the second draft of my manuscript and made important suggestions about the structure of the book. Eric Kerl did a fantastic book cover.

I couldn't have written *The Package King* without the help of many other writers and historians who wrote about UPS before me. Mary Deaton's *How to Beat the Big Brown Machine* (the first thing I ever read about UPS as a much younger man), Dan La Botz's *Rank-and-File Rebellion*, and Ken Crowe's *Collision: How the Rank and File Took Back the Teamsters* are important writings that still deserve to be read. They also serve as important documents in the struggles for democracy in the Teamsters and workplace justice at UPS. I hope *The Package King* is a modest contribution to what has been, and will undoubtedly continue to be, a tradition of books about the struggles at UPS. Though I have relied on many works for their help, guidance, and insights, I have not always drawn their conclusions.

NOTES

INTRODUCTION TO THE 2015 EDITION

1. Quoted in Kate Gutmann, "The Business of Ethics—and Why We Need a New Framework," speech, Loudonville, NY, March 6, 2015.
2. Justin Martin, "It's Murder in the Workplace," *Fortune*, August 9, 1993.
3. Over the past several years, I have explored the evolution of UPS in articles for *Socialist Worker* and *Jacobin*. Those ideas have formed the foundation of this book. See https://socialistworker.org/author/joe-allen and https://www.jacobinmag.com/author/joe-allen.
4. Carol Robinson, "UPS Shooting Victims Identified, Remembered as Kind Souls, Meticulous Workers," AL.com, September 24, 2014, updated March 7, 2019, www.al.com/news/birmingham/2014/09/ups_shooting_victims_identifie.html.
5. Robinson,"UPS Shooting Victims Identified."
6. "Pastor: UPS Gunman Was 'Troubled' over Work," *USA Today*, September 24, 2014.
7. Carol Robinson, "Funeral Set for 2 Men Gunned Down During Deadly UPS Shooting in Birmingham," AL.com, September 25, 2014, www.al.com/news/2014/09/funerals_set_for_2_men_gunned.html.
8. See, for instance, Joel Christie, "UPS Boss Who Fired Gunman Was Supposed to be On Vacation," *Daily Mail*, September 24, 2014.
9. Mark Ames, *Going Postal: Rage, Murder, and Rebellion: From Reagan's Workplaces to Clinton's Columbine and Beyond* (Brooklyn, NY: Soft Skull Press, 2005), 241.
10. Ames, *Going Postal*, 73.
11. P. Orris et al., "Stress among Package Truck Drivers," *American Journal of Industrial Medicine* 31, no. 2 (1997): 202–10.
12. Niemann, *Big Brown: The Untold Story of UPS* (San Francisco: Jossey-Bass, 2007).
13. UPS does provide a brief company history on its website; see "The History of UPS," UPS, www.ups.com/cy/en/about/history.page?.

14. Niemann, *Big Brown*, 163–64.

15. Klint Finley, "Christmas Delivery Fiasco Shows Why Amazon Wants Its Own UPS," *Wired*, December 30, 2013.

16. "'UPS Ruined My Christmas,'" *Daily Mail*, December 25, 2013.

17. "'UPS Ruined My Christmas,'" *Daily Mail*.

18. Laura Stevens, Suzanne Kapner, and Shelly Banjo, "UPS, FedEx Want Retailers to Get Real on Holiday Shipping," *Wall Street Journal*, October 2, 2014.

19. Robert Wright, "UPS to Hire up to 95,000 Temporary Workers," *Financial Times*, September 16, 2014.

20. "The World's Most Admired Companies," *Fortune*, http://fortune.com /worlds-most-admired-companies/ups/.

21. Danny Katch, "A Walkout at UPS and Labor's Old School Future," *Truthout*, April 24, 2014, www.truth-out.org/news/item/23271-a-wal kout-at-ups-and-labors-old-school-future#; Ginger Adams Otis, "UPS Re-Hires 250 Drivers Who Were Axed for Work Stoppage after Day-long Negotiations with Union," *New York Daily News*, April 10, 2014.

22. Donny Schraffenberger, "Stabbed in the Back by Hoffa," *Socialist Worker*, April 29, 2014, http://socialistworker.org/2014/04/29/stabbed-in-the -back-by-hoffa.

23. Grace Schneider, "Louisville Teamsters Chief Aims to Oust Hoffa," *Courier Journal*, February 4, 2016.

24. Upton Sinclair, *The Flivver King: A Story of Ford-America* (Pasadena, CA: Self-published/United Automobile Workers, 1937).

25. Niemann, *Big Brown*, 64.

26. Margot Roosevelt, "Why a Logistics Whiz Will Never Go Hungry," *Orange County Register*, August 6, 2014.

27. "UPS Fact Sheet," UPS, https://pressroom.ups.com/assets/pdf/pressroom /fact%20sheet/UPS_Fact_Sheet.pdf.

28. Alex Frankel, *Punching In: One Man's Undercover Adventures on the Front Lines of America's Best-Known Companies* (New York: Harper Collins, 2007), 44.

29. Claude Barfield, "High Noon for the Trans-Pacific Trade Pact," *Longitudes*, UPS, April 26, 2014, https://longitudes.ups.com/crunch-time-for -the-transpacific-trade-deal/.

30. Dan Campbell. Interview by Joe Allen. May 8, 2015.

31. Steven Rosenbush and Laura Stevens, "At UPS, the Algorithm Is the Driver," *Wall Street Journal*, February 16, 2015.

CHAPTER 1: THE PACKAGE KING

1. "UPS's Values, Mission, and Strategy," UPS Pressroom, https://pressroom
   .ups.com/pressroom/ContentDetailsViewer.page?ConceptType=FactSheets
   &id=1426321650156-161.
2. Philip Hamburger, "Ah, Packages," *New Yorker*, May 10, 1947.
3. David Remnick, "Postscript: Philip Hamburger," *New Yorker*, April 25,
   2004.
4. "Errand Boy," *New Yorker*, December 8, 1934, 18.
5. "Errand Boy," *New Yorker*, 18.
6. Hamburger, "Ah, Packages," *New Yorker*.
7. Hamburger, "Ah, Packages," *New Yorker*.
8. Hamburger, "Ah, Packages," *New Yorker*.
9. Hamburger, "Ah, Packages," *New Yorker*.
10. Harvey O'Connor, *Revolution in Seattle: A Memoir* (Chicago: Haymarket
    Books, 2009), 19.
11. O'Connor, *Revolution in Seattle*, 19.
12. Greg Niemann, *Big Brown: The Untold Story of UPS* (San Francisco:
    Jossey-Bass, 2007), 20.
13. Niemann, *Big Brown*, 20.
14. Niemann, *Big Brown*, 64.
15. Sharon Smith, *Subterranean Fire: A History of Working-Class Radicalism in
    the United States* (Chicago: Haymarket Books, 2006).
16. See Andrea Gabor, *The Capitalist Philosophers* (New York: Times Busi-
    ness, 2000).
17. See Niemann, 87 and 71.
18. Mike Brewster and Frederick Dalzell, *Driving Change: The UPS Approach
    to Business* (New York: Hyperion, 2007), 42.
19. Brewster and Dalzell, *Driving Change*, 42.
20. Brewster and Dalzell, *Driving Change*, 42.
21. John Balzar, "Ex-Teamsters Boss Dave Beck Is Dead at 99," *Los Angeles
    Times*, December 28, 1993.
22. Nard Jones, *Seattle* (New York: Doubleday & Company, 1972), 179.
23. Jones, *Seattle*, 179.
24. Donald Garnel, *The Rise of Teamster Power in the West* (Berkeley and Los
    Angeles: University of California Press, 1972), 65.
25. Quoted in Dan La Botz, *Rank-and-File Rebellion: Teamsters for a Demo-
    cratic Union* (London: Verso Books, 1991), 104.
26. La Botz, *Rank-and-File Rebellion*, 105.
27. Niemann, *Big Brown*, 64.
28. John D. McCallum, *Dave Beck* (Mercer Island, WA: The Writing Works,

Inc., 1978), 226.

29. McCallum, *Dave Beck,* 227.

30. Bryan Palmer, *Revolutionary Teamsters: The Minneapolis Truckers' Strikes of 1934* (Chicago: Haymarket Books, 2014).

31. Balzar, "Ex-Teamsters Boss Dave Beck Is Dead at 99," *Los Angeles Times.*

32. Ross Rieder, "Beck, Dave (1894–1993)," HistoryLink.org, www.historylink.org/index.cfm?DisplayPage=output.cfm&file_id=2972.

CHAPTER 2: UPRISING IN NEW YORK

1. "Stores Ask Writ In Parcel Strike," *New York Times,* October 3, 1946.

2. Susan Porter Benson, *Counter Cultures: Saleswomen, Managers, and Customers in American Department Stores, 1890–1940* (Urbana/Chicago: University of Illinois Press, 1986), 93.

3. Niemann, *Big Brown,* 23.

4. "Walkout of 1,800 in Parcel Service Ends; Deliveries From 350 Stores Resume Today," *New York Times,* November 13, 1939.

5. Niemann, *Big Brown,* 23.

6. Steven Brill, *The Teamsters* (New York: Pocket Books, 1978), 157.

7. "Walkout of 1,800," *New York Times.*

8. For more about this period, see chapter 5 of Brill's *The Teamsters.*

9. See Farrell Dobbs's *Teamster Rebellion, Teamster Power, Teamster Politics,* and *Teamster Bureaucracy,* a four-volume history published between 1972 and 1977 by Pathfinder Press. See also Bryan D. Palmer's *Revolutionary Teamsters: The Minneapolis Truckers' Strikes of 1934* (Chicago: Haymarket Books, 2013).

10. Niemann, *Big Brown,* 21.

11. "Walkout of 1,800 in Parcel Service Ends; Deliveries From 350 Stores Resume Today," *New York Times,* November 13, 1939.

12. "Parcel Service Case Up," *New York Times,* June 8, 1942.

13. "Strike Parley Halted," *New York Times,* June 14, 1942; "Delivery Strike Ended by Mayor," *New York Times,* June 25, 1942.

14. "WLB Seeks Accord in Delivery Strike," *New York Times,* May 18, 1945.

15. "Delivery Strikers Call Off Walkout," *New York Times,* May 19, 1945.

16. Smith, *Subterranean Fire,* 170–71.

17. Joshua B. Freeman, "Chapter One: *Working-Class New York: Life and Labor since World War II,"* New York Times archive nytimes.com/books /first/f/freeman-newyork.html.

18. Freeman, "Chapter One: *Working-Class New York.*"

19. Macy's held wide cultural significance for its annual Macy's Thanksgiving's

Day Parade and as the setting of such films as *Miracle on 34th Street*.

20. Daniel J. Opler, *For All White-Collar Workers: The Possibilities of Radicalism in New York City's Department Store Unions, 1934–1953* (Columbus: Ohio State University Press, 2007), 150.

21. Freeman, "Chapter One, *Working-Class New York.*"

22. "Drivers' Outlaw Walkout Affects 375 Large Stores," *New York Times*, September 14, 1946.

23. "Drivers' Outlaw," *New York Times*.

24. "14,000 Idle, 781 Shops Shut; More Delivery Crews Quit," *New York Times*, September 15, 1946.

25. "14,000 Idle," *New York Times*.

26. "14,000 Idle," *New York Times*.

27. "Stores Ask Writ in Parcel Strike," *New York Times*.

28. "Parcel Service Strike Ends As City Wins Compromise," *New York Times*, November 3, 1946.

29. "Parcel Service Vote Ends 12-Week Strike," *New York Times*, December 10, 1976.

30. Emanuel Perlmutter, "Teamsters Here Bar $1 Increase in Dues, Vent Anger on Beck," *New York Times*, April 1, 1957.

31. Emanuel Perlmutter, "Rivals of Hoffa Bar Compromise," *New York Times*, December 2, 1957.

32. Brill, *The Teamsters*; see chapter 5, "Ron Carey."

33. Stan Weir, "USA: The Labor Revolt," in *Singlejack Solidarity*, George Lipsitz, ed. (Minneapolis: University of Minnesota Press, 2004), 294.

34. See Dan Moldea, *The Hoffa Wars* (New York and London: Paddington Press, 1978).

35. Perlmutter, "Rivals of Hoffa Bar Compromise."

36. A. H. Raskin, "One Cost of Democracy: Parcel Strike Is Viewed in the Light of Strong Rank-And-File Voice in Local," *New York Times*, April 21, 1959.

37. Raskin, "One Cost of Democracy."

38. Raskin, "One Cost of Democracy."

39. Stanley Levey, "Drivers on Strike at United Parcel; Service Is Halted," *New York Times*, May 14, 1962.

40. Levey, "Drivers On Strike."

41. Levey, "Drivers On Strike."

42. Levey, "Drivers On Strike."

43. Ralph Katz, "Parcel Drivers Turn Down Pact; Younger Members Oppose Plan—Fear Extended Use of Part-Time Help," *New York Times*, June 21, 1962.

44. "Normal Operations in Parcel Delivery Expected Thursday," *New York*

Times, July 3, 1962.

45. For a history of Ron Carey's first reform campaign for the general presidency of the Teamsters, see Kenneth Crowe, *Collision: How the Rank and File Took Back the Teamsters* (New York: Charles Scribner's Sons, 1993).

46. Brill, *The Teamsters,* 156.

47. Brill, *The Teamsters,* 156.

48. Brill, *The Teamsters,* 156.

49. "United Parcel Ends Philadelphia Service over 3-Month Strike," *New York Times,* July 13, 1967.

50. Weir, "USA: The Labor Revolt," in *Singlejack Solidarity,* 294.

51. La Botz, *Rank-and-File Rebellion,* 62–64.

52. Faith C. Christmas, "Striking Workers Picket Parcel Co," *Chicago Tribune,* April 15, 1969; Robert Bruno, *Reforming the Chicago Teamsters: The Story of Local 705* (DeKalb: Northern Illinois University Press, 2003).

CHAPTER 3: THE RISE OF THE "QUIET GIANT"

1. "The Quiet Giant of Shipping," *Forbes,* January 15, 1970.

2. Christmas, "Striking Workers Picket"; Bruno, *Reforming the Chicago Teamsters.*

3. Brewster and Dalzell, *Driving Change,* 58–59.

4. Lizabeth Cohen, *A Consumers' Republic: The Politics of Mass Consumption in Postwar America* (New York: Alfred A. Knopf, 2003), 257.

5. Brewster and Dalzell, *Driving Change,* 59.

6. Niemann, *Big Brown,* 100.

7. Niemann, *Big Brown,* 103.

8. One of the few histories available of the Railway Express Agency is Klink Garrett and Toby Smith's *Ten Turtles to Tucumcari: A Personal History of the Railway Express Agency* (Albuquerque: University of New Mexico Press, 2003).

9. Brewster and Dalzell, *Driving Change,* 62.

10. Dan La Botz, "The Tumultuous Teamsters in the 1970s," in *Rebel Rank and File,* ed. Aaron Brenner, Robert Brenner, and Cal Winslow (London: Verso, 2010).

11. Christopher Lydon, "Abolition of I.C.C. Urged in Report by Nader Unit," *New York Times,* March 17, 1970.

12. Brewster and Dalzell, *Driving Change,* 62.

13. "United Parcel Service Observes 25th Year in Metropolitan Area," *New York Times,* July 14, 1955.

14. "The Interstate Highway System," June 7, 2019, History.com,

www.history.com/topics/us-states/interstate-highway-system.

15. Kelly Barron, "Logistics in Brown," *Forbes*, January 10, 2000.

16. "UPS Chicago Area Consolidation Hub (CACH)," Geography of Transport Systems, https://transportgeography.org/?page_id=4586.

17. "The Quiet Giant," *Forbes*.

18. "The Quiet Giant," *Forbes*.

19. "The Quiet Giant," *Forbes*.

20. Brill, *The Teamsters*, 167.

21. See Moldea, *The Hoffa Wars*.

22. Brill, *The Teamsters*, 167.

23. Brill, *The Teamsters*, 168.

24. "Teamster Walkout Stops Deliveries by United Parcel," *New York Times*, May 3, 1968.

25. Kim Moody, Mike Pflug, and Fred Eppsteiner, "Towards the Working Class: An SDS Convention Position Paper,"appendix in Kim Moody, *In Solidarity: Essays on Working-Class Organization and Strategy in the United States* (Chicago: Haymarket Books, 2014). The paper was submitted by the International Socialist Committee (Berkeley) for the 1966 SDS convention.

26. Lichtenstein is quoted in Cal Winslow's "Overview: The Rebellion from Below, 1965–81," in *Rebel Rank and File*, 6.

27. "United Parcel Strike Is Ended by Lifting of Ban on Flags Pins," *New York Times*, August 11, 1970.

28. Brill, *The Teamsters*, 180.

29. "United Parcel Strike Is Ended," *New York Times*.

30. "United Parcel Strike Is Ended," *New York Times*.

31. Brill, *The Teamsters*, 180–81.

32. Robert Putnam and Lewis Feldstein, *Better Together: Restoring the American Community* (New York: Simon and Schuster, 2003), 206.

33. Niemann, *Big Brown*, 120.

34. Niemann, *Big Brown*, 121.

35. Putnam and Feldstein, *Better Together*, 207.

36. Niemann, *Big Brown*, 123.

37. "Milestones: 1973," EEOC, www.eeoc.gov/eeoc/history/35th/milestones/1973.html.

38. Niemann, *Big Brown*, 124.

39. Robert Mcg. Thomas Jr., "Bernard G. Segal Dies at 89; Lawyer for Rich and Poor," *New York Times*, June 5, 1997.

40. *Evening Bulletin*, November 10, 1967.

41. Niemann, *Big Brown*, 124.

42. Margot Hornblower, "Backlash Hits 'Vigilante,'" *Washington Post*, March 2, 1985.

CHAPTER 4: UPSURGE AT THE TIGHTEST SHIP

1. La Botz, "The Tumultuous Teamsters in the 1970s," in *Rebel Rank and File.*
2. Anne Mackie, a presentation on the history of UPSurge before the Chicago district of the International Socialist Organization, March 22, 2014.
3. Mackie, presentation.
4. La Botz, *Rank-and-File Rebellion*, 62.
5. La Botz, *Rank-and-File Rebellion*, 63.
6. La Botz, *Rank-and-File Rebellion*, 63.
7. La Botz, *Rank-and-File Rebellion*, 63–64.
8. La Botz, *Rank-and-File Rebellion*, 64.
9. Mackie, presentation.
10. La Botz, *Rank-and-File Rebellion*, 63.
11. "Hal Draper: 1914–1990," Marxists Internet Archive, www.marxists.org /archive/draper/.
12. Kim Moody, "Understanding the Rank and File Rebellion in the Long 1970s," in *Rebel Rank and File*, 105–45.
13. Mackie, presentation.
14. Mackie, presentation.
15. Winslow, "Overview," in *Rebel Rank and File*, 25.
16. Mackie, presentation.
17. Winslow, "Overview," in *Rebel Rank and File*, 25.
18. *UPSurge* newspaper, September 1975.
19. Mackie, presentation.
20. Lee Sustar, "UPSurge: Rank and File Led the Way," *Socialist Worker* special supplement, June–July 1997.
21. Sustar, "UPSurge," *Socialist Worker.*
22. Sustar, "UPSurge," *Socialist Worker.*
23. Mackie, presentation.
24. Winslow, "Overview: The Rebellion from Below," 26. The location of the meeting was actually the Marriott Hotel, according to Anne Mackie.
25. All quotations in this paragraph are drawn from "Indy '500' Says Shove It UPS," *UPSurge,* February 1976.
26. "Indy '500' Says Shove it UPS," *UPSurge.*
27. "Our Big Idea," *UPSurge*, September 1975.
28. Mackie, presentation.
29. Mackie, presentation.
30. Kenneth Labich, "Big Changes at Big Brown," *Fortune*, January 18, 1988.
31. "UPS the Tightest Ship in the Shipping Business 1985," YouTube video, 0:30, posted by Kevin Noonan, February 19, 2014, www.youtube.com /watch?v=f-qtenyZu0k.

32. Kim Moody, *An Injury to All: The Decline of American Unionism* (London: Verso Books, 1988).

33. Niemann, *Big Brown*, 115.

34. Niemann, *Big Brown*, 115.

35. La Botz, *Rank-and-File Rebellion*, 212.

36. "UPS Secret Document Plots Speedup, Mass Firings," *Workers' Power*, July 26, 1976.

37. Mary Deaton, *How to Beat the Big Brown Machine* (Cleveland: Hera Press, 1979), 9.

38. Deaton, *How to Beat*, 9.

39. "The 'Casual' Issue at UPS," *Newsweek*, November 1, 1976.

40. "The 'Casual' Issue," *Newsweek*.

41. "The 'Casual' Issue," *Newsweek*.

42. Deaton, *How to Beat*, 9.

43. Deaton, *How to Beat*, 9.

44. La Botz, *Rank-and-File Rebellion*, 207.

45. La Botz, *Rank-and-File Rebellion*, 207.

46. Quoted in Kyle Smith, "How Democrats Abandoned the Working Class and Spurred Rise of Donald Trump," *New York Post*, March 12, 2016.

47. Dorothy Robyn, *Braking the Special Interests: Trucking Deregulation and the Politics of Policy Reform* (Chicago: University of Chicago Press, 1987), 78.

48. Michael H. Belzer, *Sweatshops on Wheels: Winner and Losers in Trucking Deregulation* (New York: Oxford University Press, 2000).

49. Arthur A. Sloane, *Hoffa* (Cambridge, MA: MIT Press, 1991), 193.

50. Sloane, *Hoffa*, 193.

51. Ruth Marcus and Ben White, "UPS PAC Fined $9,000," *Washington Post*, December 28, 1997.

52. La Botz, *Rank-and-File Rebellion*, 211.

53. Labich, "Big Changes at Big Brown," *Fortune*.

54. La Botz, *Rank-and-File Rebellion*, 209.

55. Labich, "Big Changes at Big Brown," *Fortune*.

56. Labich, "Big Changes at Big Brown," *Fortune*.

57. Christopher Drew, "In the Productivity Push, How Much Is Too Much?" *New York Times*, December 17, 1995.

58. Drew, "In the Productivity Push," *New York Times*.

59. Drew, "In the Productivity Push," *New York Times*.

60. P. Orris et al., "Stress among Package Truck Drivers," *American Journal of Industrial Medicine*, 202–10.

61. La Botz, *Rank-and-File Rebellion*, 211.

62. La Botz, *Rank-and-File Rebellion*, 211.

63. La Botz, *Rank-and-File Rebellion*, 211.

64. Niemann, *Big Brown*, 10.
65. Don Cohen and Laurence Prusak, *In Good Company: How Social Capital Makes Organizations Work* (Boston: Harvard Business School Press, 2001), 2.
66. Cohen and Prusak, *In Good Company*, 122.

CHAPTER 5: AIR WAR: TAKING ON FEDEX

1. Niemann, *Big Brown*, 139.
2. John D. Kasarda and Greg Lindsay, *Aerotropolis: The Way We'll Live Next* (New York: Farrar, Strauss & Giroux, 2012), 62.
3. Brewster and Dalzell, *Driving Change*, 77.
4. Brewster and Dalzell, *Driving Change*, 77.
5. Larry Reibstein, "Federal Express Faces Challenges to Its Grip on Overnight Delivery," *Wall Street Journal*, January 8, 1988.
6. Niemann, *Big Brown*, 150–51.
7. Brewster and Dalzell, *Driving Change*, 76.
8. Niemann, *Big Brown*, 151.
9. Niemann, *Big Brown*, 151.
10. Niemann, *Big Brown*, 152.
11. Reibstein, "Federal Express Faces Challenges," *Wall Street Journal*.
12. Niemann, *Big Brown*, 139.
13. Niemann, *Big Brown*, 154.
14. Leonard Sloane, "Chief Executive Named at United Parcel Service," *New York Times*, June 3, 1980.
15. Greg Winter, "George C. Lamb Jr., 75, Ex-Chief of United Parcel," *New York Times*, April 7, 2001.
16. Kasarda and Lindsay, *Aerotropolis*, 61.
17. Dave Healy, interview by Joe Allen, Chicago, April 4, 2015.
18. "1981–1990, UPS Airlines," UPS, www.ups.com/bm/en/about/history/1981-1990.page.
19. Niemann, *Big Brown*, 154.
20. Teamsters for a Democratic Union, "UPS Contract Bulletin #4," June 27, 1990.
21. Merrill Goozner, "Teamsters Postpone UPS Strike," *Chicago Tribune*, July 27, 1990.
22. Teamsters for a Democratic Union, "UPS Contract Bulletin #4," June 27, 1990.
23. Michael Schiavone, "Rank-and-File Militancy and Power: Revisiting the Teamster Struggle with United Parcel Service Ten Years Later," *WorkingUSA* 10 (June 2007).

24. Nick Ravo, "Labor Pact Is Ratified at U.P.S.," *New York Times*, August 14, 1990.
25. Ravo, "Labor Pact."
26. Goozner, "Teamsters Postpone UPS Strike."
27. Nick Ravo, "Unusual Labor Tensions at U.P.S.," *New York Times*, July 28, 1990.
28. Federal Express changed its name to FedEx in 2000.
29. La Botz, *Rank-and-File Rebellion*, 212.
30. Labich, "Big Changes."
31. Labich, "Big Changes."
32. Labich, "Big Changes."
33. Labich, "Big Changes."

CHAPTER 6: DEMOCRACY COMES TO THE TEAMSTERS

1. La Botz, *Rank-and-File Rebellion*, 291.
2. "Old guard" became the pejorative term for the reactionary, mob-connected officers of the union.
3. La Botz, *Rank-and-File Rebellion*, 195–207.
4. Kenneth Crowe, *Collision: How the Rank and File Took Back the Teamsters* (New York: Charles Scribner's Sons, 1993), 37.
5. Gerald R. Boyd, "Teamsters Vote to Endorse Reagan," *New York Times*, August 31, 1984.
6. La Botz, *Rank-and-File Rebellion*, 285. For an examination of Jackie Presser's life as an FBI informer, see James Neff, *Mobbed Up* (New York: Atlantic Monthly Press, 1989).
7. A. H. Raskin, "A Health-Care Union Returns to Good Health," *New York Times*, May 19, 1986.
8. Raskin, "A Health-Care Union."
9. Raskin, "A Health-Care Union."
10. La Botz, *Rank-and-File Rebellion*, 286.
11. La Botz, *Rank-and-File Rebellion*, 286.
12. For a complete account of the 1986 Teamster convention, see Crowe, *Collision*, 37–45.
13. Leslie Maitland Werner, "U.S. Seeks Control of Teamster Union," *New York Times*, July 11, 1987.
14. La Botz, *Rank-and-File Rebellion*, 288.
15. La Botz, *Rank-and-File Rebellion*, 293.
16. These changes in the Teamster election process demanded by the consent decree were later enshrined in the Teamster constitution.

17. For a profile of Kilmury, see La Botz, *Rank-and-File Rebellion*, 221–26.
18. For a profile of Eddie Burke, see Crowe, *Collision*, 1–12.
19. TDU staff, "How a Grassroots Movement Made History: An Analysis of the 1991 IBT Election," 1992.
20. Peter T. Kilborn, "Teamsters' New Chief Vows to Put Members First, *New York Times*, December 13, 1991.
21. Niemann, *Big Brown*, 64.
22. "Reform Slate Takes Teamsters Union Office," *Los Angeles Times*, February 2, 1992.
23. Quoted in Crowe, *Collision*, 262.
24. Peter T. Kilborn, "Reformer Takes Oath as Teamster Chief," *New York Times*, February 2, 1992.

CHAPTER 7: A WAR ON EVERY FRONT

1. Jesus Sanchez, "Short-Lived Strike against UPS Has Little Impact on Deliveries," *Los Angeles Times*, February 8, 1994.
2. United States, National Labor Relations Board, *Decisions and Orders of the National Labor Relations Board*, vol. 318, 781, www.nlrb.gov/cases-decisions/decisions/board-decisions?volume=318&slipnumber_i=&page_number; "Teamsters Reach UPS Pact," *New York Times*, September 28, 1993.
3. Sheila Cohen and Kim Moody, "Unions, Strikes, and Class Consciousness Today" chapter 2 in Moody, *In Solidarity*, 34.
4. "People Before Packages," *The New Teamster*, April–May, 1993, 12–15.
5. "People Before Packages," *The New Teamster*, 12–15.
6. Crowe, *Collision*, 180.
7. "3,000 Workers Strike United Parcel; Union Tells Them to Return," *New York Times*, January 6, 1980.
8. "Court Order Defied by U.P.S. Strikers," *New York Times*, September 15, 1982.
9. Maira Perrucci, interview by Joe Allen, April 16, 2015.
10. Dan Campbell, interview by Joe Allen, April 13, 2015.
11. Maria Perrucci, interview by Joe Allen, April 16, 2015.
12. Maria Perrucci, interview by Joe Allen, April 16, 2015.
13. Dan Campbell, interview by Joe Allen, April 13, 2015.
14. Dan Campbell, interview by Joe Allen, April 13, 2015.
15. Quoted in Schiavione, "Rank-and-File Militancy and Power."
16. Laurie M. Grossman, "UPS's Talks with Teamsters Heat Up as Company Moves to Stave Off Strikes," *Wall Street Journal*, June 15, 1993.

17. "UPS Workers to Be Polled by Teamsters on a Strike," *Wall Street Journal*, August 26, 1993.
18. Aaron Bernstein, "In the Line of Fire at the Teamsters," *Bloomberg*, August 30, 1993, www.bloomberg.com/news/articles/1993-08-29/in-the-line-of-fire-at-the-teamsters.
19. Bernstein, "In the Line of Fire."
20. "UPS, Teamsters Agree to Extend Their Talks; Union Lines Up Funds, *Wall Street Journal*, August 3, 1993.
21. "Teamsters at UPS Authorize Walkout If Negotiations Fail," *Wall Street Journal*, September 7, 1993.
22. Dan La Botz, "The Fight at UPS: The Teamsters Victory and the Future of the 'New Labor Movement,'" December 10, 2019, Solidarity, http://solidarity-us.org/ups.
23. National Master United Parcel Service Agreement, August 1, 1993 to July 31, 1997, 45.
24. Schiavione, "Rank-and-File Militancy and Power."
25. Dan Campbell, interview by Joe Allen, April 21, 2015.
26. Frank Stanfield, "UPS Drivers Join Strike in Protest against Heavier Loads," *Orlando Sentinel*, February 8, 1994; Jesus Sanchez, "Short-Lived Strike," *Los Angeles Times*.
27. "Strike Victory Turns to Struggle on Job," *Convoy Dispatch*, March 1994.
28. "Package-Handling Dispute Settled at UPS; Teamsters Win Concession on Parcel Weight," *Chicago Tribune*, February 8, 1994.
29. Bob Hasegawa, interview by Joe Allen, May 21, 2015.
30. La Botz, "The Fight at UPS."
31. Jesus Sanchez, "Short-Lived Strike," *Los Angeles Times*.
32. "Suit Tossed," *Chicago Tribune*, July 2, 1994; "Federal Court Dismisses $50 Million UPS Lawsuit," *Convoy Dispatch*, August 1994.
33. "Package-Handling Dispute Settled," *Chicago Tribune*.
34. "Federal Court Dismisses," *Convoy Dispatch*.
35. Ken Patt, interview by Joe Allen, April 8, 2015.
36. "Strike Victory Turns," *Convoy Dispatch*.
37. National Labor Relations Board, *Decisions and Orders of the National Labor Relations Board*, 2007.
38. United States, National Labor Relations Board, https://www.nlrb.gov/rights-we-protect/whats-law/employers/interfering-or-dominating-union-section-8a2
39. Cohen and Moody, "Unions, Strikes, and Class Consciousness Today," in *In Solidarity*, 35.
40. Matt Witt and Rand Wilson, "Part-Time America Won't Work: The Teamsters' Fight for Good Jobs at UPS," in *Not Your Father's Union*

Movement: Inside the AFL-CIO, ed. Jo-Ann Mort (New York: Verso Books, 1998), 182.

41. Witt and Wilson, "Part-Time America," in *Not Your Father's Union*, 182.

CHAPTER 8: THE CAMPAIGN TO DESTROY OSHA

1. Quoted in Michael Weisskopf and David Maraniss, "The Hill May Be a Health Hazard for Safety Agency," *Washington Post*, July 23, 1995.
2. "Lobbyists at Home in Another House," *USA Today*, May 7, 1996.
3. Aaron Freeman, "Congress: The Chief Worker-Safety Threat," *Multinational Monitor* 16, no. 10 (October 1995).
4. Drew, "In the Productivity Push."
5. John Greenwald, "Hauling UPS's Freight," *Time*, January 29, 1996.
6. Arthur Brice and Rodney Ho, "Delivering the Bucks: United Parcel Service Hikes Political Contributions in What Some See as an Attempt to Buy Influence in Its Battle to Curb Health and Safety Regulations," *Atlanta Journal-Constitution*, February 17, 1996.
7. Carey Gillam, "UPS Piles Up Safety Complaints," *Atlanta Business Chronicle*, August 4–10, 1995.
8. Gillam, "UPS Piles Up Safety Complaints."
9. Gillam, "UPS Piles Up Safety Complaints."
10. Michael Weisskopf and David Maraniss, *Tell Newt to Shut Up* (New York: Simon & Schuster, 1996), 62.
11. "Background on Ergonomic Problems at UPS," Teamsters Communications Department, January 31, 1997.
12. Freeman, "Congress: The Chief Worker-Safety Threat."
13. Quoted in Freeman, "Congress: The Chief Worker-Safety Threat."
14. Weisskopf and Maraniss, *Tell Newt to Shut Up*, 63.
15. Weisskopf and Maraniss, *Tell Newt to Shut Up*, 62.
16. Clifford Krauss, "House Passes Bill to Ban Replacement of Strikers," *New York Times*, June 6, 1993; Lance Selfa, *The Democrats: A Critical History* (Chicago: Haymarket Books, 2008).
17. Greenwald, "Hauling UPS's Freight."
18. Greenwald, "Hauling UPS's Freight."
19. Greenwald, "Hauling UPS's Freight."
20. Quoted in Weisskopf and Maraniss, "The Hill May Be."
21. Peter T. Kilborn, "Saving Money or Saving Lives," *New York Times*, September 19, 1995.
22. "Food Plant Fire Kills 25; Exits Blocked," *Los Angeles Times*, September 4, 1991.

23. Greg Lacour and Emma Way, "Requiem for a Cage Rattler," *Charlotte Magazine*, February 19, 2015.

24. Weisskopf and Maraniss, "The Hill May Be a Health Hazard."

25. "Cass Ballenger," OpenSecrets.org, www.opensecrets.org/members-of-congress//summary?cid=N00002377.

26. Quoted in Freeman, "Congress: The Chief Worker-Safety Threat," *Multinational Monitor.*

27. Weisskopf and Maraniss, *Tell Newt To Shut Up*, 60.

28. Freeman, "Congress: The Chief Worker-Safety Threat."

29. Weisskopf and Maraniss, *Tell Newt To Shut Up*, 64.

30. Freeman, "Congress: The Chief Worker-Safety Threat."

31. Greenwald, "Hauling UPS's Freight."

32. Drew, "In the Productivity Push."

33. Selfa, *The Democrats*, 80.

34. Selfa, *The Democrats*, 80.

35. Lou Dubose and Jan Reid, *The Hammer: Tom DeLay, God, Money, and the Rise of the Republican Congress* (New York: Public Affairs, 2004), 113.

36. Dubose and Reid, *The Hammer*, 115.

CHAPTER 9: LAST, BEST, AND FINAL OFFER?

1. Quoted in George Saavedra, "'Little Nobodies' Ready to Take On UPS for a Good Contract," *Convoy Dispatch*, July–August, 1997.

2. "Cleaning Up the Teamsters Union: A Three-Year Progress Report," International Brotherhood of Teamsters, Washington, DC, February 1995.

3. "Employers Long for Past, Fear the Future," *Convoy Dispatch*, December 1996.

4. Steven Greenhouse, "Once Again, the Hoffa Name Rouses the Teamsters' Union," *New York Times*, November 17, 1996.

5. Chris Bohner, "Jimmy Hoffa Junior: A Study of His Connections to Corrupt Elements in the Labor Movement," Labor-Community Research Consulting, commissioned on behalf of the Ron Carey Reform Campaign, Summer 1996.

6. See William Serrin's "Hacks and Hatchet Jobs," *In These Times*, February 19, 1996, for information on the media smear campaign against Carey.

7. Glenn Burkins, "Teamster Watchers Ponder a Hoffa Win," *Wall Street Journal*, December 9, 1996.

8. "Battling the Old Guard: UPS Vote Is Crucial Test for Reform-Minded Union Leader," *Atlanta Journal-Constitution*, October 16, 1993.

9. See Robert Bruno, *Reforming the Chicago Teamsters: The Story of Local 705*

(DeKalb: Northeastern Illinois University Press, 2003).

10. Steven Greenhouse, "Yearlong Effort Key to Success for Teamsters," *New York Times*, August 25, 1997.

11. "Wilson, Rand," Our Campaigns, www.ourcampaigns.com /CandidateDetail.html?CandidateID=129664.

12. Rand Wilson, interview by Joe Allen, April 29, 2015.

13. Greenhouse, "Yearlong Effort," *New York Times*.

14. Witt and Wilson, "Part-Time America," in *Not Your Father's Union*, 182.

15. Rand Wilson, interview by Joe Allen, May 5, 2015.

16. Greenhouse, "Yearlong Effort," *New York Times*.

17. International Brotherhood of Teamsters Research Department, "Half a Job Is Not Enough" (Washington, DC, June 1997), 3.

18. International Brotherhood of Teamsters, "Half a Job Is Not Enough," 3.

19. "Teamsters Suspend Useless Talk," *Convoy Dispatch*, June–July 1997, 6.

20. Deepa Kumar, *Outside the Box: Corporate Media, Globalization, and the UPS Strike* (Urbana/Chicago: University of Illinois Press, 2007), 135.

21. Witt and Wilson, "Part-Time America," in *Not Your Father's Union*, 182.

22. David Eckstein, interview by Joe Allen, May 5, 2015.

23. David Eckstein, interview by Joe Allen, May 5, 2015.

24. David Eckstein, interview by Joe Allen, May 5, 2015.

25. David Eckstein, interview by Joe Allen, May 5, 2015.

26. These flyers and brochures are in the possession of the author.

27. Steven Greenhouse, "Teamsters Chief, Despite Victory, Is Remaining Defiant," *New York Times*, December 16, 1996.

28. "Teamster Ballot Certified, January 11, 1997"; "Report from the Election Officer," *Teamster*, July 1997.

29. Quoted in Charlotte Ryan, "It Takes a Movement to Raise an Issue: Media Lessons from the 1997 U.P.S. Strike," in *Culture, Power, and History: Studies in Critical Sociology*, ed. Patricia Arend et al. (Boston: Brill, 2006), 436.

30. Ken Paff, interview by Joe Allen, April 1, 2015; "Ken Hall—Proven Track Record of Union Leadership," *Convoy Dispatch*, April 1998, 6.

31. Witt and Wilson, "Part-Time America," in *Not Your Father's Union*, 183.

32. Witt and Wilson, "Part-Time America," in *Not Your Father's Union*, 183.

33. Dave Dethrow, "What It Was Like to Bargain with UPS: A Rank and Filer's Report," *Convoy Dispatch*, October 1997, 5.

34. Dan Campbell, interview by Joe Allen, April 28, 2015.

35. "Collusion Fails—Teamsters United," *Convoy Dispatch*, June–July 1997.

36. "Collusion Fails," *Convoy Dispatch*.

37. "Carey to Locals: Get in the Act," *Convoy Dispatch*, July–August 1997, 6.

38. Tim Buban, interview by Joe Allen, May 3, 2015.

39. Tim Buban, interview by Joe Allen, May 3, 2015.

40. Nicholas Johnson's letter, *The New Teamster*, April–May 1994, 2–33; Sarah Nordgren, "Teamsters Suspend Four Officials; Officials Deny Wrongdoing," Associated Press, April 17, 1996.

41. Tim Buban, interview by Joe Allen. May 3, 2015.

42. Tim Buban, interview by Joe Allen. May 3, 2015.

43. Kumar, *Outside the Box*, 136–37.

44. "Teamsters Suspend Useless Talk," *Convoy Dispatch*, 6.

45. "Teamsters Suspend Useless Talk," *Convoy Dispatch*.

46. "UPS's Early Missteps in Assessing Teamsters Help Explain How Union Won Gains in Fight," *Wall Street Journal*, August 21, 1997.

47. John Russo and Andy Banks, "How Teamsters Took the UPS Strike Overseas," *WorkingUSA* 2 (January–February 1999): 78.

48. David Eckstein, interview by Joe Allen, May 5, 2015.

49. Chris Hudson, interview by Joe Allen, September 5, 2015.

50. Dethrow, "What It Was Like," 5.

51. Dan Campbell, interview by Joe Allen, May 8, 2015.

52. Dan Campbell, interview by Joe Allen, May 8, 2015.

53. Witt and Wilson, "Part-Time America," in *Not Your Father's Union*, 184.

54. Murray's letter to Ron Carey and the tape "From the Horse's Mouth" are in the possession of the author.

55. See "America's Victory: The 1997 UPS Strike," YouTube video, 9.31, July 27, 2007, www.youtube.com/watch?v=NbYqoGM0GX8.

56. Quoted in Saavedra, "'Little Nobodies,'" *Convoy Dispatch*.

57. Dethrow, "What It Was Like," 5.

58. Author's notes on the 1997 strike.

59. Steven Greenhouse, "U.P.S. Struck by Teamsters as Talks Fail," *New York Times*, August 4, 1997.

60. David Eckstein, interview by Joe Allen, May 5, 2015.

CHAPTER 10: PART-TIME AMERICA WON'T WORK

1. Kumar, *Outside the Box*, 76.

2. Greenhouse, "U.P.S. Struck by Teamsters."

3. "UPS's Early Missteps," *Wall Street Journal*.

4. Smith, *Subterranean Fire*, 280.

5. Kumar, *Outside the Box*, 87.

6. David Stout, "Shippers Scramble as Strike Hits U.P.S," *New York Times*, August 5, 1997.

7. Stout, "Shippers Scramble."

8. Louis Uchitelle, "Strike Points to Inequality in 2-Tier Job Market," *New York Times,* August 8, 1997.

9. "Study: Strike Has Big Impact," Scripps Howard News Service, *Gainesville Sun*, August 6, 1997.

10. Shaun Harkin, "When Big Brown Was Shut Down," *Socialist Worker*, August 3, 2007.

11. Quoted in Kumar, *Outside the Box,* 141.

12. Author's notes on the UPS strike.

13. "Angry Voices of Pickets Reflect Sense of Concern," *New York Times*, August 6, 1997.

14. "Angry Voices," *New York Times.*

15. Steven Greenhouse, "No Bargaining in Strike, and Very Few Deliveries," *New York Times*, August 6, 1997.

16. *The NewsHour with Jim Lehrer*, August 4, 1997, transcript, American Archive of Public Broadcasting, https://americanarchive.org/catalog/cpb-aacip_507-7s7hq3sk03.

17. Kumar, *Outside the Box,* 148.

18. For a complete account of the media coverage of the strike, see Kumar, *Outside the Box.*

19. Bob Herbert, "Workers' Rebellion," *New York Times*, August 7, 1997.

20. Herbert, "Workers' Rebellion."

21. Dennis Byrne, "Little Guy Still Waiting for His Due," *Sun-Times*, August 5, 1997.

22. David Eckstein, interview by Joe Allen, May 5, 2015.

23. When I was a part-time air and package car driver in Chicago, I participated in many pre-work communication meetings that hammered home this point time and time again.

24. Kumar, *Outside the Box,* 76.

25. Bruno, *Reforming the Chicago Teamsters*, 64–65.

26. Author's notes on the UPS strike.

27. Chuck McWhinnie and Jim Casey, "Strikers Block UPS Deliveries," *Chicago Sun-Times,* August 14, 1997, 1–2.

28. Author's notes on the UPS strike.

29. Kumar, *Outside the Box*, 125.

30. Quoted in Smith, *Subterranean Fire*, 280.

31. Carey and Sweeney quotes from the Chicago rally are drawn from "Chicago UPS–Teamster Strike '97," *Labor Beat*, produced by William Jenkins, 1997.

32. Leon Pitt, "UPS Hurt More Than It Says," *Chicago Sun-Times*, August 1997.

33. Ken Paff, interview by Joe Allen, May 12, 2015.

34. David Eckstein, interview by Joe Allen, May 12, 2015.

35. Dan Campbell, interview by Joe Allen, May 12, 2015.

36. This according to Jodi Budenaers, UPS pilot/IPA member, Support UPS Workers Solidarity Rally, Chicago, August 9, 1997.

37. Jack Spiegel and Vicki Starr ("Stella Nowicki"), both CIO veterans, were present; also in attendance were '70s Teamster rebel Pete Camarata, Staley "Road Warrior" Dan Lane, and UPS pilot Jodi Budenaers.

38. According to veteran Chicago UPS worker Dave Healy, Bennie Jackson is probably referring to a letter attached to their paychecks four days into the strike. The letter contained "the last, best, and final offer" and urged the local union to vote on it; Dave Healy, interview by Joe Allen, May 13, 2015.

39. Bennie Jackson, Support UPS Workers Solidarity Rally, Chicago, August 9, 1997. An audiotape of the event is in the possession of the author.

40. Greenhouse, "U.P.S. Struck by Teamsters."

41. Greenhouse, "U.P.S. Struck by Teamsters."

42. Greenhouse, "U.P.S. Struck by Teamsters."

43. *The NewsHour with Jim Lehrer*, August 4, 1997, transcript, American Archive of Public Broadcasting.

44. Steven Greenhouse, "High Stakes for 2 Titans," *New York Times*, August 5, 1997.

45. Kumar, *Outside the Box*, 98; see page 99 for the Teamsters' press release on Sonnenfeld.

46. "Teamsters, UPS Hold Firm as Strike Begins," CNN.com, August 4, 1997, http://edition.cnn.com/US/9708/04/ups.update/index.html.

47. Steven Greenhouse, "U.P.S. Urges Vote on Deal; Union Chief Sees a Ploy," *New York Times*, August 11, 1997.

48. Pitt, "UPS Hurt More."

49. Greenhouse, "U.P.S. Urges Vote."

50. "Ron Carey's Weird Strike," *Wall Street Journal*, August 14, 1997.

51. Glenn Burkins and Glenn R. Simpson, "Teamsters Chief Takes Big Risk, While He's Already Under Fire," *Wall Street Journal*, August 5, 1997.

52. Francine Knowles, "Strikers Feeling Big Strain on Wallets and Marriages," *Chicago Sun-Times*, August, 1997.

53. "Chicago Locals Still on Strike against UPS," *Chicago Tribune*, August 19, 1997.

54. Tim Buban, inteview by Joe Allen, May 10, 2015.

55. Tim Buban, inteview by Joe Allen, May 10, 2015.

56. Tim Buban, inteview by Joe Allen, May 10, 2015.

57. Russo and Banks, "How Teamsters Took the UPS Strike Overseas," *WorkingUSA*, 83.

58. Joan Campbell, ed., *European Labor Unions* (Westport, CT: Greenwood

Press, 1992), 181.

59. Russo and Banks, "How Teamsters Took the UPS Strike Overseas," 84.

60. Russo and Banks, "How Teamsters Took the UPS Strike Overseas," 85.

61. The strike continued for a few more days in Chicago to resolve specific issues that applied to the Teamsters 705 contract.

62. "Teamster Unity Wins UPS Victory," *The Teamster*, October 1997, 2–3.

63. Steven Greenhouse, "Teamsters and U.P.S. Agree on a 5-Year Contract Plan to End Strike After 15 Days," *New York Times*, August 19, 1997.

64. "The Return of the Two-Sided Class Struggle," *International Socialist Review*, Fall 1997.

CHAPTER 11: THE "GET CAREY" CAMPAIGN

1. United States, Congress, Opening Statement of Congressman Pete Hoekstra, Chairman, Subcommittee and Investigations, House Education and the Workforce Committee, March 28, 2000, "The International Brotherhood of Teamsters, One Year After the Election of James P. Hoffa," 4.

2. Ken Crowe, "The Vindication of Ron Carey," *Union Democracy Review*, December 2001–January 2002; Carey also recounts this story in Kumar, *Outside the Box*.

3. "A New Vote for the Teamsters," *New York Times*, August 23, 1997.

4. Steve Early, "What Went Wrong?" *In These Times*, December 14, 1997, https://inthesetimes.com/article/4602/what_went_wrong.

5. Early, "What Went Wrong?" *In These Times*.

6. Steven Greenhouse, "Teamsters' Head Returns More Disputed Campaign Donations," *New York Times*, March 21, 1997.

7. Early, "What Went Wrong?" *In These Times*.

8. Alexander Cockburn, "The Teamsters and the Journal," *The Nation*, August 11–17, 1997.

9. Early, "What Went Wrong?" *In These Times*.

10. James Gerstenzang, "Hoffa Calls for Carey to Quit Teamster Post," *Los Angeles Times*, August 25, 1997.

11. "Federal Judge Appoints a New Overseer for Teamsters' Election," Associated Press, September 30, 1997.

12. The exchange between Quindel and UPS is recounted in Frank Swoboda, "UPS Accuses Federal Officer of Favoring Union," *Washington Post*, September 4, 1997.

13. Independent Review Board, "Report of Investigation of General President Ronald Carey," July 11, 1994; report is in possession of the author.

14. This number was reached by my calculation. See Independent Review Board, "Report of Investigation of General President Ronald Carey."

15. "Federal Official Reconsiders Letting Teamsters Chief Run," *Boston Globe*, September 12, 1997.

16. Kenneth C. Crowe, "New Info Resurrects Carey Probe," *Newsday*, September 12, 1997.

17. "Federal Official Reconsiders," *Boston Globe*; Steven Greenhouse, "Doubt on Carey Spot on Teamster Ballot," *New York Times*, September 12, 1997.

18. "Federal Official Reconsiders," *Boston Globe*; Greenhouse, "Doubt on Carey Spot."

19. Greenhouse, "Doubt on Carey Spot," *New York Times*. For political history of Lyndon LaRouche and Richard Leebove's role in supporting the Teamster old guard, see Dennis King, *Lyndon LaRouche and the New American Fascism* (New York: Doubleday, 1989).

20. Steven Greenhouse, "3 Teamster Aides Make Guilty Pleas and Hint at Plot," *New York Times*, September 19, 1997.

21. "The Ron Carey Campaign Investigations," www.angelfire.com/ga /careywatch/bzqquits.html.

22. Early, "What Went Wrong?"; Stephen Labaton, "Teamsters Election Monitor Is Reported Planning to Quit," *New York Times*, August 30, 1997.

23. House Committee on Education and the Workforce, Subcommittee on Oversight and Investigations, "Report on the Financial, Operating and Political Affairs of the International Brotherhood of Teamsters," 1999. https://librarycatalog.dol.gov/client/en_US/msha/search/de-tailnonmodal/ent:$002f$002fSD_ILS$002f0$002fSD_ILS:27138/ one?qu=United+States.+Congress.+House.+Committee+on+Educa-tion+and+the+Workforce.+Subcommittee+on+Oversight+and+Investiga-tions.&qf=PUBDATE%09Publication+Date%092016%092016&ic=true.

24. Steven Greenhouse, "Teamsters' Chief Lobbyist Quits, Calling U.S. Inquiry a 'Circus,'" *New York Times*, July 31, 1997.

25. Early, "What Went Wrong?"

26. Greenhouse, "Teamsters' Chief Lobbyist Quits."

27. Mark Maremont, "Hoffa Operative Used 'Moles," False Identity in Teamsters Probe," *Wall Street Journal*, December 23, 1997.

28. Maremont, "Hoffa Operative Used 'Moles.'"

29. Steven Greenhouse, "Teamsters Union Members Cite Pressure for Donations," *New York Times*, October 15, 1997.

30. "The Second-Term Representative Will Head the House Subcommittee on Oversight and Investigations," *Grand Rapids Press*, December 13, 1994.

31. Leedham campaign leaflet, 1998; in possession of the author.

32. "Corporate Response to Corporate Campaigns: If We Can't Beat 'Em,

Let's Ban 'Em," Corporate Campaign, Inc., www.corporatecampaign
.org/corporate_response.php.

33. "National Press Club Newsmaker Luncheon with Teamsters President
Ron Carey," Washington, DC, October 20, 1997, Transcript by Federal
News Service, www.c-span.org/video/?c8209/clip-labor-issues.

34. Dirk Johnson, "A New Grinch Turns Up at the Mall," *New York Times*,
December 18, 1995.

35. Stephen Franklin, "Teamsters' Reform Image Tested," *Chicago Tribune*,
October 15, 1997.

36. Ron Carey to Peter Hoekstra, October 10, 1997; in possession of the
author. The letter was entered into the subcommittee record.

37. United States, Congress, Subcommittee on Oversight and Investigations of the House of Representatives Committee on Education and the
Workforce, 105th Congress, 1st Sess., October 14, 1997.

38. Glenn R. Simpson, "Teamsters Officials Tell House Panel of Coercion,
Beatings by Carey Backers," *Wall Street Journal*, October 15, 1997.

39. United States, Congress, Subcommittee on Oversight and Investigations of the House of Representatives Committee on Education and the
Workforce, 105th Congress, 1st Sess., October 14, 1997.

40. Terry Wilson, "Jury Acquits Daniel Ligurotis in Son's Shooting Death,"
Chicago Tribune, September 2, 1992.

41. Bruno, *Reforming the Chicago Teamsters*, 41.

42. Bruno, *Reforming the Chicago Teamsters*, 41.

43. "Carey Supporter Beats Hoffa Backer in Chicago Loser Challenging
Teamster Victory by Reform Candidate," *Boston Globe*, December 9,
1997; International Brotherhood of Teamsters (IBC), 25th International
Convention, Philadelphia, July 1996, 74–75.

44. Stephen Franklin, "Upset in Teamster Elections," *Chicago Tribune*, December 8, 2003.

45. Bruno, *Reforming the Chicago Teamsters*, 96.

46. "For Teamsters, Local Victory in Chicago Be Sign," Associated Press,
December 8, 1997.

47. Stephen Franklin, "Union Panel Votes Out 2 Teamsters for Life," *Chicago
Tribune*, May 31, 2002.

48. Greenhouse, "Teamsters Union Members Cite Pressure."

49. Greenhouse, "Teamsters Union Members Cite Pressure."

50. Maremont, "Hoffa Operative Used 'Moles.'"

51. Maremont, "Hoffa Operative Used 'Moles.'"

52. TDU press release, October 31, 1997, in possession of the author.

53. David Eckstein, interview by Joe Allen, May 24, 2015.

54. Franklin, "Teamsters' Reform Image Tested."

55. "What's Become of Labor?," *Wall Street Journal*, October 17, 1997.

56. National Press Club Newsmaker Luncheon with Teamsters President Ron Carey, Washington, DC, October 20, 1997, transcript available at www.c-span.org/video/?c8209/user-clip-clip-labor-issues.

57. National Press Club Newsmaker Luncheon, October 20, 1997.

58. Quoted in Kenneth Crowe, "UPS Ordered to Butt Out," *Newsday*, November 6, 1997.

59. Crowe, "UPS Ordered to Butt Out."

60. Steven Greenhouse, "An Overseer Bars Teamster Leader from Re-Election," *New York Times*, November 18, 1997.

61. Greenhouse, "Overseer Bars Teamster Leader."

62. Alexander Cockburn, "Reform Is Bigger than One Man," *Los Angeles Times*, November 19, 1997, www.latimes.com/archives/la-xpm-1997-nov-19-me-55269-story.html

63. "Ron Carey's Sad Fall," *New York Times*, November 18, 1997.

64. Steven Greenhouse, "Beleagured Carey Steps Aside as President of the Teamsters," *New York Times*, November 26, 1997.

65. Steven Greenhouse, "Teamster Camp Hails Fallen Carey Even as it Scans the Room for His Successor," *New York Times*, November 24, 1997.

66. David W. Chen, "Judge Upholds Ban on Race by Teamster," *New York Times*, January 2, 1998.

67. "Company News; Teamsters Told That Promised Jobs Are Halted," *New York Times*, July 11, 1998.

68. Steven Greenhouse, "Board Expels Ron Carey from Teamsters for Life," *New York Times*, July 28, 1998.

69. United States Congress, Opening Statement of Congressman Pete Hoekstra, Chairman, Subcommittee and Investigations, House Education and the Workforce Committee, March 28, 2000, "The International Brotherhood of Teamsters, One Year after the Election of James P. Hoffa," 4.

70. Steven Greenhouse, "Ex-President of Teamsters Is Charged with Lying," *New York Times*, January 26, 2001.

71. Ken Crowe, "The Vindication of Ron Carey," *Union Democracy Review*, December 2001–January 2002.

72. Ron Carey, "Labor Won't Be Silenced," *Verdict*, January 2003.

73. John D. Schulz, "In Love with Hoffa," *Traffic World*, May 1, 2000.

74. "In Re: Leedham Slate, Protestor," IBT Vote, www.ibtvote.org/Protest-Decisions/esd2005/2006esd381.

75. Mark Brenner, "*Labor Notes* Interviews Former Teamsters General President Ron Carey on the UPS Contract," *Labor Notes*, October 31, 2007.

76. Ken Paff, interview by Joe Allen, August 1, 2015.

CHAPTER 12: WE LOVE LOGISTICS

1. General Omar Bradley quoted in T. Pierce, *Proceedings of the US Naval Institute* 122, no. 9 (September 1996): 74

2. There are surprisingly few popular histories of FedEx or DHL. Among them are Robert A. Sigafoos and Roger R. Easson, *Absolutely Positively Overnight! The Unofficial Corporate History of Federal Express* (Memphis: St. Luke's Press, 1988); and James D. Scurlock, *King Larry: The Life and Ruins of a Billionaire Genius* (New York: Scribner, 2012).

3. "Ogilvy Ad for UPS—'That's Logistics,'" YouTube video, 0:31, September 10, 2010, www.youtube.com/watch?v=IAsxuSwKjRU.

4. Edna Bonacich and Khaleelah Hardie, "Wal-Mart and the Logistics Revolution," in *Wal-Mart: The Face of Twenty-First Century Capitalism*, ed. Nelson Lichtenstein (New York: New Press, 2006), 163.

5. Vicki Howard, *From Main Street to Mall: The Rise and Fall of the American Department Store* (Philadelphia: University of Pennsylvania Press, 2015), 10.

6. Quoted in Nelson Lichtenstein, *The Retail Revolution: How Wal-Mart Created a Brave New World of Business* (New York: Henry Holt and Company, 2009), 34.

7. Howard, *From Main Street*, 10.

8. Philip S. Foner, *The Great Labor Uprising of 1877* (New York: Pathfinder Press, 1977); Shelton Stromquist, *A Generation of Boomers* (Urbana/Chicago: University of Illinois Press, 1987); and Ray Ginger, *The Bending Cross: A Biography of Eugene V. Debs* (Chicago: Haymarket Books, 2007).

9. See Pete Davies, *American Road: The Story of an Epic Transcontinental Journey at the Dawn of the Motor Age* (New York: Henry Holt and Company, 2002).

10. The four-volume history of the Minneapolis Teamsters by Farrell Dobbs remains the best history of the Teamsters during that era; the works are available through Pathfinder Press.

11. Marc Levinson, *The Box: How the Shipping Container Made the World Smaller and the World Economy Bigger* (Princeton, NJ: Princeton University Press, 2008).

12. Quoted in Kim Moody, *US Labor in Trouble and Transition* (London: Verso Books, 2007), 50.

13. Deborah Cowen, *The Deadly Life of Logistics: Mapping Violence in Global Trade* (Minneapolis: University of Minnesota Press, 2014). If Bradley is remembered at all today, it is because of the 1970 film *Patton* starring George C. Scott as Patton and Karl Malden as Bradley.

14. Cowen, *Deadly Life of Logistics*, 3.

15. Cowen, *Deadly Life of Logistics*, 3.

16. Quoted in Lichtenstein, *The Retail Revolution*, 26.

17. Lichtenstein, *Retail Revolution*, 35.

18. Lichtenstein, *Retail Revolution*, 5.

19. Cowen, *Deadly Life of Logistics*, 1.

20. Cowen, *Deadly Life of Logistics*, 2.

21. Cowen, *Deadly Life of Logistics*, 2.

22. Lichtenstein, *Retail Revolution*, 39.

23. Mark Brenner, "As Cargo Chains Grow, So Does Workers' Leverage," *Labor Notes*, January 29, 2008.

24. Moody, *US Labor in Trouble and Transition*, 107.

25. Greg Bensinger and Laura Stevens, "Amazon, in Threat to UPS, Tries Its Own Deliveries," Steve Babson, ed. *Wall Street Journal*, April 24, 2014.

26. "Data: GDP," The World Bank, https://data.worldbank.org/indicator /NY.GDP.MKTP.CD?end=2013&start=2010.

27. "Logistics and Transportation Spotlight," SelectUSA, www.selectusa.gov /logistics-and-transportation-industry-united-states.

28. Megan Woolhouse, "Truck Driving Jobs Plentiful as Economy Recovers," *Boston Globe*, October 12, 2014.

29. Scurlock, *King Larry*, 2012.

30. "Failure to Deliver: DHL Gives Up on Its American Dream," *Economist*, November 13, 2008.

31. Kasarda and Lindsay, *Aerotropolis*, 64, 80.

32. Kasarda and Lindsay, *Aerotropolis*, 66, 65.

33. Kasarda and Lindsay, *Aerotropolis*, 82.

34. Michael Honey, *Going Down Jericho Road: The Memphis Strike, Martin Luther King's Last Campaign* (New York: W.W. Norton & Company, 2008).

35. Kasarda and Lindsay, *Aerotropolis*, 61.

36. Jeffrey F. Rayport, "The Miracle of Memphis," *MIT Technology Review*, December 20, 2010.

37. Rayport, "Miracle of Memphis."

38. Rayport, "Miracle of Memphis."

39. Kasarda and Lindsay, *Aerotropolis*, 62.

40. Joe Bates, "ACI Reveals the World's Busiest Passenger and Cargo Airports," *Airport World*, April 9, 2018.

41. Kasarda and Lindsay, *Aerotropolis*, 62.

42. Kasarda and Lindsay, *Aerotropolis*, 62.

43. Cowen, *Deadly Life of Logistics*, 73–75.

44. Kevin Coyne, *A Day in the Night of America* (New York: Random House, 1992), 101.

45. Coyne, *A Day in the Night*, 102.

46. "UPS Worldport Facts," UPS Pressroom, https://pressroom.ups.com /pressroom/ContentDetailsViewer.page?ConceptType=FactSheets&id

=1426321566696-701.

47. John McPhee, "Out in the Sort," *New Yorker*, April 18, 2005.

48. Kasarda and Lindsay, *Aerotropolis*, 62–63.

49. "UPS Worldport Facts," UPS Pressroom.

50. Kasarda and Lindsay, *Aerotropolis*, 65.

51. "UPS Aircraft Fleet Fact Sheet," UPS Pressroom, www.pressroom.ups
.com/pressroom/ContentDetailsViewer.page?ConceptType=FactSheets
&id=1426321565529-534; UPS Air Operations Facts, UPS Pressroom,
www.pressroom.ups.com/pressroom/ContentDetailsViewer.page
?ConceptType=FactSheets&id=1426321563773-779.

52. Kasarda and Lindsay, *Aerotropolis*, 66.

53. Kasarda and Lindsay, *Aerotropolis*, 68.

54. Teamsters, Local 89, "Basic Info," www.unionfacts.com/lu/20926/IBT/89/.

55. Donald L. Barlett and James B. Steele, "Corporate Welfare," *Time*,
November 9, 1998.

56. Kasarda and Lindsay, *Aerotropolis*, 68.

57. Kasarda and Lindsay, *Aerotropolis*, 69.

58. McPhee, "Out in the Sort."

59. Kasarda and Lindsay, *Aerotropolis*, 69.

60. David A. Mann, "UPS's Growing Supply Chain Division Has Expanded
into Shepherdsville," *Business Journals*, December 19, 2014, www
.bizjournals.com/louisville/news/2014/12/19/upss-growing-supply
-chain-division-has-expanded.html?s=print.

61. Kasarda and Lindsay, *Aerotropolis*, 69.

62. "UPS Plays Hardball, Louisville Members Say No," TDU, March 14,
2014, www.tdu.org/news/ups-plays-hardball-louisville-members-say-no.

63. Philip Siekman, "The New Wave in Giant Ships Vessels Too Big for the
Panama Canal, Carrying Enough Containers to Stretch 27 Miles, Are
Slashing Costs," *CNN Money*, November 12, 2001, https://money.cnn
.com/magazines/fortune/fortune_archive/2001/11/12/313317/index.htm.

64. "Fact Sheet: Chicago Area Consolidation Hub (CACH)," 2015, ITS
Midwest, www.itsmidwest.org/2015AnnualMeeting/factsheet.pdf.

65. "Fact Sheet: Chicago Area Consolidation Hub (CACH)," ITS Midwest,
2015.

66. Matt Van Hattem, "Inside Willow Springs," *Trains*, July 6, 2006.

67. Melissa Harris, "Amazon to Open Its 1st Illinois Warehouse," *Chicago
Tribune*, October 28, 2014.

68. Patrick Sisson, "9 Facts about Amazon's Unprecedented Warehouse
Empire," Curbed, November 19, 2018, www.curbed.com/2017/11
/21/16686150/black-friday-2018-amazon-warehouse-fulfillment.

CONCLUSION: WHO WILL MOVE THE WORLD?

1. Quoted in Diana Jones, "UPS: A Technology Company with Trucks," Drexel University LeBow College of Business, www.lebow.drexel.edu /news/ups-technology-company-trucks.

2. Jessica Bruder, "These Workers Have a New Demand: Stop Watching Us," *Nation*, May 27, 2015.

3. Erica Pandey, "Amazon, the New King of Shipping," Axios, June 27, 2019, www.axios.com/amazon-shipping-chart-fedex-ups-usps -0dc6bab1-2169-42a8-9e56-0e85c590eb89.html.

4. James Vincent and Chaim Gartenberg, "Here's Amazon's New Transforming Prime Air Delivery Drone," The Verge, June 5, 2019, www.theverge.com/2019/6/5/18654044/amazon-prime-air-delivery -drone-new-design-safety-transforming-flight-video.

5. "UPS Completes $1.8 Billion Coyote Logistics Acquisition," Transport Topics, August 18, 2015, www.ttnews.com/articles/basetemplate.aspx ?storyid=39202.

6. Jesse Pound, "FedEx, UPS Jockey with Amazon as Tech Giant Expands into Shipping," CNBC, September 1, 2019, www.cnbc.com/2019/09/01 /fedex-ups-jockey-with-amazon-as-tech-giant-expands-into-shipping.html.

7. Mary Schlangenstein, Richard Weiss, and Elco van Groningen, "FedEx Bids $4.8 Billion for TNT Two Years after UPS Deal," *Bloomberg,* April 7, 2015.

8. Robbie Whelan, "FedEx Aiming to Build New Hub in Connecticut," *Post & Parcel*, July 24, 2015; James Fink, "FedEx to Start $50 Million Hamburg Project," *Buffalo Business News*, March 17, 2015.

9. Robbie Whelan, "DHL to Spend $108 Million to Expand Cincinnati Air Hub," *Wall Street Journal,* May 31, 2015.

10. "DHL and KTZ Express Sign MOU to Enhance China-Kazakhstan Rail Freight Link," *Post & Parcel*," July 1, 2015, https://postandparcel .info/65963/news/dhl-and-ktz-express-sign-mou-to-enhance-china -kazakhstan-rail-freight-link/.

11. "Press Release: Deutsche Post DHL Announces 'Strategy 2020,'" DHL, April 2, 2014, www.dhl.com/en/press/releases/releases_2014/group /dp_dhl_strategy_2020.html#.Xa9MHZNKjOR.

12. "Strategy 2025: We Deliver Excellence in a Digital World," DHL, www.logistics.dhl/us-en/home/about-us/strategy-2025.html.

13. Matthew Weigelt, "USPS Looking to Modernize Mail Truck Delivery Fleet," *Washington Technology*, April 9, 2015.

14. Andy Medici, "Postal Service Wants to Buy a High-Tech, Flexible Fleet," *Federal Times*, April 7, 2015.

15. Devin Leonard, "It's Amazon's World. The USPS Just Delivers in It," *Bloomberg Businessweek*, July 30, 2015.

16. Natalie Gagliordi, ZDNet, August 9, 2019, www.zdnet.com/article /usps-reports-decline-in-package-shipments-as-amazon-brings-more -deliveries-in-house/.

17. Harry Braverman, *Labor and Monopoly Capital: The Degradation of Work in the Twentieth Century* (New York: Monthly Review Press, 1974), 125.

18. "ORION Backgrounder," UPS Pressroom, www.pressroom.ups.com /pressroom/ContentDetailsViewer.page?ConceptType=Factsheets&id =1426321616277-282.

19. Rosenbush and Stevens, "At UPS, the Algorithm Is the Drive."

20. Bruder, "These Workers Have a New Demand."

21. Bruder, "These Workers Have a New Demand."

22. Mark Brenner, "Union Faces Fresh Questions in West Coast Longshore Standoff," *Labor Notes*, January 22, 2015.

23. "Small but Powerful Union Is at Center of Port Dispute," *Los Angeles Times*, February 17, 2015.

24. Darrin Hoop, "Will the New Agreement Weaken the ILWU?" *Socialist Worker,* April 1, 2015, https://socialistworker.org/2015/04/01/will-the -new-deal-weaken-the-ilwu.

25. Josh Dzieza, "'Beat the Machine': Amazon Warehouse Workers Strike to Protest Inhumane Conditions," The Verge, July 16, 2019, www.theverge .com/2019/7/16/20696154/amazon-prime-day-2019-strike-warehouse -workers-inhumane-conditions-the-rate-productivity.

26. Bruder, "The Great Debate."

27. Spencer Soper, "Inside Amazon's Warehouse," *Morning Call*, August 17, 2015.

28. Noam Scheiber and Stephanie Strom, "Labor Board Ruling Eases Way for Fast-Food Unions' Efforts," *New York Times,* August 27, 2015.

29. "Amazon Workers Strike in Germany as Christmas Orders Peak," Reuters, December 15, 2014.

30. "A Message from the General President: Building a Stronger Union," *Teamster Magazine*, July/August 2002, www.teamster.org/sites/teamster .org/files/mag_julaug2002.pdf.

31. "Florida Department of Corrections Officer Vote to Join Teamsters," Teamsters press release, November 17, 2011, https://teamster.org/content /florida-department-corrections-officers-vote-join-teamsters.

32. Bill Kaczor, "Florida Prison Guards Dump PBA, Go with Teamsters," Associated Press, November 17, 2011.

INDEX

238

ABOUT THE AUTHOR

© Jared Rodriguez, jaredrodriguez.com

Joe Allen is the author of *Vietnam: The (Last) War the U.S. Lost* and *People Wasn't Made to Burn: A True Story of Race, Murder, and Justice in Chicago*. Allen is a former member of the Teamsters and worked for several years at United Parcel Service. He has written extensively on the Teamsters at UPS. Joe Allen was born and raised in Stoughton, Massachusetts, and is the son and nephew of United States Marines. He attended the University of Massachusetts at Boston and currently lives in Chicago.

ALSO AVAILABLE FROM HAYMARKET BOOKS

Bit Tyrants: The Political Economy of Silicon Valley
Rob Larson

Disposable Domestics: Immigrant Women Workers in the Global Economy
Grace Chang, foreword by Alicia Garza, afterword by Ai-jen Poo

Dying for an iPhone: Apple, Foxconn, and the Lives of China's Workers
Jenny Chan, Ngai Pun, and Mark Selden

The Long Deep Grudge: A Story of Big Capital, Radical Labor, and Class War in the American Heartland
Toni Gilpin

On New Terrain: How Capital is Reshaping the Battleground of Class War
Kim Moody

Radicals in the Barrio: Magonistas, Socialists, Wobblies, and Communists in the Mexican-American Working Class
Justin Akers Chacón

Rank and File: Personal Histories by Working-Class Organizers
Alice and Staughton Lynd

Song of the Stubborn One Thousand:
The Watsonville Canning Strike, 1985–87
Peter Shapiro

Striking to Survive: Workers' Resistance to Factory Relocations in China
Fan Shigang, introduction by Sam Austin and Pun Ngai

ABOUT HAYMARKET BOOKS

Haymarket Books is a radical, independent, nonprofit book publisher based in Chicago. Our mission is to publish books that contribute to struggles for social and economic justice. We strive to make our books a vibrant and organic part of social movements and the education and development of a critical, engaged, international left.

We take inspiration and courage from our namesakes, the Haymarket martyrs, who gave their lives fighting for a better world. Their 1886 struggle for the eight-hour day—which gave us May Day, the international workers' holiday—reminds workers around the world that ordinary people can organize and struggle for their own liberation. These struggles continue today across the globe—struggles against oppression, exploitation, poverty, and war.

Since our founding in 2001, Haymarket Books has published more than five hundred titles. Radically independent, we seek to drive a wedge into the risk-averse world of corporate book publishing. Our authors include Noam Chomsky, Arundhati Roy, Rebecca Solnit, Angela Y. Davis, Howard Zinn, Amy Goodman, Wallace Shawn, Mike Davis, Winona LaDuke, Ilan Pappé, Richard Wolff, Dave Zirin, Keeanga-Yamahtta Taylor, Nick Turse, Dahr Jamail, David Barsamian, Elizabeth Laird, Amira Hass, Mark Steel, Avi Lewis, Naomi Klein, and Neil Davidson. We are also the trade publishers of the acclaimed Historical Materialism Book Series and of Dispatch Books.